KU-221-503

THE

SUPERPOWERS

IN

CRISIS

Pergamon Titles of Related Interest

Deibel & Gaddis CONTAINING THE SOVIET UNION

Denoon CONSTRAINTS ON STRATEGY

Eliot & Pfaltzgraff THE RED ARMY ON PAKISTAN'S BORDER

Levchenko ON THE WRONG SIDE

Ludwikowski THE CRISIS OF COMMUNISM

Perry & Pfaltzgraff SELLING THE ROPE TO HANG CAPITALISM?

Pfaltzgraff & Eliot NATIONAL SECURITY

Sejna & Douglass DECISION-MAKING IN COMMUNIST COUNTRIES

Weeks BRASSEY'S SOVIET AND COMMUNIST QUOTATIONS

Whelan & Dixon THE SOVIET UNION IN THE THIRD WORLD

Related Journals*

DEFENSE ANALYSIS

DEFENCE ATTACHE

*Free specimen copies available upon request

0296939   KRICKUS R.J.
          BW 9.88

327.47

The Superpowers
In Crisis.
21.50

-0 SEP 1988

HERTFORDSHIRE LIBRARY SERVICE

Please renew/return this item by the last date shown.

So that your telephone call is charged at local rate, please call the numbers as set out below:

	From Area codes 01923 or 0208:	From the rest of Herts:
Renewals:	01923 471373	01438 737373
Enquiries:	01923 471333	01438 737333
Minicom:	01923 471599	01438 737599

L32b   Checked 15/9/11

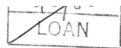

LOAN   14 JUL 2003

18 JAN 1996

2 3 APR 2002

THE
SUPERPOWERS
IN
CRISIS

Implications of Domestic Discord

RICHARD J. KRICKUS

PERGAMON-BRASSEY'S

International Defense Publishers, Inc.

WASHINGTON · NEW YORK · LONDON · OXFORD · BEIJING
FRANKFURT · SÃO PAULO · SYDNEY · TOKYO · TORONTO

U.S.A. (Editorial)	Pergamon-Brassey's International Defense Publishers, 8000 Westpark Drive, Fourth Floor, McLean, Virginia 22102, U.S.A.
(Orders)	Pergamon Press, Maxwell House, Fairview Park, Elmsford, New York 10523, U.S.A.
U.K. (Editorial)	Brassey's Defence Publishers, 24 Gray's Inn Road, London WC1X 8HR
(Orders)	Brassey's Defence Publishers, Headington Hill Hall, Oxford OX3 0BW, England
PEOPLE'S REPUBLIC OF CHINA	Pergamon Press, Room 4037, Qianmen Hotel, Beijing, People's Republic of China
FEDERAL REPUBLIC OF GERMANY	Pergamon Press Hammerweg 6, D-6242 Kronberg, Federal Republic of Germany
BRAZIL	Pergamon Editora, Rua Eça de Queiros, 346, CEP 04011, Paraiso, São Paulo, Brazil
AUSTRALIA	Pergamon-Brassey's Defence Publishers, P.O. Box 544, Potts Point, N.S.W. 2011, Australia
JAPAN	Pergamon Press, 8th Floor, Matsuoka Central Building, 1–7–1 Nishishinjuku, Shinjuku-ku, Tokyo 160, Japan
CANADA	Pergamon Press Canada, Suite No. 271, 253 College Street, Toronto, Ontario, Canada M5T 1R5

Copyright © 1987 Pergamon-Brassey's International Defense
Publishers, Inc.

*All rights reserved. No part of this publication may be reproduced, stored
in a retrieval system or transmitted in any form or by any means:
electronic, electrostatic, magnetic tape, mechanical, photocopying,
recording or otherwise, without permission in writing from the
publishers.*

First printing 1987

Library of Congress Cataloging-in-Publication Data
Krickus, Richard J.
The superpowers in crisis.
Bibliography: p.
1. United States—Foreign relations—Soviet Union.
2. Soviet Union—Foreign relations—United States.
3. United States—Economic conditions—1981– .
4. Soviet Union—Economic conditions—1981– .
5. United States—Politics and government—1981– .
I. Title.
E183.8.S65K75   1987   327.73047   86–30293

ISBN 0–08–034705–3 (Hardcover)
ISBN 0–08–035158–1 (Flexicover)

HERTFORDSHIRE
LIBRARY SERVICE

327·47073
0296939

Printed in Great Britain

For Mary Ann Carroll

Contents

Preface

To most Americans, the words "national security" mean protecting the United States from a Soviet nuclear attack. This is justifiable: the superpowers each have 10,000 strategic nuclear weapons. Should a fraction of them be detonated, millions of Americans and Soviets would be killed, and material wonders that took centuries of toil and sacrifice to build would be destroyed in a matter of hours. Even discounting Carl Sagan's claim that the Northern Hemisphere would be gripped in a "nuclear winter," producing conditions analogous to an ice age, the ecological damage would be devastating. This spectre of a nuclear holocaust accounts for the vast outpouring of books, articles, and television programs devoted to the East–West military competition—the "First Front" of the superpower rivalry. It has been the basis for a massive buildup of U.S. military might and for a pledge by President Ronald Reagan to develop a space-based missile defense system—"Star Wars"—capable of safeguarding the country from Soviet ICBMs.

There is another dimension to national security, however—what we shall call the "Second Front"—in the titanic struggle between Washington and Moscow. It involves political, economic, and socio-cultural problems afflicting Americans and Soviets. We speak of them collectively as "predicaments" because there are no easy or ready solutions to them. For example, the soaring federal deficits that hang over the U.S. economy, or opposition to Soviet imperialism in Eastern Europe that may one day soon produce "another Hungary." A predicament is a source of grave concern because it is a precursor to a more serious condition—a "societal crisis." Sociologists define this phenomenon as one in which values, beliefs, and institutions that once produced social order are no longer capable of doing so. Indeed, they often are the source of the crisis or serve as a deterrent to its resolution.

Societal crises can be resolved when new modes of thought and action are developed and fundamental shifts in power relationships occur. This is what happened in Great Britain when the ruling classes, faced with the disruptions of industrialization and urbanization, reached an accommodation with the middle and working classes who demanded a voice in government and a larger piece of the economic pie. The failure of rulers on the continent to follow a similar path led to revolutionary upheaval, and the old social order crumbled before communist and fascist movements. The rulers of Russia, Italy, and Germany were reluctant to establish a new basis for social tranquility. They believed they could mollify popular discontent without making economic or political concessions, or they simply did not recognize how serious the crises were. By the time they learned otherwise, they were incapable of reversing the tide of internal forces that swept them from power.

Given the awesome U.S. and Soviet nuclear arsenals, one can understand preoccupation with the First Front of the superpower rivalry. Traditionally, however, writers in the opposing camps have predicted the other side's social system would self-destruct, that internal, not external, forces on the Second Front would lead to its demise. Marxists have predicted the collapse of capitalism as far back as 1848, when Marx and Engels wrote *The Communist Manifesto*. Contemporary Soviet writers assert that it is only a matter of time before this fate befalls the United States. Western analysts, in turn, have forecast the demise of the Soviet regime since the Russian Revolution. Borrowing from Karl Marx's lexicon, Ronald Reagan has said that the USSR is doomed to the "ash heap of history."

The goals of this book, therefore, are threefold. The first rests upon the thesis that the Soviet Union is in the throes of a societal crisis. This crisis represents the gravest threat to the USSR since World War II. To identify the problems responsible for it and to discuss its capacity to destroy the Leninist regime, the Russian empire, or both, is a pivotal goal of this book.

A second goal is predicated on the proposition that the U.S. predicament is not as serious as the Soviet crisis but is capable, nonetheless, of threatening U.S. national security. This goal is to identify the sources of this predicament and determine its capacity to produce a crisis that endangers the United States.

The third goal of this book is to explore what impact the Soviet crisis and the U.S. predicament will have upon East–West relations on the First Front. The superpowers' internal problems are of global significance because they can precipitate "international crises." An international crisis involves two or more powers in conflict. It is characterized by high stakes, unappealing options, and time constraints that compel the antagonists to make hasty decisions. Under severe strain and in a compressed time frame, leaders are in danger of making mistakes and taking provocative actions, ultimately leading to war.

Some analysts believe that crises at home will reduce U.S.–Soviet confrontation and lessen the prospect of a nuclear calamity. Preoccupied with internal problems, the superpowers will restrain themselves internationally and avoid trouble spots capable of embroiling them in hostilities. Under these circumstances, détente can be resurrected, arms control breakthroughs achieved, and the likelihood of war reduced.

Other commentators, however, are pessimistic. They believe that societal crises will cause one side to adopt belligerent policies in an effort to deflect domestic anger abroad. This will provoke the other side to respond in kind, heightening East–West tensions, undermining arms control talks, and spawning a new race for military dominance. Leaders in both countries will conclude that the other one is striving for a first-strike capability. Ultimately, the superpowers will be drawn into a crisis that will precipitate the nuclear calamity both wish to avoid. The nuclear scenario defense analysts in Moscow and Washington deem most plausible is predicated on just such assumptions.

Acknowledgements

Many friends and colleagues helped shape this book: Jack Albertine, Lew Fickett, Vic Fingerhut, Paul Manchester, Don McClure, and Jim Saverese. Jack Kramer, who read and commented on the manuscript, deserves special recognition. Financial support from Mary Washington College expedited its completion.

As always, my wife, Mary Ann, took time from her busy career to read the book through its various reincarnations, and her assistance was vital. Finally, my son, Anthony, and daughter, Alexi, lifted my spirits during the course of a protracted enterprise. They were an inspiration.

Introduction

The Ash Heap of History?

Soon after the Bolsheviks wrested power from the hands of their disorganized enemies, Western writers asked how long a regime built upon political oppression and economic destitution could survive. How could a movement largely dominated by Russians maintain hegemony over the more than 100 ethnic groups in the USSR? How could leaders who threatened to spread communism expect to endure the enmity of the world's most powerful capitalist countries?

In 1921, when preparing an article for *The New Republic*, Walter Lippmann discovered that between 1917 and 1920, the *New York Times* had predicted the collapse of bolshevism 91 times.[1] It was not alone in this practice. Most of Lenin's detractors underestimated him. But unlike Kerensky, Lenin provided the political acumen and personal will to subdue the mélange of enemies seeking his demise. After his death, the wily Stalin and the intellectual Trotsky embarked upon a bitter struggle to fill Lenin's shoes, prompting forecasts that the infant Bolshevik state was doomed. By late 1929, Stalin emerged the victor. In the following decade he conducted a brutal collectivization drive, costing the lives of millions of people, and liquidated tens of thousands of old Bolsheviks and Red Army commanders. His monstrous policies and the Soviet Union's poor showing in the Finnish–Russian War were perceived in Berlin as evidence that the USSR was vulnerable. Hitler concluded that if confronted with the Wehrmacht's massive military might, Stalin's regime would crumble in several months. In June

1

1941, German forces struck, imposing frightful losses upon the Red Army and compelling it to retreat over a vast front. Traumatized, Stalin sought shelter in the bowels of the Kremlin where he was afflicted by deep depression for weeks.

But he recovered, rallied his armies, and after several years of the most deadly of World War II battles, the Red Army drove the Nazis back into the rubble of the Third Reich, where they were finally beaten into submission. By the late 1940s, an "iron curtain" had rung down, separating Eastern from Western Europe.

Stalin's death in 1953 caused Kremlin-watchers to predict a power struggle, which would deny the winner the capacity to rule the vast empire he had bequeathed. The succession was not entirely tranquil, but no extensive bloodbath occurred, and by the time Khrushchev denounced "Stalin's crimes" in 1956, he was in firm control of the party and governmental apparatus.

Following Krushchev's downfall in 1964, Zbigniew Brzezinski began a heated debate among U.S. Sovietologists when he said that an accumulation of crises—economic, political, and social—was gaining momentum in the USSR. The Kremlin had to face an ominous prospect: the Soviet Union was in an advanced stage of political decay.[2] Forecasts that the Soviet Union was in decline subsided after Brezhnev consolidated his position in the party, crushed the dissidents, and embarked upon a drive to achieve nuclear parity with the United States. The massive Soviet military buildup in the 1960s and 1970s was made possible by high levels of economic growth. The economy grew fast enough to improve the living standards of the Soviet people, too.

It was in the face of these developments that Richard Nixon concluded that the superpowers had to resolve their differences through détente. Nuclear parity meant that neither side could use its nuclear arsenal to achieve international objectives at the other side's expense. Henry Kissinger, Nixon's national security adviser, argued that the West had to face the unpleasant truth that the Soviet empire was an established fact and that it was unproductive to tamper with the Soviet Union's internal affairs.

By the mid-1970s, however, confrontationists in Washington cited Soviet projections of power in Africa, the Middle East, and Afghanistan as evidence that détente was a "one-way street" allowing the Soviets to expand their influence at the free world's expense. Jimmy Carter was badly beaten in his bid for a second term in 1980—to a large degree because the American people believed that he was an inept leader and had mishandled the economy. But a significant number of voters rebuffed him because they reasoned that the time had come to get tough with the Soviets and that he was not up to the job. They believed Ronald Reagan when he pledged to rearm America and put the Soviets in their place.

Reagan appointed many outspoken critics of détente to his administration—Harvard professor Richard Pipes to a post at the National Security Council, former Henry Jackson aide Richard Perle to an important job at the Department of Defense. And Eugene Rostow, a leading figure on the Committee on the Present Danger, which had blistered SALT II, was appointed director of the Arms Control and Disarmament Agency. As he promised, Reagan dramatically increased the defense budget, with two purposes in mind. The first, to close the strategic nuclear gap that the confrontationists claimed favored the USSR, was obvious. The second one was only mentioned in passing. It hinged on the hope that if the Kremlin attempted to match the U.S. drive for nuclear supremacy, the Soviet regime would run the risk of exacerbating roblems in its empire, which might bring it crashing down.

Reagan informed the British parliament in June 1982: "What I am describing now is a plan and hope for the long term—the march of freedom and democracy which will leave Marxism–Leninism on the ash heap of history as it has left other tyrannies. . . ."[3] Moscow characterized expectations that the Soviet system would self-destruct as "wishful thinking" but cited the speech as further evidence that the Reaganites were out to destroy the USSR. Many commentators in the United States, who deemed it improper for a president to make such provocative statements, nonetheless concurred that the USSR was confronting an accumulation of crises that represented the gravest threat to the Kremlin since World War II.

Washington analysts today claim that four crises comprise the Soviet predicament:

Crisis #1: Economic Austerity

The Soviet Union will experience slow economic growth for many years due to a chronically sick agricultural sector, a labor and capital crunch, low productivity, outmoded technology, and a flawed system of centralized planning. This is bound to foster widespread discontent on the part of the Soviet people who, after making modest but steady gains over the past 20 years, will be asked to tighten their belts and accept lower living standards.

Crisis #2: Turmoil in Eastern Europe

"The Polish disease" may be in remission, but, though dormant, its bacilli are spreading through Eastern Europe. It is only a matter of time before it flares up again, and this time it may not be confined to a single country or be put down without the intervention of the Red Army. Moreover, the Kremlin fears that discontent in Eastern Europe will spill over into the USSR, afflicting segments of the Soviet population.

Crisis #3: Ethnic Discord

By 1990 the Great Russians will represent less than 50% of the Soviet population. More importantly, there is rising ethnic self-awareness on the part of non-Russians, who bitterly resent Russian dominance of major Soviet institutions—the party, government, military, and the like. This trend has helped spur Russian nationalism, which in turn feeds the anti-Russian sensibilities of the USSR's ethnic minorities. In a period of economic austerity, discord between the Russians and the other ethnic groups will escalate.

Crisis #4: A Power Struggle

Yuri Andropov and Konstantin Chernenko were replaced in smooth transfers of power, prompting many analysts to conclude that the Soviets had resolved the problem of succession. But this conclusion is premature. The real succession crisis will occur when Gorbachev attempts to grapple with the preceding crises. If he adopts the far-reaching measures needed, a power struggle will ensue, setting in motion the kind of intra-elite struggle that followed the deaths of Lenin and Stalin.

Separately, there is little doubt that the Soviets can handle these problems, but taken together they will foster widespread discontent and divide the ruling elite, producing upheaval and discord of monumental proportions—in other words, a "societal crisis." A pivotal question is whether the younger generation, in the face of this crisis, will liberalize Soviet society or cling to the status quo. James H. Billington, a prominent American student of Russian history, believes that it will adopt long overdue reforms: "There is reasonable likelihood that the forthcoming generational change of leadership may bring with it greater change in policies than at any time since Lenin moved from War Communism to his New Economic Policy in 1921."[4]

Since Gorbachev's ascendency, the media have observed that at long last the USSR has a ruler young and energetic enough to shake things up in Moscow. Journalists of this opinion and Billington may be right, but it is too early to make any firm judgments about Gorbachev's stewardship. Most Kremlinologists agree with Timothy J. Colton that one thing is evident: "The death of Leonid Brezhnev on November 10, 1982 closed a chapter of Soviet history exceptional for its stability and predictability. Now, with difficulties mounting on several fronts, little can be taken for granted about the country's prospects by the Soviet public or by foreign onlookers."[5]

American foreign policy analysts agree that the Soviet Union is in serious trouble, but disagree about whether or not the Soviet predicament will cause a societal crisis and, if so, what impact it will have upon Soviet foreign policy. Will the Soviets become more or less aggressive? What policies should the

United States adopt toward the USSR under these circumstances? We shall return to these questions in a few pages. First, let us look at Soviet claims that the United States is faced with a crisis of its own and that economic problems in Western Europe, as well as Third World debt may yet prove prophetic Marx's assertion that capitalism will eventually self-destruct.

The Other Side: U.S. Discord

Georgy Arbatov, director of the Institute of United States and Canadian Studies, has said:

> My colleagues and I think that American society has been living through a protracted, multifaceted crisis involving many spheres of American life. It is becoming increasingly clear that, unless some very serious and rational attempts are made in the United States to adapt its policies, including its foreign policy, to changing realities, America is in for a series of very strong shocks, possibly stronger than at any time in her history.[6]

Arbatov, who is a key adviser to Gorbachev on American affairs, contends that the U.S. establishment is concerned about the "ungovernability" of the United States. It has displayed alarm about "lack of consensus, fragmentation of political institutions, and overload of social demands on the political system, 'too much' democracy, and so forth."[7]

Other Soviet commentators cite the economic difficulties afflicting all capitalist countries as evidence of a serious crisis that will get worse over time. It has taken on worldwide dimensions, as witnessed by the Western Europeans' economic plight and that of debt-ridden Third World countries that are part of the U.S.-dominated neocolonialist system—Argentina, Brazil, and Mexico. Lenin recognized the importance of the developing countries to the viability of the advanced capitalist powers decades before "bourgeois" writers did. In 1916 he wrote that capitalists bought off workers in the Occident, by exploiting the colored peoples of the world but in the process set the stage for capitalism's global demise. The Asian, African, and Latin American victims of imperialism would one day turn on their tormentors, and capitalism would be consumed in the flames of a worldwide revolution.[8]

Such prophecies have been part of the Marxist writings for years, and Westerners have reasons to reject it. But even American thinkers concede that the United States faces a predicament of its own in this decade and that it will have a marked impact on U.S. society for the remainder of the century—even if it never evolves into a societal crisis.

Ironically, the best way to understand the U.S. predicament is to first review the accomplishments of the most powerful country in the free world. Consider, in this connection, the following observations. Unlike most multi-ethnic societies, the United States, with a population approaching 240 million people representing a cross section of the world's religions, races, and ethnic groups, has amalgamated them into a viable nation. It has achieved social order on the basis of consensus instead of coercion. It is one of the few industrial societies where workers and employers alike are staunch supporters of the free enterprise system. Americans have always associated change with progress and have displayed a confidence in their capacity to solve problems that perplex other nations.

Most Americans attribute these successes to the "American dream," the adhesive that binds our diverse society using a trinity of convictions that are political, cultural, and economic in nature:

- The political conviction: in spite of its limitations, the polity is essentially fair and responsive to the demands of its citizens.
- The cultural conviction: as a nation blessed with a unique heritage, we possess the know-how to grapple with problems, foreign and domestic, that threaten our cherished values and institutions; it was preordained (some say by God) that we use science and technology to build a civilization excelling all others in history.
- The economic conviction: the living standards of every generation will surpass those enjoyed by preceding generations.

As we approach the 21st century, however, the haunting fear that the American dream is unraveling has become widespread:

- Political alienation is pervasive. During his first term, Ronald Reagan's stewardship lifted the morale of the American people; but the Iran-contra fiasco in 1986 has resurrected doubts about the integrity of American public officials, and about the capacity of the political system to resolve society's problems.
- There is a crisis of confidence in American culture associated, among other things, with widespread drug abuse, family fragmentation, declining faith in American know-how, and the failure to sustain cherished values in a rapidly changing world.
- In spite of the economic recovery, there is a lapse of confidence in our economic system stemming from the knowledge that our nation's problems are serious and enduring, that millions of jobs in the manufacturing sector never will be reclaimed, and that changing international economic conditions dictate lower living standards for millions of our people.

The erosion of the American dream promises either political stalemate or political polarization, widespread economic discontent, and social divisions denying us the unity of purpose necessary to resolve pressing problems at home and abroad. On occasion there may be reason for optimism, but the problems facing the United States are deep-seated and will not be resolved quickly. On the eve of Ronald Reagan's first term, Seymour Martin Lipset and William Schneider reported:

The United States enters the 1980s . . . with a lower reserve of confidence in the ability of its institutional leaders to deal with the problems of the polity, the society, and the economy than at any time in this century. As a result of the strains produced by the experience of the last fifteen years, our institutional structure is less resilient than in the past. Should the 1980s be characterized by a major crisis, the outcome could very well be substantial support for movements seeking to change the system in a fundamental way. Serious setbacks in the economy or in foreign policy, accompanied by a failure of leadership, would raise greater risks of a loss of legitimacy now than at any time in this century. Although the evidence on the surface seems reassuring, there are disturbing signs of deep and serious discontent.[9]

There is little reason to challenge this conclusion today; yet, as with their counterparts in the Soviet Union, there is no indication that U.S. leaders are prepared to resolve the country's predicament by making sweeping changes in its major institutions. On the contrary, the point men in the conservative counterreformation are bent on reaffirming values, ideas, and power relationships that predate the New Deal.

Emboldened by the political disintegration of the FDR coalition and the sagging morale of the Democrats, they have overlooked a trenchant fact: the nation's difficulties are inextricably linked to American liberalism, the prevailing public philosophy throughout most of the nation's history.

American liberalism was first formulated in the 18th century by the founding fathers. Products of the Enlightenment, they believed in reason, human perfection, and the ability of free men to govern themselves. But they were at odds over the size and the role of government, and they split into two camps after the Revolution. The "liberals," led by Thomas Jefferson, feared government abuses of power, opposed state intervention in the private sector, and favored a constitution that diffused power. Alexander Hamilton, the leader of the "conservatives"—this term was not to enter the Anglo–American political lexicon until the 19th century—believed strong government was needed to hold the unruly masses in line and to help the new republic actualize its economic potential. Hamilton did not get the kind of strong political system he proposed at the Grand Convention of 1787, but as Washington's secretary of the treasury, he helped enact laws enhancing the prospects of U.S. enterprises to compete with foreign ones.

In the aftermath of the U.S. Civil War, American liberals and conservatives revised their earlier views of government. The liberals discovered that the new, giant business enterprises were now capable of abusing power and had to be held in check. Henceforth they looked to the state to countervail corporate power and to government to ameliorate economic and social disruptions associated with the new industrial system. The conservatives now feared the state more than the people because reformers were using public authority to interfere in commercial affairs—passing child labor, antitrust, and other laws that "violated" property rights.

European conservatives made something of a similar transformation in the face of the gathering socialist storm, but they also feared the cultural consequences of the industrial order their American cousins applauded, and they were less disturbed by strong political authority as long as it was "in the right hands." The most discerning of them realized that, while the Marxists preached revolution, the captains of industry had embarked upon the most revolutionary course in history. They were responsible for the great transformation from rural to urban life, from agricultural to industrial pursuits, from traditional to modern society.

In the 1930s the havoc wrought by the Great Depression compelled the Americans to make readjustment in the laissez-faire system that had dominated the country since the end of the Civil War. Forward-looking members of the business community and conservatives of a pragmatic bent realized that the time had come to follow the British Tories, who had adopted welfare state programs to undermine the appeal to workers of trade unionism and socialism.

From the 1930s until the 1960s, proponents of affirmative government dominated U.S. public policy, although the Right dominated the private sector. The leaders in the business and financial community acceded to liberal control of government because Keynesian policies were largely responsible for the postwar economic prosperity that had emasculated the radical left. It was only after the liberals could no longer guarantee the country's economic growth and disputes over social issues split the Democratic party that their policies lost their appeal. By the mid-1970s, moreover, power was shifting in the Republican party from the "Old Right"—led by the eastern establishment whose principal spokesman was Nelson Rockefeller—to the "New Right," which had rallied around Ronald Reagan. The eastern establishment had retained some ideas associated with the Tories—for example, the rich and powerful have an obligation to behave generously toward less fortunate members of society, individuals of means have a responsibility to serve in public affairs, and politicians should be guided by pragmatism, not dogmatism, in making policy.

The New Right—which sought to fill the intellectual and policy void left by the demoralized liberals—was ideological, not pragmatic, and its followers wished to resurrect American liberalism much as it flourished during the era of laissez-faire capitalism. In 1980 the New Right's leading spokesman was elected president. Badly shaken by the twin traumas of Vietnam and Watergate and fearful of their economic future, millions of voters were attracted to Reagan, who promised to restore America's military might and to revitalize its economy.

In pledging to restrict government intervention in people's lives, Reagan exploited deep-seated beliefs in American liberalism that had receded in the face of the New Deal but had reasserted themselves as Democratic solutions lost their luster in the 1970s. As Jeane Kirkpatrick, a formerly liberal political scientist who was appointed by Reagan to serve as U.S. ambassador to the United Nations, wrote:

> The principles reaffirmed in President Reagan's vision of the modern liberal democratic state are grounded in the conviction that the state should be subordinate to the society and not society to the state, that the market system is the most successful economic approach to stimulating production and distributing goods, and that the free individual is the source of creativity in the economic, political, and cultural spheres.[10]

This vision and the conviction that we are an "exceptional" people has long influenced American thinking, and it explains why we have rejected two alternatives to liberalism popular in Europe: socialism and conservatism. Socialism has never much appealed to Americans because the conditions that gave rise to it in the Old World—feudalism, gross social and economic inequalities, and the aristocracy's resistance to popular sovereignty—were not evident or were attenuated in the New World. At the same time, we have turned our backs on the Western conservative tradition. The American right has rejected European conservative impulses: hostility toward the industrial system and privatism, and a commitment to an organic society dominated by an elite opposed to cultural changes generated by modernity. This truism accounts for the claim that all Americans are liberals in the pure sense of the word.

Indeed, conservatives in the United States today oppose an organic view of society and a strengthening of political authority, because they deem them the twin pillars of a collectivist regime. They favor maintaining social safety-net programs to provide protection against economic disasters but oppose government attempts to reduce social and economic inequalities further because they consider them to be a natural part of the human condition. And in this respect they adhere to notions that have been part of Western conservative tradition for centuries.

To rely upon the capacity of the private sector to cope with our predicament, however, is a dangerous pretense that represents a grave threat to our national security. Thus we have arrived at one of this book's major themes: contemporary conservatives are ill-prepared to cope with the American predicament because they oppose two vital components of the conservative tradition—the belief that government is not a necessary evil but a natural part of the human condition, and the conviction that the cult of individualism denies a people the unity of purpose and cohesion essential to an orderly society.

Global Implications

Soviet analysts claim that neither the Republicans nor the Democrats can spare capitalism the crisis that will eventually consume it. When the cataclysm occurs, it will advance the cause of socialism worldwide. But Soviet theorists cannot ignore Marx's warning that the capitalists will not surrender without a fight. They must anticipate the Americans will adopt aggressive policies that will imperil the Soviet Union.

Lenin in his classic *Imperialism: The Highest State of Capitalism* wrote that the capitalists could avoid revolution by "exporting their contradictions" to other parts of the world; that is, they would dump their expensive surplus manufactured goods on the peoples of Asia, Africa, and Latin America and purchase commodities from the Third World, in turn, for deflated prices. With the handsome profits they earned from such transactions, they would pay their proletariat better wages, improve their working conditions, and provide them other amenities through the welfare state. This explanation of how Western capitalism would avoid revolution is consistent with Marxist theory, albeit updated by Lenin to reflect the changing circumstances of "mature" 20th century capitalism.

However, as Lenin noted, imperialism would only delay the disintegration of capitalism, and henceforth the struggle between socialism and capitalism would take on global dimensions. Even the *Wall Street Journal* concedes the U.S. economy is inextricably meshed with the international capitalist system and cannot escape its pitfalls, although its writers are optimistic about its prospects.

In their pronouncements Soviet officials claim that the Americans may escape the shocks of an internal crisis for years, but ultimately even the U.S. economy will succumb to its contradictions. In addition to internal dislocations, the Americans must contend with international ones. Capitalists in the Third World are now offering stiff competition to their competitors in Western Europe, North America, and even Japan. By exploiting the vast pool of low-wage labor at their command and with technology provided by the Americans and Japanese, they are undermining the economic position of working people and business firms in the Occident. To protect themselves from this competition, whatever the source, the mature capitalist countries have been resorting to neo-mercantilist policies. Witness the rise of protectionist fervor in the halls of Congress and demands on the part of business and labor leaders to "whack the Japs." Advocates of these policies claim that they be applied selectively, declaring that once the Japanese see that their anti-free-trade practices threaten all of the industrial democracies, they will come to their senses.

Observers in Moscow see these policies as symptoms of an economic system in grave crisis and that Western Europeans and North Americans will resort to full-scale economic warfare, such as preceded World War II and drove the Japanese to attack Pearl Harbor, once they see that they are incapable of sustaining a liberal international economic order. The Soviets proclaim that this is good news for the progressive and exploited peoples of the world, but that bad news goes along with it. To explain away their predicament, the Americans will point to the "communist menace."

Arbatov claims that some segments of the ruling class are prepared to embark upon a second cold war to prevent discord within America from reaching serious proportions. "It is not forgotten," he writes, "that during the Cold War the United States was a more 'organized' and 'disciplined' society, which simplified the task of governing. I suspect that many of those who have grown desperate over this 'ungovernability' expect a more tense international situation to make Americans more docile." Arbatov contends this is what prompted Washington to sabotage détente long before Moscow extended a helping hand to "progressive" movements in Angola, Ethiopia, and Afghanistan. The tough, anti-Soviet rhetoric Reagan employed his very first day in office was calculated "to provoke the Soviet Union into changing its policies, and thus justify a return to cold war."[11]

Henry Trofimenko, a colleague of Arbatov, has written that the United States is on a confrontation course with the USSR because Washington blames Moscow for revolutionary upheaval in the Third World. The United States, "by replacing the bullets of European colonialism with the dollars of neo-colonialism," has become "virtually the supreme master in the vast zone of developing countries...."[12] Under these circumstances the Americans perceive revolutionary movements in the less-developed countries (LDCs) as a threat to U.S. hegemony and are prepared to employ any means at their disposal, including military power, to crush them.

The Soviets contend, however, that military power will not prevent the victory of revolutionary forces in the Third World (as demonstrated by the U.S. war in Southeast Asia). This conclusion rests on the Marxist substructural/superstructural paradigm; that is, the substructure, or the economic base, of society determines all other institutions and values in the superstructure—the state, religion, culture, etc. This paradigm, the rationale for the definition of Marxists as economic determinists, is also the basis for the Soviet strategic concept of "correlation of forces." It involves the vast array of political, economic, military, and sociocultural factors that have a bearing on how well a country or bloc does in influencing relations with another country or bloc. Soviet strategists assert that military power (involving decisions made in a society's superstructure or political system) is one factor influencing the U.S.–Soviet rivalry. Military power is less important, however, than the economic and class-related elements at work in a country's substructure or economic realm and the equivalent forces operating on the world stage. In other words, neocolonialism is responsible for the economic exploitation in

Central America, which explains why the campesinos are picking up guns to fight the U.S.-backed oligarchies that have enslaved them for generations. Because peasants and workers in other LDCs are involved in the same struggle, the capacity of the U.S. neocolonialists to control international developments is on the decline everywhere in the world.

Consequently the collapse of "reactionary" regimes in the Third World is not the result of Kremlin policies, but rather the unfolding of historical forces beyond the control of either the United States or the USSR. Unfortunately, Americans do not think dialectically; they are thus inclined to "misperceive" the demise of pro-Western governments as part of a Soviet grand design for world conquest. While disputing such intentions, the Soviets are not hesitant in proclaiming that a change has taken place in the correlation of forces. "This change means a definite and irresistible tendency toward the increased influence of socialism on the course of world developments."[13] The declining capacity of the United States to influence international developments will deepen the domestic predicament, because U.S. exploitation of the developing countries has contributed to American economic prosperity. It is with this thought in mind that Washington has sought to change the course of history by striving to regain the dominant military position it enjoyed for several decades after World War II.

The issue of what policies the Soviets might adopt in the face of a global capitalist crisis will be treated later. As we shall see, if one occurs it may pose great dangers for the Soviet bloc—not just great opportunities. But one thing is clear: Soviet commentators claim that a U.S. military response to a change in the global correlation of forces is foolhardy because armed might cannot stop the engine of history. They lament, moreover, that it is dangerous because it will heighten East–West tensions and compel the socialist states to match the U.S. buildup. In short, it will produce a climate in which nuclear war becomes possible.

Implications for U.S.–Soviet Relations

What impact will the crisis in the Soviet Union have upon Moscow's foreign policy? And how should the United States respond to the Soviet Union in crisis? American policymakers must address these two critical questions because the outcome of the U.S.–Soviet rivalry may be decided on the second front of the competition, not the first one.

Many American Kremlin watchers are convinced that the Soviets will attempt to compensate for their internal problems by throwing their weight around abroad. Adam Ulam, perhaps the leading student of Soviet affairs in the United States, supports this proposition. He is by no means alone in this view. Seweryn Bialer, a prolific writer on the USSR, asserts:

In the 1980s Soviet leaders will need to find ways to counteract the effects of a decline in growth and possible stagnation in the standard of living, to alleviate frictions that develop among elites, to justify greater demands for sacrifice, and to mobilize the population for greater productivity.[14]

They will attempt to achieve this by stressing the "theme of external enemies," and by manipulating xenophobia among a people known to lean in that direction. Should the crises within their empire prompt the Soviets to become more aggressive abroad, there is little hope for the reduction in East–West tensions necessary to achieve arms control treaties and to negotiate a superpower code of conflict that minimizes U.S.–Soviet confrontations in the Third World.

This assessment of Soviet behavior during a period of crisis is consistent with the "window of vulnerability" scenario, which President Reagan frequently referred to in his first term. Proponents of the scenario claim it is comprised of three major elements.

First, the men in the Kremlin are bent on worldwide revolution. They may conduct summit conferences, engage in arms control discussions, and even display occasional signs of goodwill for tactical reasons, but they are as unyielding as Lenin in their quest to communize the world.

Second, and even worse, the Soviets possess a first-strike capability. By launching one-third of their massive ground-based ICBMs, they could destroy 90% of our land-based ICBM force. With their nuclear edge, they will engage us in a diplomacy of terror in the hope of destroying the Western Alliance and preventing the free world from challenging them in the LDCs. If need be, they are prepared to resort to nuclear war, and if they do, we would be forced to yield after they struck us first.

Third, the United States must close the window of vulnerability by deploying the MX missile, by upgrading our nation's C^3I—command control, communications, and intelligence—capability, by scrapping Mutual Assured Destruction in favor of a "limited nuclear war-fighting doctrine," and by deploying a "Star Wars" system.

In Reagan's second term, leading officials in Washington adopted a more upbeat mood—perhaps the window of vulnerability had been closed. Many analysts concluded that this was the finding of the Scowcroft Commission, which the president had established to explore a basing mode for the MX. Soon after Reagan's reelection, George Shultz claimed that the correlation of forces had shifted in Washington's favor, but in seeking more defense dollars Caspar Weinberger implied that the Soviets still enjoyed a nuclear edge.

Although official Washingon is at odds over the nature of the Soviet nuclear threat, there is a consensus that domestic problems have put the Soviets in peril. In *Survival is not Enough*, Richard Pipes urges that the United States wage economic warfare against the USSR, that now is the time to put pressure on the Soviet system.[15] This recommendation, along with the Soviet charge that the Reaganites hope to destroy the Soviet economy by engaging the USSR in a costly arms race, suggests the existence of a second front strategy.

Insofar as it exists, there are several problems with such a plan. First, the U.S. economy is twice as large as the Soviet economy, but Gorbachev can keep abreast of the Americans in an arms race by forcing his people to accept sacrifices that are unthinkable in the West. Second, developments within the USSR cannot be markedly affected by manipulating U.S. economic and technological resources. The dynamics of capitalism forecloses the possibility of economic warfare against the Soviets: Moscow can purchase products from the Europeans or Japanese if the United States refuses to sell them. Third, many scholars believe that faced with serious internal difficulties, Gorbachev will adopt less aggressive foreign policies and seek to reduce East–West tensions. We should welcome these initiatives because through détente we may enhance the influence of reformers in the USSR who wish to liberalize economic and political life there.

Finally, the United States has neglected its own vulnerabilities on the second front: political gridlock, economic volatility, and cultural disarray. Presently they do not constitute a grave threat to the country's security, but they can take on more lethal aspects if unresolved. Simultaneously, there are international problems—trade imbalances, monetary distortions, Third World debt, etc.—that can precipitate a global economic crisis capable of transforming the American predicament into a full-blown societal crisis. These can be avoided through the adoption of multilateral policies, but they demand a level of government intervention antithetical to the conservative ethos prevailing in the United States today.

Notes

1. John Patrick Diggins, "The New Republic and Its Times," *The New Republic*, 10 December 1984, p. 33.
2. Zbigniew Brzezinski, "The Soviet Political System: Transformation or Degeneration," in A. Brzezinski, ed., *Dilemmas of Change in Soviet Politics* (New York: Columbia University Press, 1960), pp. 1–24.
3. Alexander Dallin and Gail W. Lapidus, "Reagan and the Russians," in Kenneth Oye et al., eds. *Eagle Defiant* (Boston: Little, Brown and Co., 1983), p. 219.
4. *Washington Post*, 20 November 1983.
5. Timothy J. Colton, *The Dilemma of Reform in the Soviet Union* (New York: Council on Foreign Relations, 1984), p. 23.
6. Georgy Arbatov and William Oltmans, *The Soviet Viewpoint* (New York: Dodd, Mead, 1983), p. 24.
7. Arbatov and Oltmans, *The Soviet Viewpoint*, p. 6.
8. V. I. Lenin, *Imperialism: The Highest Stage of Capitalism* (New York: International Publishing, 1943).
9. Seymour Martin Lipset and William Schneider, *The Confidence Gap* (New York: The Free Press, 1983), pp. 411–12.

10. Jeane Kirkpatrick, *The Reagan Phenomenon* (Washington: The American Enterprise Institute, 1983), pp. 12–13.
11. Arbatov and Oltmans, *The Soviet Viewpoint*, p. 6.
12. Henry Trofimenko, "The Third World and the U.S.–Soviet Competition: A Soviet View," *Foreign Affairs* 59 (Summer 1981): 1224.
13. Quoted in Vernon Aspaturian, "Soviet Global Power and the Correlation of Forces," *Problems of Communism* (May–June 1980): 11.
14. Seweryn Bialer, *Stalin's Successors* (New York: Cambridge University Press, 1981), p. 301.
15. Richard Pipes, *Survival is Not Enough: Soviet Relations and America's Future* (New York: Simon and Schuster, 1984).

PART ONE

The Soviet Union in Crisis

CHAPTER ONE

An Economy in Crisis

We pretend to work, and they pretend to pay us. — Adage popular among Soviet workers

Socialism and the Search for Material Progress

An African delegate to an international arms control conference once told me, "The Americans and Russians claim to be different, but you aren't really all that different. You both believe there is a link between the production of pig iron and human happiness. The peoples of the Third World think otherwise."

It was difficult to take the speaker's last sentence seriously. He wore an expensive, three-piece, pin-striped suit and was making quick work of hors d'oeuvres spread over a large buffet table. Although a Muslim, he was not sipping orange juice or soda water, but Tennessee's best sour mash whiskey. Yet, like many of us who sometimes suffer from myopia when looking at our own society, he was seeing foreign countries with greater clarity than his own.

When citing similarities between the Soviet Union and the United States, it is customary to dwell upon their belonging to an elite club comprised of only two members—"the superpowers." Consequently a great deal is said about their awesome military might and their capacity to shape events in places far distant from their shores. Preoccupation with their superpower status, however, has overshadowed a vital fact about both countries that has a profound bearing upon U.S.–Soviet relations. Both share a revolutionary vision of human development—a belief in progress and the capacity of man to conquer nature and excel in every area of human endeavor.

This hubris has its roots in the Enlightenment, which provided mankind with the knowledge to manipulate the environment and lift the shroud of superstition and ignorance that had stunted human development for centuries. The Enlightenment established the intellectual framework for the industrial revolution, which in turn provided society with the prospect of material abundance. It is no wonder then that, like the American dream, "the ideological tradition of the USSR calls for unabating progress toward a more affluent society. . . ."[1] The Soviet ideologue in this sense is very bourgeois, the analogue of Sinclair Lewis' Babbitt. Soviet Marxists reject such "slander." They see little about capitalism that is worthy of emulation—at least that's what they proclaim.

This wasn't always the case. The founding fathers of "scientific socialism" did see a positive side to capitalism. In the Marxist framework, social phenomena can be either good or bad, depending upon the circumstances. Capitalism was good when it eliminated feudalism and the "idioticy of rural life." It was a progressive impulse when it produced the abundance necessary for mankind to advance to a higher state of development—socialism. Capitalism, however, became a reactionary force when the bourgeoisie resisted efforts to achieve a new social order, one that served the proletariat, the people who were responsible for capitalism's success in the first place.

Note that the Marxist vision of a socialist society was founded upon economic growth, technological innovation, and the application of science to the organization of society and the resolution of its problems. All of these elements characterize American liberalism, the public philosophy that has prevailed in the United States since its founding.

Kremlin spokesmen take exception to any implication that their worldview has much in common with the American vision of human well-being. While admitting that they are "materialists," they reject the accusation that their social vision is founded merely on economic output. People living in grinding poverty, of course, may look upon "socialism" with this prospect in mind, but educated revolutionaries who espouse Marxism–Leninism are searching for something more. They are, in the very best sense of the word, idealistic. They believe a social order can be designed where individual self-actualization and the advancement of the community are not mutually exclusive phenomena. In a socialist society, the individual can enjoy the warmth and comfort of community, a social condition shattered by capitalism, which is crassly materialistic in the worst sense of the word.

Soviet commentators assert that their citizens support the regime because it espouses a worldview superior to the one prevailing in the capitalist West. But while the Soviet people look at the world through the prism of Marxist–Leninist categories, few of them believe the USSR is about to become a communist utopia. This is no great revelation—it is common knowledge on both sides of the Iron Curtain. Ideological orthodoxy may motivate elements of the Soviet elite, and some ordinary citizens too, but they are the exception to the rule.[1] Conventional Western opinion, however, that social order in the USSR rests exclusively on fear of the KGB and "administrative" measures adopted by other state bureaucracies to crush dissidents and keep the people in line is also fallacious.

Support for the regime stems from an array of different sources: patriotism, pride in the country's superpower status, the deference to authority typical of people who have always lived in a despotic society, and a conviction that their rulers have the best interests of the people at heart. This may be truer of the Russians than of other ethnic groups, but it is by no means peculiar to the country's dominant nationality. In one poll of Soviet Jews living in Israel, 90% of the sample claimed that the Soviet authorities cared about the people's welfare.[2] While a number of factors explain why Soviet citizens deem their government legitimate, the regime's ability to raise living standards is one of the most important ones.

The Creation of the Soviet System

Under Tsar Nicholas II, the material conditions endured by the Russian masses were pitiful. Millions were illiterate and malnourished, and starvation was common in many parts of the empire. Housing conditions were abysmal, and health care was close to nonexistent in the villages where most of the people lived. Infant mortality was high, and the life expectancy of the adult population was years below that in other parts of Europe. The tsar's indifference to the ignorance and poverty of his subjects was unconscionable. It eventually led to the downfall of the Romanov dynasty.

The Bolsheviks took power promising to improve the living standards of the suffering Soviet people, and some American observers claim that their success accounts for the regime's longevity. Jerry Hough writes:

> Rule by the Communist Party was accompanied by upward mobility for a large percentage of the Soviet people. In the 1920s and early 1930s, an astonishing proportion of the skilled working class was promoted into administrative or professional positions, either directly or after having been sent to college. . . .[3]

Moreover, "rapid mobility [did not cease] after the Great Purge of 1937–38." Indeed, the purges opened up possibilities for advancement for tens of thousands of young people who normally would have to wait many years before being promoted. They acquired influential positions in the party, government, military, and industry a generation before it was possible to do so in other societies. Nikita Khrushchev, Leonid Brezhnev, Yuri Andropov, and Konstantin Chernenko all were beneficiaries of the purges; hence the origin of the appellation, "the class of '38."

Russians were not the only ones to improve their lot. Most inhabitants of the USSR, especially those who lived in Central Asia and other backwaters of the empire, benefited as well. Hough notes that, in a bid to secure the support of non-Russians, "the regime . . . from the beginning not only permitted but even promoted the movement of members of local nationalities into college, into the party, and into higher status jobs within the republics."[4]

There is no disputing that economic growth provided support for the Soviet regime, but the preceding analysis is a rather Pollyannaish portrayal of economic prosperity under Stalin's reign. There was a darker aspect to Stalin's massive economic development campaign. According to Seweryn Bialer, Stalin was committed to rapid industrial growth "regardless of the social cost." His drive to modernize and collectivize the Soviet economy had little to do with improving the people's living standards. His primary objective was twofold: to consolidate the Bolsheviks' political power and establish the industrial infrastructure necessary to build a mighty Red Army.

Economic policy, from the outset of the Soviet regime, was inextricably linked with its ability to govern. Little thought was given to the people's welfare per se. Stalin was aware that improved living conditions would spur the masses to work harder, but he looked to the stick with greater expectations. Terror was the defining feature of Stalinism, and the major instrument of terror was the secret police.

> Far from acting as an autonomous, discrete, and secret force, the "secret" police was an open and recognized political force, glorified and praised in the media, highly visible at all official ceremonies and political assemblies, and extolled by Soviet propaganda as a prime example for emulation.[5]

Stalin's use of terror to telescope economic growth in the USSR in decades rather than centuries has been discussed often and at length. We need only recall that millions were killed and equally large numbers imprisoned in labor camps to "build socialism" in the Soviet Union. Yet there is no question that Stalin's unstinting commitment to heavy industry and rapid economic expansion enabled the Soviet Union to absorb the German blitzkrieg in June 1941.

After the Germans surrendered, many American commentators assumed that he would reward his people by improving their living standards. They had suffered unspeakable hardships during the "Great Patriotic War" and had displayed great courage in fighting the Germans. With a buffer zone in Eastern Europe and no serious threat to the USSR on the continent, Stalin surely could channel some investments from the Soviet war machine into agriculture and the production of consumer goods. Stalin, however, persisted in emphasizing heavy industry, gigantic enterprises, and sheer volume of output, and ignored the needs of the Soviet people who lived close to subsistence. The centralization of economic decisionmaking militated against innovation and enterprise at the local level. Stalin's "command economy" was well suited for a Soviet Union in the takeoff stage of development but inappropriate for a society whose future development depended upon quality, precision, and flexibility. The consumer goods made available were not only meager but shoddy.

With Stalin's passing in 1953, his successors sought to circumscribe the Stalinist network of terror, largely because it was people like themselves—the visible members of society—who were most likely candidates for liquidation or imprisonment in the gulag. They neither permitted political dissent nor tolerated intellectual freedom, but they sought to win the people's cooperation by meeting workers' and peasants' basic needs and providing the "middle class" with some of the amenities Westerners enjoyed.

It was with these goals in mind that Nikita Khrushchev embarked upon a course of "goulash communism." He realized that the regime could not survive if the Soviet people had to endure the hardships Stalin had imposed upon them. They wanted more and better food, labor-saving devices, decent housing, and other amenities that made life more bearable. Consequently, Khrushchev reduced investment in heavy industry and increased funding for agriculture and light manufacturing. He also sought to moderate defense spending. He moved erratically, however, so that when he encountered resistance to a proposed reform—such as the decentralization of economic decisionmaking—he backed down. But during most of his stewardship, the Soviet GNP grew about five percent annually, and living conditions of the Soviet people improved.

In visits to capitalist countries in the late 1950s, Khrushchev boasted that the Soviet Union would "bury" the West in the race for economic growth and technological innovation. He told the Twenty-Second Party Congress:

> Comrades, the Communist Party is advancing a great task—to achieve in the coming 20 years a living standard higher than that of any capitalist country and to create the necessary conditions for achieving an abundance of material and cultural values.[6]

Soon after he made this proclamation, he was deposed—in part because his economic policies were not as successful as he claimed they were.

The military and the managers of heavy industry helped topple Khrushchev; they could not forgive him for cutting their budgets. His successors, therefore, realized that they had to pacify the generals and neo-Stalinists. They did just that in the second half of the 1960s when the Soviet Union began a massive military buildup. Nonetheless, the collegial leadership in the Kremlin remained committed to improving the people's living standards. High rates of economic growth enabled them to pursue a policy of "guns and butter" simultaneously.

Leonid Brezhnev, who would emerge as "the first among equals," was especially interested in agriculture because as a young man he had been a land use specialist and had later presided over the Virgin Lands program. As his grip over the centers of power tightened, Brezhnev fought for heavier investments in agriculture, and he pressed for increased meat production in particular. He adroitly defended this shift in emphasis by claiming that he was seeking to free the USSR from its dependency upon foreign food sources. In other words, he induced hard-liners to perceive his farm reforms as vital to the country's "national security." Careful not to alienate the military, he funded his agricultural programs by cutting the budgets of civilian transport, health care, and other sectors of the economy lacking powerful friends in Moscow. He left the military budget intact.

After Brezhnev died in 1982, he was replaced by Yuri Andropov, who according to some accounts was a lover of American jazz and Scotch whiskey; an intelligent, cosmopolitan man who spoke English and was something of a liberal. A liberal he was not: he had served as Soviet ambassador to Hungary in the fateful year of 1956; later, as head of the KGB, he helped crush the dissident movement. But he was pragmatic and forthright. The time had come, he said, to recognize that the economy was in grave difficulty and that concrete measures had to be taken to restore it to health. Failure to do so would place the security of the USSR in grave jeopardy. In the 1970s GNP growth had slipped to 3.7% during the 1971–1975 plan and to 2.7% during the 1976–1980 plan.[7]

Andropov refuted Brezhnev's claim that the Soviet Union had become a "developed socialist society." The Soviet Union, he said, had a long way to go, and the process of development was uneven, not linear. "In some areas we will be able to move more quickly, in other areas more slowly. This is what the real map of social progress is like. It cannot be smoothed out into a straight line."[8] He warned Soviet managers and workers alike that he meant business, that he would replace dead wood in the bureaucracy and that he would enforce labor discipline. To underscore Andropov's resolve, the Soviet press reported that shirkers were being pulled out of the bathhouses and diverted from other activities when they were supposed to be at work.

Andropov did not live long enough to put his policies into effect. Konstantin Chernenko, a Brezhnev protégé who replaced Andropov, said he would move along these lines. But he was sick and frail, and not up to taking on the bureaucrats and some colleagues in the Politburo who preferred stagnation to the uncertainties of change.

Mikhail Gorbachev was groomed by Andropov to replace the former KGB chief, and it is alleged that Gorbachev was really the power behind the throne during Chernenko's short reign. It is no wonder, therefore, that he has pledged to follow Andropov's policies. He has fired inept officials in the party and government and has removed managers for their poor performance. He has instituted programs to increase worker productivity and has warned shirkers that they will lose their jobs if they do not labor in earnest.

It will be years before one can determine the success of Gorbachev's policies. They may never be implemented but disappear into the vast black hole of the Soviet bureaucracy, or they may only modestly improve an economy that is in deep trouble. One thing is clear: Gorbachev realizes that the regime's viability rests upon its ability to close the economic gap between East and West and to improve the Soviet people's living standards through growth and innovation.

Macroeconomic Perspectives

Since the mid-1970s, the Soviet economy has not matched the growth rates of the 1960s and early 1970s, and there is some doubt whether it can provide both guns and butter in the future as it has in the past. The Western media have devoted a great deal of time to details of the USSR's economic troubles, so we need not dwell on them here, but merely outline some major features.

The sad state of agriculture exemplifies the serious obstacles that Gorbachev will have to overcome if he is going to revitalize the Soviet economy. Stalin's policies did lasting damage to Soviet agriculture. From 1928 to 1953, "livestock and grain production dropped. Collectivized agriculture resulted in the over-extension of the state bureaucracy into agriculture and the loss of peasant incentives to increase production beyond subsistence levels."[9] The peasants had, in effect, underwritten Stalin's Grand Transformation, and they suffered grievously for the privilege. The Soviet consumer paid dearly for Stalin's mishandling of agriculture, too. Meat, eggs, milk, fruit, and vegetables were scarce for many years after his death. "Facing an agricultural crisis," Krushchev "took immediate steps to reform Stalin's policies and increase output. He raised state procurement prices, reduced compulsory sales to the state, cut taxes on private plots, and cut transport and marketing costs."[10] To revitalize private agriculture, peasants were encouraged to increase the size of their plots and herds. In 1954 the ambitious Virgin Land program began, "which added some 74 million acres of land to production in Southern Russia, Kazakhstan, and Siberia over a 3-year period."[11]

For a while, Khrushchev's economic policies were successful. From 1953 to 1958, agricultural production increased by 40%. But then he returned to more rigid policies hostile to private incentives, which had increased output. The Virgin Land campaign, moreover, proved a failure, and from 1959 to 1964, agriculture grew by only 13%.[12] This turnabout in the fortunes of agriculture clearly contributed to Khrushchev's downfall in October 1964.

As indicated, Brezhnev devoted even more money to upgrading Soviet agriculture than Khrushchev did. "From 1961 to 1969 some 19% of national investment was allocated to agriculture; between 1976 and 1980 this figure increased to 27%."[13] It appeared that this massive injection of rubles into agriculture would help resolve the USSR's farm problem. From 1964 to 1970, agricultural output increased annually by an average of 3.9%, but in the early 1970s, farm production plunged to 1.2% and deteriorated even further in the mid-1970s. By the end of the decade, the Soviets withheld agricultural production statistics, presumably because the Kremlin did not want to share bad news with its people and with foreigners. In the late 1970s, the USSR had to import grain to compensate for several years of bad harvests. By 1981 Soviet imports exceeded exports by $16 billion, largely because of these circumstances.

The USSR lags far behind the United States in agricultural production. U.S. specialists estimate that output per Soviet farm worker is 11% that of the U.S. farm worker. The Soviet estimate is higher — 20 to 25% of the U.S. figure — but it clearly demonstrates how poor the Soviets' agricultural performance is. Soviet inefficiency in agriculture is illustrated by another comparison with the United States: 22.7% of the Soviet labor force is in agriculture, compared to 3.2% for the United States.[14]

One explanation for this discrepancy is that the United States enjoys an advantage in the mechanization of its agricultural sector. Another is that the USSR encompasses the world's largest land mass, but most of it lies north of the 45th parallel, where growing seasons are short and the soil is poor. Furthermore, the Soviet Union does not enjoy adequate rainfall for its crops. "Only 1 percent of the Soviet farmland receives 28 inches of rainfall a year, an amount that nearly all American states receive in one year."[15]

Finally, analysts cite centralized decision-making as a factor contributing to low farm output. Farm managers complain about nonsensical instructions from bureaucrats, who live and work in cities far distant from the Soviet heartland. Brezhnev recognized this problem and often made speeches pledging to allow local managers to have a greater voice in their operations. But in face of the awesome power of the Soviet bureaucracy, he never implemented such reforms.

Turning to manufacturing, productivity in the Soviet Union is half that of the United States. Soviet planners have sought to compensate for this deficiency by pumping massive sums of capital into the economy. Over the years, they had typically invested the equivalent of 30% of their GNP to sustain economic growth. By comparison, the United States has contributed about 16% of its GNP for this purpose.[16] Indications are that the Soviet economy will not generate sufficient capital to upgrade and modernize its industrial base. This means Moscow's reliance on Western credits and hard cash will rise. In 1981, for example, 40% of Soviet hard currency came from trade with the West, amounting to $38 billion.

Soviet planners cannot look upon this dependence with pleasure. It is another indication that the Soviet economy is becoming more closely integrated into a world economy dominated by capitalists. There is still justification for the claim that the Soviet economy is self-sufficient, but it is based on the Kremlin's long-term acceptance of slow economic growth rates. If the USSR wants to close the economic gap with the West, it must look forward to even more intimate economic relations with capitalist economies than is the case today.

Another way the Soviets have sought to compensate for low productivity has been through a massive infusion of labor into the economy. By putting more people to work, the Soviets compensate for low productivity and outmoded technology. They will not be able to do so in the future. The CIA reports:

> Additions to the working-age population have been falling since the mid-1970s because of the lower birth rates of the 1960s, an increase in the number of workers reaching retirement age, and a rising mortality rate among males in the 25 to 44 age range. These increments will be lower in the next several years than at any time in the last several decades. In fact, they will be less than one-third of the annual additions to the work force in the first half of the 1970s.[17]

This condition, together with an investment crunch, will seriously hamper economic growth rates for the rest of the 1980s and perhaps well into the next decade.

To make matters worse, declining economic output will depress living standards, which, in turn, will provide a disincentive for young couples to have children. As is true of the United States, there is a correlation between child-bearing women in the labor force and low birth rates, but the Soviet economy needs these women, and they need to work because a single breadwinner cannot support the average Soviet family. The Soviets, therefore, are in a Catch-22 situation. In European areas of the USSR, families will not grow without expanded income, but living standards will not increase without steady, massive infusion of labor into the economy.

The Achilles' heel of all Soviet bloc countries, of course, continues to be centralized planning. The command economy has hampered industrial and agricultural output because "it is nothing like the rational command mechanism it is supposed to be. Rather, it is an exercise in log rolling and pork barreling that would evoke envy on Capitol Hill. . . ."[18] Some brave soul in the USSR have said as much for years, but to no avail. To strip the power of the Moscow bureaucrats and pass it on to their counterparts at the regional and local levels represents grave political risks in the eyes of the Soviet managerial and party elite. As good Marxists, they know that political power flows from economic influence, so pronouncements to the contrary, they have not adopted reforms that diffuse power from the center to the system's extremities.

Recently the Kremlin has provided a new excuse for remaining wedded to the command economy—the computer. High-speed computers can gather and process the kind of information that a free market system makes available. Thus one can have the benefits of a free market without the limitations of political pluralism. As British economist Martin Cave has observed, "the computer encourages Party and planning officials to believe there is a central solution" to their economic problems, that they need not adopt reforms that will jeopardize their political prerogatives.[19] This is wishful thinking, of course. It is a flight from reality; the latter dictates that improvements in the Soviet economy can occur only through economic decentralization, the introduction of free market mechanisms, and other reforms threatening to the political hegemony of the party and to the technocrats and bureaucrats serving it.

In addition, the Soviet Union is far behind the United States in computer technology. In 1977, the last year for which reliable data is available, the USSR had an estimated 20,000 computers as compared with 325,000 in the United States.[20] Moreover, millions of Americans are computer literate, and the computer has been integrated into U.S. society to a degree that the Soviets are unlikely to match until the 21st century (perhaps not even then, given the fear that computers can be used by "anti-Soviet" elements against the regime).

Finally, massive defense spending has contributed to Soviet economic problems. The Cuban Missile Crisis and Brezhnev's ascendency to the post of general secretary precipitated a dramatic increase in the military budget. Between 1965 and 1976, defense spending grew an average of 4 to 5% per year. Afterward, it declined to a rate of 2% annually, but the CIA estimates that the Soviets devote 13 to 14% of their GNP to the armed forces:

> [This] is considerably higher than the comparable 7-percent figure for the United States. The defense share of the Soviet GNP has remained roughly constant since 1965 because the growth of defense spending has matched overall economic growth. [Consequently,] when economic growth slowed after 1975, defense spending growth slowed correspondingly.[21]

But huge defense outlays alone do not explain the relationship between defense spending and the Soviet crisis. The Soviet defense industry attracts the best-qualified scientists, engineers, technicians, and managers. It has a priority over other sectors of the economy when it comes to equipment, raw materials, etc. It demands and gets the best Soviet society has to offer.

This situation accounts for an anomaly that has captured the attention of many Westerners. How can a society produce the latest and deadliest nuclear weapons, yet not build adequate housing for its citizens and provide them with appliances that work, quality clothing, and decent food? The answer is that the most developed sector of the Soviet economy is closely tied to the defense industry and that only second-rate workers, and managers, are assigned to civilian purposes.

This assessment of the Soviet Union's macroeconomic problems, though brief, provides background for two related questions. First, to what extent is the economic predicament harming the Soviet people? Second, if the economic crisis worsens, will it spawn political discontent capable of endangering the regime? Because there are many factors bearing on a people's political consciousness, this is a difficult question to answer under the best of circumstances. It is an especially difficult task when it is directed at a closed society where there is little reliable information about public attitudes. Nonetheless, since the link between the USSR's economic plight and political discontent is a focal point of our inquiry, we cannot ignore it.

Class Division in Soviet Society

There are classes in the Soviet Union, just as there are in capitalist countries. At the very pinnacle of Soviet society perch the leading members of the communist party, government, industry, military, and the arts. Émigré Soviet journalist and historian Alexander Yanov calls them the Soviet aristocracy. Other writers refer to them as the *nomenklatura*—people who obtain high office through a secret selection system. They are privileged members of the Soviet Union who earn dramatically more money than the average citizen and have access to special stores where Western goods, unobtainable elsewhere, can be purchased. They own summer homes and are allowed to travel freely throughout the Soviet empire. The most privileged of all can even visit the West. Like their counterparts in other parts of the world, the Soviet elite want to pass their prerogatives of power, money, and status on to their children. Because of their influence, they can be rest assured that even if the economy stagnates, their living standards will not suffer much, if at all.

But what about the people who really make the system work, those who belong to the growing army of energetic and hard-working men and women we in the West call the middle class? In the USSR, the middle-level office functionaries, doctors, dentists, engineers, and agronomists, as well as members of the intellectual professions, have served as an adhesive holding Soviet society together even during periods of social disintegration like the collectivization and industrialization drive prior to World War II. Beginning in the 1950s, the middle class experienced economic gains, and conditions improved further in the 1960s. Consumer goods the average American took for granted—televisions, telephones, labor-saving appliances, and even automobiles—were made available to a growing number of people. By U.S. standards, they were of poor quality, but for the Soviet middle class, they were concrete evidence that things were getting better.

In the mid-1970s, however, the faltering economy began to affect the middle class. Its members were earning larger salaries than in the past, but with shrinkage in economic output and curtailment in the production of consumer goods, all of these cherished items were exceedingly more difficult to purchase. What good was having money if one could not buy items that one desired? The general scarcity of consumer goods, quality food, and the like, compounding the drabness of life, is a source of concern to the Soviet middle class. What troubles them most about the system is not the absence of political liberty but its inefficiency, its corruptness, and the belief that the economy is no longer working on their behalf. This, by the way, is the conclusion of an American scholar who believes that reports about rising discontent rooted in the economic predicament have been greatly exaggerated.[22]

Perhaps he is right, but he concedes that the Soviet middle class has grave doubts about its economic future. And all Kremlinologists in the West agree that materialism has become a way of life in the USSR. The transcendent vision that had attracted millions of idealists to Marxism for over 100 years has been replaced in the first Marxist society by the promise of material well-being—the holy grail of bourgeois life that Marx so scathingly attacked.

Some scholars claim there is "a residue of optimism about the system" in the middle class, but these scientists, managers, and technocrats are in a position to cause the authorities serious problems.[23] The Soviet rulers know this, for the middle class has the expertise the Kremlin badly needs to reduce the East–West economic gap. Time, therefore, is not on the regime's side. Indeed, the younger members of the middle class, having been spared the privations of the past, are more likely than their elders to be impatient. Their economic expectations, of course, are not measured in terms of Western living standards, but rather by the quality of life that millions of them have observed in Eastern Europe firsthand. Nonetheless, the Soviet Union suffers as a result of this comparison. How galling it must be to the Russian professional who travels to East Berlin or Budapest to discover that even ordinary people there have the opportunity to purchase consumer goods unavailable back home. How maddening it must be to ponder the disconcerting truth that in social systems much like their own, Czechs, East Germans, and Hungarians enjoy higher living standards than they do.

The ruling elite in the USSR knows it cannot allow the middle class's living standards to slip too far, and it is likely that the Kremlin will make an effort to preclude dramatic economic setbacks. This has been the case for years. Westerners who have had the opportunity to compare life styles in the cosmopolitan areas of the Soviet Union—Leningrad, Kiev, and Moscow—with those in smaller cities and provincial towns have reported that the authorities have made a concerted effort to stock the stores in the large cities with goods unobtainable elsewhere in the country. In the "workers' paradise," then, the ruling elite will strive to protect the middle class from setbacks linked to slow rates of economic growth, passing the burden of sacrifice on to the workers and peasants instead.

How will the workers and peasants, who represent a majority of the Soviet population, respond to a reversal in their living standards? Material conditions have improved for all strata in the USSR, including the urban proletariat and the farm workers. But gains achieved during an era of economic growth may work against the regime during a period of economic decline. Students of social change have found that social upheaval usually occurs in the wake of a period of prosperity followed by economic hard times. The Soviet masses, who have improved their living standards, therefore, may not suffer setbacks in silence. There are a number of reasons why they may become disgruntled.

Discontent, Dissent and the Potential for Protest

The major complaint of Soviet consumers is about food. The average Soviet family spends about half its income on food, and this observation vividly underscores why its availability is so important to the Soviet people. Workers in the Soviet Union have enough to eat, but quantity is not at issue here— quality is. Specifically, they want more meat on the supper table and fewer starches and crude vegetables like cabbage. This may strike Americans as a rather mundane issue—especially as more of them are eating less steak today than in the past—but it is no laughing matter in the USSR, where workers consume less red meat than do the poor in the United States.

In a survey of Soviet émigrés conducted by Radio Free Europe, the respondents painted a bleak picture. A former Muscovite reported that "in order to buy milk, meat and butter, one had to get up at dawn and travel to the outskirts of the city." An artist from Leningrad complained, "butter sometimes disappeared for two days in a row. . . . Milk was on sale in the morning, but sold out in two or three hours." Finally, a teacher from Central Asia revealed that food was such a treasured item that "it was better to be paid with food than with money."[24]

After food, housing is the largest issue to Soviet consumers. Many people must share apartments with other families, and in spite of past progress, there will not be a great deal of improvement in the future, especially as Kremlin planners struggle to invest in activities that promote foreign exchange, such as energy, or that safeguard the nation, such as missiles and tanks. Under Soviet law, the state is bound to provide 9 square meters of shelter per person. In spite of improvements in the 1960s and 1970s, the best the government could do in 1977 was to provide 8.2 square meters per person. A U.S. economist has concluded:

> Perhaps the most telling reflection of the problem is that in 1980, 20 percent of the Soviet population still live in communal apartments. This means that one or more families each have a room in what would normally be a one-family apartment, and that toilets and kitchens are shared.[25]

Westerners who write about Soviet workers agree that the declining opportunity for advancement is another source of discontent. It is ironic that in a "workers' state" the ruling elite has inspired workers to move beyond that position, but such is the case. The promise that one could rise above the station in life to which one was born—and perhaps of larger importance, that one's children could move from the ranks of the working class to the exalted heights of the Soviet middle class—has enhanced the status of the regime in the people's eyes. Yet it is no longer true that men and women from modest backgrounds can move from the bottom to higher rungs of the social ladder as their parents and grandparents did. As one commentator, who thinks it unlikely that worker discontent will ever reach significant proportions, concedes, "The son of a worker cannot assume that, down the line, an engineer's job waits" for him.[26]

Recently American demographers have found health statistics that provide shocking evidence of decreased quality of life in the USSR. In the 1930s and 1940s, the government improved health care so that by the late 1950s, "the average Soviet citizen could expect to live 68.7 years; longer than his American counterpart, who had begun the century with a seventeen-year lead." Moreover, "By 1960, the Soviet infant mortality rate, higher than any in Europe as late as the Twenties, was lower than that of Italy, Austria, or East Germany. . . ." Since the mid-1960s, however, life expectancy in the USSR is six years lower than in Western Europe, and infant mortality three times as high. "Measured by the health of its people, the Soviet Union is no longer a developed nation. . . . In the realm of health, the Soviet Union's peers are to be found in Latin America and Asia."[27]

Because most Westerners are discouraged by the government to travel extensively in the Soviet countryside, we know less about the plight of the peasants than we do about the industrial proletariat. On the basis of available reports, the people who till the soil on collective and state farms, or those few who work their own private plots, are generally worse off than the urban population. There may be exceptions, for example, in parts of Central Asia and the Caucasus and areas where agricultural output is high. But living conditions in European areas of the Soviet Union, where most Russians live, are especially grim.

Émigrés from the USSR paint an even bleaker picture than the one portrayed by Western scholars. Alexandr Solzhenitsyn, for example, claims that economic conditions in the Soviet Union are declining and that the lowest living standards of all are to be found in the Russian Republic:

> [T]oday the most poverty-stricken rural areas of the USSR are the Russian villages. The same is true of Russian provincial towns, which have not seen meat, butter or eggs for decades and which can only dream of even such simple fare as macaroni and margarine.[28]

One indication of just how bad things are for the Russian peasant is that some Western analysts refuse to acknowledge that declining living standards will foster political discontent among urban workers because so many of them recall just how awful things were, and are, back on the farm. It can be assumed that if health care and other critical services have slipped in the cities, conditions must be even worse in the countryside. Solzhenitsyn claims that living conditions have so deteriorated in the Soviet Union that bread strikes and other violent signs of discontent are on the rise. Although most writers in the United States believe he has exaggerated the situation, they admit that worker discontent is on the upswing. It takes many forms.

The Soviet media do not try to hide the fact that alcohol abuse is rampant and represents a serious threat to productivity. Reducing the consumption of alcohol is one of Gorbachev's top priorities, but in spite of his crackdown, signs of public drunkenness are common and widespread. Because of drinking bouts that last long into the night (as long as the vodka is available), many workers are unable to report to work. Others arrive so inebriated they can barely stand up. Consequently, the quantity and quality of their output suffers. Alcohol abuse also accounts for a high incidence of industrial accidents.

Other symptoms of worker discontent are illustrated by high rates of absenteeism unrelated to drinking, the practice of expropriating "socialist property" for one's own private use, and high rates of crime and juvenile delinquency among working people. One of the most telling signs of worker discontent is the widely expressed view that "we pretend to work, and they pretend to pay us." This aphorism may amuse editors at the *Wall Street Journal*, but it is no joke to the economic writers at *Pravda*.

The single most important indicator of worker and consumer discontent, however, is exemplified by the flourishing underground economy, which is so vital that the regime could not squelch it without doing grave damage to the economy. The underground economy is run for private gain in violation of Soviet law. It takes many forms. For example, a manager who is behind his production quotas may purchase goods from a private entrepreneur or manager from another plant, via a barter arrangement. Or, unable to get his car fixed quickly through proper channels, a consumer exchanges parts (filched from his factory) in payment to a mechanic servicing his car. Although it is difficult to estimate the ruble amounts involved, both Western and Soviet observers indicate that the underground economy has become an integral part of economic activity in the Soviet Union. Whatever the precise magnitude of the practice and the money involved, a flourishing underground economy is further proof that the Soviet economic system is in deep trouble. For tens of millions of people, the only way to cope with economic dislocations is to operate outside the system.

Nevertheless, Kremlinologists caution us not to jump to the conclusion that these economic conditions will lead to political protest. Soviet workers, we are told, are preoccupied with "gradual minor improvements rather than with sweeping changes in income, status and other social indicators." They have endured hardships in the past and are prepared to do the same in the future. Moreover, "the workers' basic perceptions are generally positive and pro-system."[29] They passively accept the autocratic rule of the Soviet elite, a condition of powerlessness at work and in the polity that would be intolerable to U.S. workers. Displaying a traditional Russian aversion to anarchy, many of them speak favorably about Stalin because when he ran things, no one dared to rock the boat. Consequently, intellectual dissidents, whom many Soviet workers perceive as "boat rockers," have had little luck attracting the Soviet proletariat to their cause for democratic reform. It is unthinkable, according to American Sovietologists, that a significant number of them would conduct the kind of strikes which have occurred in Poland, or complain about phony, state-controlled unions, much less demand the expulsion of corrupt public officials from office.

Bialer cautions against confusing dissent, which is politically significant, and discontent, which is not. In this connection, he makes a distinction between "high" and "low" politics. High politics involve issues with which intellectual dissidents like Andrei Sakharov have been associated—freedom of speech and assembly, the rule of law, and the like. Low politics is associated with issues that are important to ordinary people in their communities and work places—overcrowded apartments, the availability of food, working conditions, pay scales, etc. Economic hard times may cause disgruntlement among workers, compelling them to speak out about matters that can be categorized as "low politics," but they will not join the tiny minority in the USSR that realizes such issues are linked to "high politics."[30]

In spite of this, and other conditions that serve as deterrents to organized protest on the part of the Soviet workers, their declining economic fortunes are a potential source of unrest. There is no disputing that the Soviet regime will be faced with serious economic problems in the 1980s, and even if millions of disgruntled Soviet citizens do not press their government for relief in an organized fashion—as occurred in Poland—they will take measures at work that will deepen the economic crisis. They will work less, drink and steal more, and sabotage efforts to improve output. Moreover, to predict future worker discontent by employing criteria from previous generations (such as fear of authority or low expectations)—as most American analysts of the Soviet Union are inclined to do—is to ignore the fact that younger workers in the Soviet Union, who have tasted a better way of life, are unlikely to endure a protracted period of economic hard times in silence. And once the silence is broken, history instructs us that pent-up forces can be set into motion and take on unpredictable forms—perhaps massive strikes, violent clashes with the police, and organized protests, which would prompt the authorities to respond in a manner that are only likely to exacerbate the people's discontent.

There is little reason, on the basis of past behavior, to forecast that popular disgruntlement with living standards will spawn widespread violence or organized protest. But economic stagnation is only one of several problems that may arouse the Soviet people from their slumber. The Soviet authorities must worry about three other problems in particular: persistent and widespread demands on the part of ethnic minorities in the USSR for a greater voice in matters affecting their lives, turmoil in Eastern Europe, and the uncertainty associated with a changing of the guard from the older to the younger generation.

In short, Gorbachev and his colleagues are confronting an accumulation of interrelated problems which, together, may create a critical mass, thus producing a cumulative effect greater than the sum of its parts. Soviet spokespersons and Western commentators would have us believe that the Soviet empire will be spared the upheaval and insurrection that have destroyed other great empires. No one can predict with certainty that this fate awaits the USSR—but neither can one declare that it does not.

Notes

1. Jerry F. Hough and Merle Fainsod, *How the Soviet Union is Governed* (Cambridge, MA: Harvard University Press, 1979), pp. 561–2.
2. John Bushnell, "The New Soviet Man Turns Pessimist," *Survey*, no. 24 (September 1979), p. 6.
3. Hough and Fainsod, *How the Soviet Union*, pp. 561–2.
4. Hough and Fainsod, *How the Soviet Union*, p. 562.
5. Seweryn Bialer, *Stalin's Successors* (New York: Cambridge University Press, 1981), p. 15.
6. James R. Millar, "A Economic Overview," in James Cracraft, ed., *The Soviet Union Today* (Chicago: University of Chicago Press, 1983), p. 173.
7. Millar, "An Economic Overview," p. 175.
8. Timothy J. Colton, *The Dilemma of Reform in the Soviet Union* (New York: Council on Foreign Relations, 1984), p. 14.
9. David N. Balaam and Michael J. Carey, "Agri-Policy in the Soviet Union and Eastern Europe," in Balaam and Carey, eds., *Food Politics: The Regional Conflict* (Montclair, NJ: Allanheld, Osman, 1983), p. 53.
10. Balaam and Carey, "Agri-Policy in the Soviet Union," p. 53.
11. Balaam and Carey, "Agri-Policy in the Soviet Union," p. 53.
12. Balaam and Carey, "Agri-Policy in the Soviet Union," p. 54.
13. D. Gale Johnson, "Agriculture," in Cracraft, *The Soviet Union Today*, (Chicago: University of Chicago Press, 1983), p. 197.
14. Herbert Block, "The Economic Basis of Soviet Power," in Edward Luttwak, ed., *The Grand Strategy of the Soviet Union* (New York: St. Martin's Press, 1983), p. 153.
15. Balaam and Carey, "Agri-Policy in the Soviet Union," p. 49.
16. *Business Week*, 1 October, 1981, p. 78.
17. Robert Gates, "The Allocation of Resources in the Soviet Union and China—1984," statement before the U.S. Joint Economic Committee (November 21, 1984), p. 17.
18. *Business Week*, 1 October, 1981, p. 78.
19. *Business Week*, 1 October, 1981, p. 78.
20. Seweryn Bialer, *The Soviet Paradox* (New York: Alfred A. Knopf, 1986), p. 77.
21. Gates, "The Allocation of Resources," pp. 11–12.
22. Walter D. Connor, "Workers, Politics, and Class Consciousness," in Arcadius Kahan and Blair A. Ruble, eds., *Industrial Labor in the USSR* (Elmsford, NY: Pergamon Press, 1979), pp. 313–29.
23. For example, Bushnell, "The New Soviet Man."

24. *Washington Post*, 7 May, 1982.
25. Marshal I. Goldman, "The Economy and the Consumer," in Cracraft, *The Soviet Union Today*, p. 189.
26. Connor, "Workers, Politics, and Class Consciousness," p. 317.
27. Nick Eberstadt, "The Health Crisis in the USSR," in *The New York Review of Books*, 19 February, 1981, p. 23.
28. Alexandr Solzhenitsyn, "Misconceptions about Russia Are a Threat to America," *Foreign Affairs* 4 (Spring 1980): 981.
29. Connor, "Workers, Politics, and Class Consciousness," p. 317.
30. Bialer, *Stalin's Successors*, pp. 166–7.

CHAPTER TWO

A Minority In Their "Own Country": The Russians and the Nationalities Question

"Just wait until the Chinese come; they'll show you what's what."—Attributed to angry Soviet Central Asian

It is customary for American commentators to use the word *Russian* when referring to inhabitants of the Soviet Union. But this practice distorts our perception of Soviet society in a number of very important ways:

- Russia is merely one of fifteen national republics, and although the Russians are the single largest ethnic group in the USSR, they represent less than half of the population.
- Birth rates among certain ethnic minorities (e.g., the Asians) are much higher than those of the Russians, so that by the 21st century, the Russians will represent an even smaller percentage of the population than they do today.
- Most non-Russians continue to display strong ethnic-group self-awareness, which in some cases is on the rise—for example, among the Muslims of Central Asia and the Caucasus. Moreover, many of them are demanding a more prominent voice in a range of matters that heretofore have been dominated by their Russian comrades.

For all of the preceding reasons, displays of Russian nationalism are on the upswing, and Russian chauvinism, in turn, is fanning the flames of ethnic group discord in the USSR. In light of the serious nature of this problem, it is puzzling that U.S. policymakers ignored it for so many years. How can we account for this situation? What has been the Kremlin's policies toward the ethnic minorities? Why do most ethnic minorities in the USSR continue to display a strong attachment to ethnic values and loyalties? What are the reasons for some of them displaying a stronger sense of ethnic self-awareness than ever before in spite of the Kremlin's Russification drive? And finally, what bearing does the nationality question have upon Soviet society in the 1980s?

Ethnicity and Soviet History

Neglect of the Soviet nationality question stems from a major intellectual error of which both Western democratic and Marxist social theorists are guilty.

In the aftermath of World War II, most Western scholars shortchanged the ethnic factor in explaining human behavior—at least as it pertained to the advanced industrial societies.[1] It was conventional wisdom that although ethnic ties and values were not altogether dead, they were rapidly declining under the pressures of industrialization, urbanization, and secularization. In modern societies it was senseless to pay much attention to ethnic groups because the common bond of self-interest—be it defined by economics, education, or life-style—had relegated ethnic factors such as race, nationality, and religion to a secondary place in the lives of most people. During certain holidays, religious holy days, and cultural celebrations, traditional ethnic customs and folkways flourished, but for most of the year people were preoccupied with their jobs, businesses, careers, and other facets of modern life.

This empirical downplaying of ethnicity was reinforced by the normative judgment that the ethnic ties and values that had survived the crucible of modernization were repugnant. They were, after all, the source of intergroup conflict, nationalism, and ultimately war. In the wake of World War II, as the awful dimensions of the Holocaust became common knowledge, ethnicity was characterized as a parochial impulse responsible for Hitler's genocidal policies. The lesson was clear: this primitive impulse had to be superseded by universalistic values celebrating the brotherhood of mankind, not those dividing the human family.

Against this background it was little wonder that most U.S. policymakers and opinion-molders ignored the importance of the non-Russians residing in the USSR and exaggerated the Kremlin's capacity to "Russify" the more than 100 ethnic groups living there. This tendency was reinforced by the success of the United States in integrating succeeding waves of immigrants from all parts of the world into its political community. Ethnicity continued to have a bearing on political behavior in the United States, but no ethnic group was demanding the establishment of its own independent state. With the exception of some minority groups, such as the blacks, ethnicity was on the decline.

Finally, even Western detractors of Marxism were influenced by Marxist social theory, which minimized the importance of ethnic groups in advanced industrial societies. Marx and his benefactor, Friedrich Engels, in *The Communist Manifesto*, argued that the industrial revolution was destroying cultural values and social arrangements rooted in rural life. Since ethnic groups were an integral part of rural society, their days were numbered.[2] On empirical grounds then, Marxists agreed with "bourgeois" writers that modernization was destroying the influence of ethnicity.

The Marxists also attacked ethnicity on normative grounds. The capitalists had traditionally manipulated ethnic differences to divine workers, preventing them from appreciating that their bosses, and not members of other ethnic groups, were their real enemies. There was an anomaly here: capitalism was objectively destroying the viability of ethnic groups, while subjectively the capitalists exploited ethnic ties to split the proletariat.[3] The capitalists would succeed for a while, but over time the workers would see that shared ethnic ties were secondary to the overriding fact that they belonged to a larger international fraternity—"wage slaves" exploited by bosses who treated them like draft animals. It was in the face of such inhumanity that the proletariat would gain a revolutionary consciousness transcending parochial affinities and national boundaries.

Although Marx appreciated that certain ethnic groups (for example, the Irish) had legitimate grievances, and their plight might have a bearing on revolutionary programs, most of his followers associated ethnicity with the forces of reaction. But early in the 20th century, when many "mini-nations" in Europe were demanding the right of national self-determination, the issue became a hot topic of debate among Marxists: should they oppose or assist ethnic nationalists in the Russian and Austro-Hungarian empires in their struggle for independence? Otto Bauer, an Austrian Marxist, forcefully argued in favor of the radical left siding with the nationalists of Eastern and Central Europe. More orthodox comrades, such as the Pole Rosa Luxembourg, disagreed. She contended that to do so would encourage ethnic chauvinism and undermine working class solidarity. Her position was not altogether divorced from her Jewish background; she could not forget that the Polish aristocracy frequently manipulated anti-Semitism to facilitate their brutal exploitation of the Polish masses. To legitimize the nationalists in their quest for independence, therefore, was to set loose forces of reaction that traditionally had been hostile to socialism.[4]

It was at this point that Lenin entered the fray and threw his weight behind those who followed Bauer's line. "Can a nation be free if it oppressed other nations?" Lenin pondered. The answer was no. It was in the Great Russians' interest to "struggle against such oppression. In Russia, the creation of an independent national state so far remains the privilege of one nation, the Great Russian nation. We, the Great Russian proletarians, defend no privileges. . . ."[5]

Lenin wrote this prior to the 1917 revolution, but after the Bolsheviks seized power, a new set of circumstances arose: the "submerged" ethnic minorities he once portrayed as "prisoners" of Russia were not pivotal actors in the Soviet drama. If they joined the "counterrevolutionaries," the Bolshevik regime might fall. Another prospect, less dramatic but of grave concern to Lenin, was that they might split off from the new state as the Balts, Finns, and Poles had done, denying the USSR considerable human and material resources and precious strategic territory. Lenin was especially worried about the Ukrainians who, although Slavs, thought of themselves as a nation with a distinct culture, history, and language. And then there were the backward tribes of Central Asia, led by "reactionary" mullahs—whom would they support?

To win the non-Russian's allegiance, Lenin agreed to the formation of a federal system, rather than a unitary one where political power would be centralized. The adoption of a federal system placated the ethnic minorities, but ever since, some Soviet leaders have rued the day Lenin made the compromise. All of the major ethnic groups—the Russians, Ukrainians, Armenians, Georgians, etc.,—would have their own national republics. The Russians would dominate the party and polity, but Soviet federalism would provide an institutional and administrative framework by which the people living in the national republic could oppose the very Russian chauvinism Lenin once bitterly attacked.

Although Lenin's nationalities policy was largely governed by the imperative of power politics, many Bolsheviks in the early 1920s subscribed to the principle of "national equality" and believed the Muslims who had lived under tsarist despotism were grateful that a new, progressive government had replaced it. So when Lenin called a "Congress of Oppressed Peoples of the East" in September 1920 at Baku, the Russians were astounded when the "Asiatic comrades" spoke favorably of self-determination. "They pointed out that there existed a world of Asian peoples enslaved by Europe, that these people feared being subjugated by Europe's revolution just as they had been subjugated by its imperialism. . . ."[6] To leaders like the Sultan Galiev, Marxism meant "national emancipation" and not "class struggle"; it meant securing his people's release from the embrace of the mighty Russian bear. Galiev, who was arrested for his involvement in the Basmachi guerrilla movement in 1932, argued that the real objective of the Asiatic people should not be the dictatorship of the proletariat but "the dictatorship of the colonies and semi-colonies over the metropolitan countries."[7]

The Bolsheviks' permissive treatment of non-Russians changed dramatically once the wily old Georgian, Joseph Stalin, had the reins of power firmly in his grasp—by late 1929. Perhaps because he was a member of an ethnic minority that cherished its language and culture (and Lenin had appointed him to oversee the nationality question for the new Bolshevik regime), he knew better than his Russian comrades how powerful a force nationalism was and how the various ethnic minorities pulling in different directions could wreck the Soviet state. Stalin declared his nationality policy as being national in form but socialist in content, masking his conviction that it was impossible to rule a society where myriad ethnic groups would have a voice in affairs of state. He made quick work of those non-Russian comrades who displayed a keen sense of nationalism, even if they were steadfast Marxist-Leninists.

Stalin, in an effort to undercut the ability of other groups to challenge his regime, promoted the dominant role of the Russian nation, which he held up as a model for the other ethnic groups to emulate. The threat of another German invasion gave him further cause to encourage Russian nationalism. In the mid-1930s Stalin's writings and public utterances prepared the masses for war by appealing to their national élan. Now Russian nationalism overshadowed the international motif of Soviet literature and art. Under Stalin's direction, filmmakers, playwrights, and novelists resurrected Peter the Great and Ivan the Terrible from the misty past to be gloriously displayed before the people as great patriots, true heroes of the motherland. The Russian people, he reasoned, might not fight to preserve the Soviet regime, but they would die bravely to save Mother Russia from Hitler's invading armies.

The war's outcome demonstrated the wisdom of employing Russian nationalism in defense of the Soviet regime. Acts of collaboration on the part of Crimean Tartars, the Chechens, and the Ingush fed Stalin's distrust of ethnic minorities. These peoples from the Caucasus and Central Asia consequently were transported, under duress, into the vast heartland of the USSR. They were not the only ones to collaborate with the enemy: Khrushchev contended that Stalin probably would have exiled the Ukrainians for the same reason, but there were too many of them to treat in this fashion.[8]

One of the biggest "ifs" of the war is what would have happened had Hitler listened to his leading authority on race, Alfred Rosenberg, who wanted to court the Ukrainians and Byelorussians, rather than treat them as subhuman as Hitler had. The German generals were surprised when they invaded the Soviet Union and were welcomed by Byelorussians and Ukrainians as liberators, not oppressors. Had Hitler ordered the SS in particular to treat the captive Slavs with greater decency, perhaps more of them would have gone over to the Nazis. But after they observed that the Germans were more brutal than their Russian masters, they joined partisan groups and plagued the German forces until the war's conclusion. The collaboration of many non-Russian groups in the Soviet Union, however, underscored Stalin's conviction that they could not be trusted and had to be treated harshly if they were to be kept in line.

In a victory speech on May 24, 1945, Stalin forewarned all ethnic minorities hoping for greater liberty to celebrate their cultures in the postwar years when he intoned: "Russia is the leading nation of the USSR," and that "in this war she had won the right to be recognized as the guide for the whole Union."[9] Other peoples residing in the USSR would have to follow the lead of their "elder brothers"—that is, learn their language and embrace their culture— for Stalin was committed to the Russification of the entire Soviet population.

It is not clear whether Stalin felt any real affinity for the Russians. He probably reasoned that by favoring them, he would facilitate the integration of the ethnic minorities into "mainstream" Russian society, thereby undercutting their sense of identity. This would help him consolidate his control over the world's last remaining empire. He would cover his bloody tracks with the universalistic precepts of Marxism–Leninism.

Since Stalin's death, his heirs have alternated their ethnic policy by shifting back and forth between permissiveness and oppression. Presently Kremlin spokesmen claim publicly that they have resolved the "nationality problem": values, folkways, and loyalties associated with the country's ethnic minorities persist, but they are secondary to a powerful and ascendant Soviet consciousness.

The claim that the Soviet Union has resolved the nationality question is nonsense, and the Soviet elite know this. Indeed, Michael Suslov, the Politburo's leading theoretician for decades, deemed it to be one of the major threats to the regime. The persistence of this problem has its roots in three sources: Russian chauvinism, the vitality of ethnicity, and the impact of modernization upon the least developed areas of the USSR.

Contemporary Ethnic Politics: The Ukraine

Claims to national equality aside, Russians dominate the major power centers in the USSR: the party, the government, and the military. The dominant group has allowed members of other ethnic groups to gain access to influential positions in their own areas, and in some cases to hold high posts in Moscow, too; however, harsh measures persist against colleagues who display "nationalist" tendencies. The Ukrainians, for example, Slavs whom the Russians call the "second elder brothers," have done very well for themselves—they are one of the few non-Russian nations adequately represented in Soviet institutions. Still, their "elder brothers" keep reminding them that energetic displays of Ukrainian nationalism will not be tolerated regardless of the credentials, or official positions, of the people involved. The fate of Petro Shelest is especially instructive in this connection.

The first secretary of the Ukrainian Communist party and a member of the

Presidium of the Central Committee of the Communist Party of the Soviet Union (CPSU), Shelest was well connnected in both Kiev and Moscow in the 1960s; and ". . . up until 1970, nothing about this good administrator . . . gave him away as a fervent nationalist."[10] Indeed, Shelest could be cited as a person who had disguarded his parochial identity for a more universalistic Soviet one. But in 1970 he alarmed his Russian comrades when he published a book, *Our Soviet Ukraine*. Shelest wrote that the Ukraine was an integral part of the USSR, but he devoted many pages to the glorification of Ukrainian history, culture, and development. Most specifically, he ignored the party line that the Ukrainians, like other ethnic minorities, were becoming "fused" into Soviet society, eschewing narrow, parochial loyalties and values for a larger Soviet worldview. Shelest's heresy was especially displeasing to the Russians because nationalist stirrings among Ukrainian intellectuals were on the rise. Indeed, one of the reasons the Soviets crushed the Dubček regime in 1968 was the Kremlin's fear that Czechoslovak nationalism might excite the Ukrainians and inspire them to even bolder displays of discontent with Russian chauvinism.[11]

Shelest's book won him the label of "ardent nationalist," a proponent of anti-Soviet (read "anti-Russian") views that could not be tolerated, and he was stripped of his posts. But that was not all. To remind the Ukrainians that their "elder brothers" were in control, "Shelest was removed from his Ukrainian functions in Moscow, not in Kiev."[12] Rubbing salt in the raw wound, a Russian was selected as second secretary of the Ukrainian Communist party. This was common practice in other republics, but not in the Ukraine, where an indigenous comrade had always filled this slot.

The Ukrainians, numbering fifty million, are the second largest ethnic group in the USSR; although it is not clear how many of them are prepared to offer organized resistance to Russian hegemony, many Ukrainians have not surrendered their dreams of an independent country. The actions of people like Shelest, and the knowledge that millions of his fellow countrymen favor national independence, is a source of concern to the Russian leadership. They must be asking themselves, "If we cannot trust fellow Slavs, whom can we trust?"

Insofar as they acknowledge their nationality problem, the Soviets imply that it involves the struggle between particularistic nationalism and universalistic socialism. This line has an appealing humanistic ring to it and strikes a responsive chord in the hearts and minds of many Westerners who associate ethnicity with nationalism, "which after all contributed to two world wars in this century alone." But to a growing number of people in the USSR, the real problem is not one of particularism versus universalism, but Russian chauvinism and the Kremlim's refusal to abide by the pluralistic (and universalistic) precepts that have a legal basis in Soviet law.

In addition to Russian chauvinism, the nationalities question continues to plague the Russian-dominated regime because ethnicity is not a transitory phenomenon linked to a peculiar period in history, but rather is basic to the human condition. The Lithuanian experience in the USSR is instructive here.

Contemporary Ethnic Politics: Lithuania

In contrast to Stalin's heavy-handed attempt to crush ethnic minorities, his successors have sought to win them over by allowing the talented and energetic to ride the escalator of success if they do not question the Soviet regime or challenge Russian domination of the USSR. Recent émigrés from the USSR testify to the truth of this assertion. Jonas Jurasas, for example, was a theatrical director in Kaunas, who had directed Shakespeare in Moscow and was allowed unusually broad artistic latitude in his homeland, Lithuania. There were several reasons he was granted such privileges: he was deemed politically reliable because his parents were killed by Lithuanian fascists when he was a boy, he attended the University of Moscow, and he had demonstrated that he was a person of real talent, someone the authorities could show off as an example that capable Soviet citizens were rewarded even if they were not Russians.

But, by the mid-1970s, Jurasas wanted to direct bolder, more innovative plays; in every instance he was denied permission. Finally, out of frustration and in the name of artistic freedom, he wrote a letter of protest to the Lithuanian minister of culture. He was immediately fired and threatened, along with his wife, Ausra, with the prospect of being incarcerated in a psychiatric hospital. His son, he was told, would become a ward of the state. Later he was allowed to leave the country, and today he is living and working in the United States.

Despite his experience, Jurasas concedes that the Russians are seeking to integrate Lithuanians into Soviet society by treating them equitably and fairly—but only until they celebrate their own culture and history with too much zeal. According to Jurasas, the lure of a higher living standard than the average citizen enjoys, the ability to travel and the opportunity to pursue a career, albeit with restrictions, explains why many intellectuals in Lithuania have not joined in protests against Russian domination of their country. In contrast to the Russian dissidents, vocal opponents of the regime in the Baltic states are often working men and women who bravely resist Russian efforts to destroy their culture and the values that are a cherished part of Lithuanian life. Indeed, after he lost his job, he discovered that old friends avoided him, and he and his family would have had a difficult time surviving if it had not been for the fact that "invisible people" (most of them ordinary Lithuanians) emerged to lend them assistance.[13]

The Lithuanians have demonstrated how important ethnicity is to non-

Russians in the USSR and how traditional ethnic values and loyalties have survived attempts to destroy them.

Lithuania was incorporated into the USSR as part of a secret protocol to the 1939 Molotov–Ribbentrop Pact. In the summer of 1940, as Russian troops marched into the country, rigged elections were held establishing a pro-Soviet government. Several weeks later the new People's Diet unanimously declared Lithuania a Soviet socialist republic. In June 1941, just prior to the *Wehrmacht*'s invasion of the USSR, 35,000 Lithuanian political leaders, intellectuals, and clergy were rounded up and shipped to concentration camps in the Soviet Union. When the Russians returned in 1945, they began a six-year deportation of an estimated 350,000 people; many Lithuanian leaders were executed. Included in this number were Roman Catholic clergy. Stalin clearly intended to destroy the Roman Catholic church in Lithuania, which like the church in Poland has always been closely associated with nationalism. He outlawed all religious orders, closed and demolished churches, and those priests who escaped execution or arrest were exiled or denied the opportunity to perform their pastoral duties. His draconian methods forced priests and nuns underground, to conduct religious activities in private homes and wherever they could be performed undetected by the KGB.

Since Stalin's death, the Krelim's policy toward the Catholic church in Lithuania has varied; at times the authorities have adopted a more tolerant policy, while at others it has supported a harsher line. Even though the Soviet and Lithuanian constitutions provide for freedom of speech and religion, Lithuania's Catholics (who represent 85% of a population of 3.5 million) have not been allowed to practice their religion. By the mid-1960s, the anti-Catholic campaign had achieved considerable progress in crushing organized religion in the country and in intimidating devout Catholics there. At this point, some Lithuanian Catholics parted company with moderates (who argued that even though the Soviets' anti-Catholic campaign had done grevious harm to the church's infrastructure and had demoralized lay Catholics, it was better to exist under these conditions than to offer resistance and risk extinction altogether) and banded together to fight the Kremlin's campaign. They were emboldened by the Prague Spring of 1968, the activities of Russian intellectuals like Solzhenitsyn and Sakharov, and protests by Jewish and other ethnic activists. They circulated petitions, wrote letters demanding that their right of freedom of conscience be honored, and resisted the orders of superiors who kowtowed to the authorities. It was only after such requests were brushed aside or ignored that the militants decided to publish the samizdat *Chronicle of the Catholic Church in Lithuania*, which documented the government's illegal anti-Catholic activities. In spite of persistent KGB attempts to stop the *Chronicle*'s publication, including numerous arrests, the incarceration of people in mental institutions, and mysterious deaths, it continues to be circulated through the country.

In contrast with the Russian intellectual dissidents, the Lithuanian Catholic civil rights activitists have attracted mass support for their cause. People from all walks of life, rural and urban, young and old, workers and scholars, have lent their support to it. In a two-year period early in the 1970s, over 50,000 Lithuanians courageously signed petitions protesting the government's religious persecution. On several occasions, militant Catholics, workers, and students have taken to the streets, and in the spring of 1972 several protest suicides occurred.

The self-immolation of Romas Kalanta, a Catholic student-worker, had a particularly profound, traumatic impact upon Lithuanians in all parts of the country. After the young martyr killed himself in a Kaunas park, muted discontent was channeled into purposeful public resistance to state oppression. The anniversary of Kalanta's death has resulted in annual public protests conducted by Catholics and non-Catholics alike. He has become a symbol for both groups, and his martyrdom has helped link people who previously thought they had little in common and often were at odds with one another. It is believed, for example, that some of the first protest documents produced by Catholic priests to reach the West were carried out by emigrating Lithuanian Jews. A Jew, Eitan Finkelstein, along with the son of a prominent communist, Thomas Venclova, and a priest, Father Karolis Garuckas, formed the Lithuanian Helsinki Watch Group to document human rights violations in Lithuania.

The Catholic militants in Lithuania also have received support from prominent Russian dissidents, such as Sergei Kovalev, who is in prison for his "anti-Soviet" activities. The Moscow dissident's help has had a marked impact upon the Lithuanians' perception of Russians. In October 1975, when Sakharov received the Nobel Peace Prize, the editors of the *Chronicle* wrote: "All the people of good will in Lithuania are truly happy that your courageous struggle for justice, freedom and the dignity of man"—including Lithuanians—"did not go unnoticed."[14] In the fall of 1979, when representatives from the three Baltic republics gathered in Moscow and distributed to Western newsmen a declaration protesting the Soviet Union's illegal occupation of their countries, Sakharov, in "A Statement of Russian Democrats," endorsed the petition. "Lithuania, Estonia and Latvia have been annexed into the Soviet Union ... essentially as a result of the occupation of the Baltic States by the Red Army."[15]

To characterize the Lithuanian human rights movement as a clique of reactionaries as Moscow has, then, is ludicrous. Indeed, the fact that so many people involved are men and women who were born and raised during the "Soviet era" is a source of special concern to the Kremlin; it demonstrates that despite their best efforts, the Russians have been unable to crush the Lithuanians' national spirit.

Organized resistance to Russian imperialism in Lithuania clearly illustrates the tenacity of ethnicity in the face of rapid social change, in spite of policies designed to eradicate it. As Harold Isaacs has written, an ethnic group's language, culture, and shared historical experiences (the components of what he calls basic group identity) are vital to the psychic and social well-being of its members.[16] An individual's identity, the formation of his or her personality, and the values that give meaning to his or her life are shaped by group affinities, religious beliefs, and other phenomena that sociologists on both sides of the Iron Curtain have deemed "premodern." In every society in the world today, capitalist and communist, developed and developing, people are fighting to preserve values and life-styles that give purpose to their existence, in the same fashion (possibly with even greater zeal) that they are struggling to protect their property and resist economic exploitation. It is for similar reasons that Ukrainians and Lithuanians, including Marxists, are prepared to risk imprisonment and even death to preserve their national cultures.

The strength of ethnic values and loyalties in Lithuania and the Ukraine can be attributed to the fact that they once were independent countries and even under tsarist hegemony celebrated distinctive cultures. But what about expressions of ethnic pride on the part of minorities in the USSR that did not display a strong sense of identity in the past, but are doing so today? Expressions of ethnic self-awareness on the parts of previously quiescent groups have been detected worldwide, and there is evidence that the very factors once believed to undermine ethnicity—industrialization, urbanization, and secularization—may have the opposite result. Developments unfolding in Soviet Central Asia, for example, are bringing the relationship between modernization and rising ethnic self-awareness into sharp focus.

Contemporary Ethnic Politics: The "Muslim Problem"

Although the Kremlin is unhappy about the KGB's failure to crush the Lithuanian human rights movement, size dictates that the Lithuanians are incapable of posing a serious threat to the regime. A different set of demographic, cultural, religious, and economic factors compel the Kremlin, however, to acknowledge that their "Muslim problem" is potentially a grave one that by itself can cause it serious and enduring difficulties.

Over 40 million people live in areas of the USSR bordering Turkey, Iran, Afghanistan, Pakistan, India, and China. Birth rates in Central Asia and Transcaucasia, where most Soviet Muslims live, are much higher than comparable ones in European areas of the USSR. In the Russian federation, the birth rate is 15.5 per thousand, whereas in Kirghizia, Uzbekistan, and the Turkmen Republic, it runs 30.5 to 37 per thousand. By the year 2000, Russians will number 147 million (47.2% of the population), while the Central Asians and Caucasians (not all of whom are Muslims) will amount to over 92 million; that is, about 30% of the Soviet population.[17]

If these people were dispersed throughout the Soviet Union, their numbers would be less significant; however, in contrast to the Russians, who have migrated to all corners of the USSR, the Muslims have displayed a keen attachment to their homelands. Those who are moving "are emigrating toward neighboring republics that share the same civilization."[18] To make matters worse for Soviet authorities, who deem language the single most important source of ethnic self-identity, "the groups most attached to their native tongues are those in the Moslem borderlands or the Caucasus."[19] In European areas of the USSR, the campaign to impose Russian as a second language has been relatively successful. But only 19% of the Kirghis, 16% of the Tadzhiks, 14.9% of the Azeris, 14.8% of the Turkmen, and 13% of the Uzbeks, respectively, speak Russian.[20] It is significant that not too long ago there was a movement toward the use of Russian on the part of the Muslims themselves, but they have recently turned away from this practice.

Along with their size and concentration, the common culture shared by Soviet Muslims represents another factor contributing to their sense of unity. Through the schools, the party, the military, and other institutions, the Russians have sought to inculcate the ethnic minorities with a Soviet (Russian) mindset. They, in particular, have placed great stock in the notion that men and women belonging to such groups who enter the professions, or who aspire to high party or governmental posts, will have to eschew traditional ways of thinking if they are going to further their careers. But there is a cultural revival among the Soviet Union's Muslims, and the people in the vanguard of that movement are the same ones who have benefited most from a Soviet education—the intellectuals.

The Muslim intellectual community is large and growing; it has been characterized as "well educated, comparable in quality to the Russian intelligentsia, devoted to its people, and well prepared to assume full responsibility of power in its republics."[21] Alexandre Benningsen, a prominent French scholar of Soviet ethnicity, has observed:

> It is also extremely proud of its recently discovered national culture [and] increasingly respectful of Islam. This in turn has led to a growing sense of kinship—even unity—with the Muslim world in the rest of the USSR and abroad, and to a corresponding growth in the sense of difference from Russians and Europeans in general.[22]

A key word here is "unity," for the Bolsheviks in the 1920s encouraged the tribes of Central Asia to adopt their own distinctive languages, hoping thereby to divide them. If they employed different languages over a period of time, it was reasoned, they would lose the ability and the incentive to perceive themselves as a single nation. But today the Kremlin's worst fears appear to be materializing: The Muslims in the USSR are beginning to think of themselves as a single people. Whatever differences divide them, they pale in importance to the characteristics that set them off from the Slavs, the Russians in particular.

A crucial question is whether this trend will persist, reaching more and more people, and ultimately take the form of a full-blown nationalist movement. Although strong, it may be only temporary in nature. There are numerous examples in other parts of the world where members of an ethnic group, upon making it into mainstream society, displayed a heightened sense of group self-awareness, reviving values and folkways their poorly educated parents could not articulate with the same élan or intellectual verve. But as the course of ethnic development in the United States indicates, once ascendant members of an ethnic group realize that there are no barriers to social and economic advancement, deep feelings of ethnic discontent subside.

This may be the course Soviet Muslims will follow; on the other hand, the ethnic experience in America is dramatically different from its counterpart in the USSR. The vast majority of immigrants to the United States left their homelands to start a new life, and only a handful ever thought of establishing nation-states in the New World. Outside of the Native Americans and Mexicans, most of them voluntarily joined the new political community. Finally, Russian chauvinism has encouraged Muslims to think of themselves as different, because their "elder brothers" treat them that way.

Religion has also contributed to this heightened sense of ethnic self-awareness. Despite efforts to crush Islam, there is a religious revival among the USSR's Muslims, and the state's atheistic campaign may be contributing to religious sentiment. There are only 143 mosques and Koranic schools operating in all of Central Asia. These figures support Muslim claims that the regime (contrary to Moscow's propaganda) does not allow Islam to function fully in the USSR. How can a religious institution function if there are insufficient places in which to worship or train clergy?[23] A selected group of Muslim clergy is allowed to conduct its own affairs in the Islamic republics, and even to travel abroad. But these clerics dare not speak their minds about the state's anti-Islamic practices; to do so would be tantamount to quitting the clergy.

In the final analysis, the Kremlin's atheistic campaign seeks to crush religion at the grass roots. If ordinary believers, young people in particular, can be induced to stay away from the mosques and to turn their backs on religion altogether, then it makes little difference whether the clergy survives or not. But the government's anti-religion campaign has failed in the Islamic areas; what it has done, rather, is to drive religion underground. Thus, the task of crushing religion becomes even more difficult, because it is harder than before to identify believers and religious leaders.

This is certainly true in the case of the Sufi brotherhoods, which are flourishing in the USSR today. Because their members are part of tightly knit groups organized along kinship lines, the KGB has had trouble infiltrating them. The threat they pose to the authorities is manifested in the fact that they "are not small underground chapels, but rather illegal mass organizations. In the Checheno–Ingush Republic alone, it is estimated that out of a population of 442,000 believers, 150,000 to 200,000 belong to the Brotherhoods. . . . They are neither heretical nor schismatic and belong to the mainstream of Muslim religion."[24]

It is also noteworthy that the Muslim clergy has adroitly combated the state's anti-Islamic campaign. They are taking two especially significant measures. First, they have not clung to orthodox religious practices that directly clash with the Soviet regime, but have sought rather to work with the authorities and to adapt their religion to the real world. To cite just one example, believers need not be held to the rule that they pray five times daily if doing so means that they interfere with work schedules or other secular duties. Secondly, they have urged the faithful to join communist organizations—the youngsters the Komsomol, the adults the Communist Party. (By contrast, Catholic militants in Lithuania have discouraged the faithful from joining these organizations.) From the KGB's perspective, efforts to destroy Islam would be facilitated were the clergy to openly resist communism and to confront the state.

It is noteworthy, moreover, that devout Muslims are influencing secular-minded members of their community. In contrast to most Christian sects, which celebrate the individual in his divine relationship with God, Islam deems it impossible to separate the individual from the larger religious community to which he is linked. "Islam in the USSR," therefore, "is not an aggregate of different religions, but primarily a community, the 'Ummah.' Whether orthodox or heterodox, all Moslems who declare themselves such are members of the community of believers."[25]

The resurgence of Islam in the USSR takes on even greater significance when one turns to the economic implications associated with it. According to one estimate, by the year 2000, 40% of the teenagers and young adults in the USSR will be non-Europeans, most of them Central Asians and Caucasians.[26] To provide this bulging segment of the population with food, clothing, housing, education, and health care, the state will have to invest heavily in those areas where they live. Also, estimates of potential active workers in the 1980s show that the percentage rate of new people entering the labor force will be 2.4% annually in Central Asia, but −0.2% in the Russian federation.[27] These estimates have important consequences for economic policy. Planners in the 1980s either must invest large sums of capital in "Asian" republics where the manpower exists, or encourage millions of Asians to relocate in European areas where it does not.

There are a number of reasons why the Soviet leadership will be reluctant to choose the first alternative. Economic logic dictates investing where the industrial infrastructure already is in place. To construct in Central Asia the kind of massive industrial sites to which the Soviets are partial means starting from scratch and violating long-held notions about economic development and political control. Also, there are good reasons for concentrating investments in Siberia, where untapped resources are abundant and demographics are in the Russians' favor.

The Russian-dominated Politburo has striven to narrow the economic gap between the poorer Asiatic republics and their more affluent European counterparts. But if the Kremlin earmarks massive sums of money for non-European areas of the USSR during a period of austerity, hard-pressed Slavic workers, technicians, planners, managers, and party and government cadres will protest because their employment prospects "at home" are being restricted. Moreover, the practice of filling slots in non-European areas of the USSR with Russians no longer can be justified. Today there are an ample number of well-qualified indigenous people able to perform at all levels—professional, managerial, and skilled workers, not just manual laborers. As the size of the Muslim labor force grows, discontent among the Islamic peoples will escalate if the Kremlin does not provide them with economic opportunities congruent with their rising expectations. The irony here is that the Kremlin's campaign to modernize Central Asia—with the thought in mind that urbanization and industrialization will facilitate the fusion of these people with the general population—will probably produce just the opposite result.

The second alternative, relocating more Muslims to European areas of the USSR, would neither be welcomed by the Muslims nor highly favored by the Russians. The Uzbeks, Kazakhs, and other Muslim peoples have demonstrated an unwillingness to leave their homelands. (This attachment is not only peculiar to Muslims in the USSR. The Yugoslavs most disinclined to emigrate for jobs in West Germany are Muslims.) Growing ethnic consciousness will serve as an additional deterrent to Muslims relocating to "alien" areas of the USSR. Relations between Muslims and Russians are not good. The former resent the influence wielded by Russians in their republics, and a British scholar reports, "In one recent demonstration of nationalist anger, 10,000 Central Asians came together in Dushanbe to protest against their treatment by Russian colons and to chant anti-Russian slogans, a breach of Soviet etiquette which required the intervention of Russian troops. . . ."[28] The émigré Russian dissident Igor Shafarevich says that Central Asians have been known to taunt Russians with the observation, "Just wait until the Chinese come; they'll show you what's what!"[29]

Russians who are targets of such remarks do not think much of the "natives" either. In Central Asia, they display pictures of Stalin in their cars conveying the message, "At least one Russian leader knew how to deal with troublesome and recalcitrant minorities."[30] Were millions of Muslims to settle in European areas of the USSR—the Soviet equivalent of *Gastarbeiter* (guest workers)—they would not be greeted with open arms. Despite official claims to the contrary, many Russians are racist, and are especially hostile to dark-skinned peoples, like the Asians who are called "blacks" (*chernye*). Russian–Central Asian relations are not likely to get better soon; on the contrary, they are likely to get worse.

Bitter interethnic competition in the USSR, associated with declining economic activity, will give impetus to a phenomenon that until recently has been neglected by the Western media—Russian nationalism. As Alexander Yanov has observed, Soviet newspapers and journals now carry articles by writers blatantly calling for the Russian leadership to take care of its own, whereas not too long ago such material had to be published "unofficially."[31] Yanov claims that Russian leaders in the party, the government, and the military, are becoming less coy about displaying their own nationalistic predelictions. Indeed, he believes that to compensate for the regime's inability to solve a host of difficult problems, it will encourage Russian nationalism. Like Stalin, the Soviet elite will seek to maintain its power by mobilizing the Russian people behind it. To achieve this objective, however, it will run the risk of abetting non-Russian nationalists who are seeking to organize their people in opposition to Russian chauvinism.

In spite of growing self-awareness, the Muslims in the USSR have not yet begun to function as an organized political opposition to Russian rule. But as they become more industrialized and urbanized and better educated, they may develop a new political consciousness. Indeed, cognizant of the relationship between rapid social change in Iran and the rise of Islamic militancy, the Soviet authorities—in addition to reasons already mentioned—have political reasons for not accelerating economic development in Central Asia and the Caucasus.

The Muslims have only recently begun to enter the mainstream of Soviet society, but as this trend gains momentum, their level of political awareness and their desire to have a voice in economic, political, and cultural affairs will escalate. This is likely to foster confrontations with the Russians or indigenous leaders in their republics who meekly accept Russian direction. As rising ethnic self-awareness throughout the world suggests, younger members of the Islamic community will rebel against acts of discrimination their parents accepted, and the Kremlin will encounter stiff resistance to its policy of handpicking religious leaders, controlling education curricula, or determining the expression of cultural impulses—just as it has in the Baltic, the Ukraine, Armenia, and Georgia.

Furthermore, developments outside of the Soviet Union's borders are likely to have an impact upon the formation of Islamic nationalism in the USSR. Islamic fundamentalism in countries bordering the Soviet Union is most significant in this respect. For many years Soviet Muslims were employed by the Kremlin to get the Turks, Iranians, Pakistanis, and Afghans to look upon the USSR as a progressive, friendly neighbor. But the formation of the Islamic Republic in Iran and the Soviet invasion of Afghanistan have set into motion a new set of circumstances. The Soviets no longer dwell upon how "their Muslims" can be used for propaganda purposes abroad but how Islamic fundamentalists might stir up Muslims in the Soviet Union.

"Iran has always enjoyed, and still enjoys, an immense prestige in the Turco–Iranian world, not only because of the country's unique and advanced culture but also because of its long tradition of statesmanship."[32] For members of the Sufi brotherhoods, the Iranian revolution has inspired young Muslims "to draw a parallel between the 'foreign imperialism' of the Americans in Iran and the 'imperialism' of the Russians in the Caucasus and in Central Asia."[33] The reaffirmation of Islamic culture as manifested by fundamentalists in Iran has heightened "the innate sense of superiority that the Caucasian Muslims feel with regard to their non-Muslim (Russian or Armenian) neighbors. . . . Where once Iranians listened to propaganda broadcasts from Radio Baku, today it is the Soviet Azeris and Turkmen who follow with interest the broadcasts from Tabriz and Teheran."[34]

The Soviet invasion of Afghanistan poses even graver problems for the USSR. For many years Soviet Muslims played a minor role as diplomats in Islamic countries, but in an effort to prevent administrative chaos in Afghanistan, the Kremlin sent in Uzbek, Tadzhik and Turkmen administrators after the April 1978 pro-Soviet coup in Kabul. With the Soviet invasion in December 1979, their numbers grew, and many of them welcomed the opportunity to "liberate" their brothers from "feudal rule." Their Russian superiors hoped that by employing them, they could portray the invasion to the outside world as an intra-Islamic affair. "But the operation did not prove a success. In February 1980, the USSR began to systematically pull out units with Central Asian soldiers and replace them with purely Slav units."[35] Simultaneously Soviet Muslims were replaced by East German administrators and Russians. Finally, even those Soviet Muslims who were "willing to assist their Russian 'elder brothers' in the mission of 'liberation' cooled off when ideology had to be translated into action. . . ."[36] Although most Soviet Muslims obeyed their Russian commanders, the latter, especially as the conflict escalated, doubted the reliability of their Muslim soldiers.

The Politburo is having second thoughts about the wisdom of invading Afghanistan. A lengthy war may awaken Islamic nationalism in the USSR. Benningsen asserts that whatever the outcome, "the iron curtain between Muslim brethren on opposite sides of the Soviet–Afghan border has already crumbled," and ideas and information are freely flowing in both directions.[37] The Soviets cannot view this development with complacency; they cannot forget that when the Japanese defeated the tsar's armies in 1905, this victory for people of color fostered the rise of Islamic nationalist parties in imperial Russia.

Even if the Soviets defeat the Afghan freedom fighters, this victory abroad may presage serious problems at home—that is, generate nationalist sentiment in Central Asia that will build over time, culminating one day in a violent clash between the Russians and their Muslim subjects.

Ethnic Divisions in the Military

Two Rand Corporation researchers, S. Enders Wimbush and Alex Alexiev, have discovered revealing information about ethnic discord in the Red Army through interviews with Soviet émigrés. All recruits carry military identity cards with their nationality on them. Quotas are enforced to prevent members of certain ethnic groups from serving in "critical units," and it is policy to adhere to them in other instances. One respondent reported that only Russians, Ukrainians, and Byelorussians served in his division, which was responsible for protecting government offices during periods of emergency. Another interviewee reported that no more than 5% of an ethnic minority can serve in air force units, and another one revealed that when it was discovered that a disproportionate number of new recruits were of German origin, they were immediately transferred.

Central Asians, or "Churkas" as the Russians call them, have a reputation for shirking the draft, so they are usually 3 to 5 years older than recruits from European areas of the USSR. The Churkas do not deem it a privilege to serve in the Red Army. They enjoy a reputation for resorting to bribes (*blat*) to get deferments, secure preferred posts, or avoid the draft altogether. "In Azerbaidzhan," one respondent said, "our officers often had to circle the train in order to keep the relatives of the recruits away. Time and again, relatives took recruits from the railway cars and ran away with them. They were not always caught and brought back home."[38]

There are still some "national divisions" in the Soviet armed forces—units comprised of a single non-Russian nationality—but they are on the decline because of the principle of "extraterritoriality." "In the simplest terms, this means that Soviet soldiers are not allowed to serve in their native regions but instead are stationed in geographically distant and ethnically different areas of the country." Balts, Caucasians, and Central Asians, in particular, are sent to areas remote from their homelands out of fear that in the event of a clash they will side with their own people. This is why they are never used for border patrol duties, and even Ukrainians and Byelorrusians, who often do so, are not allowed to patrol the borders of their own republics. One interviewee explained the policy of extraterritoriality in a few words. "A Russian soldier probably would not shoot a Russian woman, but a Kazakh would. He would say, 'They are Russians. Let's get them.'"[39]

Wimbush and Alexiev report, "The most dramatic difference in ethnic ratios among draftees can be observed between combat and noncombat units. . . . All our evidence to date shows conclusively that Soviet combat units are staffed by a clear majority of representatives of the Slavic nationalities."[40] Conversely, construction units may have as many as 90% or more troops from non-Slavic groups. In such units, one may find an exception to the rule that members of an ethnic minority do not serve in their home area. Moreover, the principal of extraterritoriality does not apply to emergency mobilization: With most Soviet divisions at half strength, local recruits may be used to fill them in crisis situations.

The authorities prefer to staff the most critical combat units, such as the Strategic Rocket Forces, exclusively with Slavs. It is not always possible to do so—because of their technical skills one may find Balts in such "critical units." In other combat units, the ethnic ratio is usually 80% Slavic and 20% non-Slavic. It is noteworthy that minority group members often do not receive combat training. Indeed, Jews, western Ukrainians, Balts, and other groups with "anti-Soviet" reputations are frequently placed in traveling construction battalions. They are deemed the least prestigious units in the Red Army. Russians may wind up in such units for individual misbehavior, but if you are a Jew or Lithuanian, you may find yourself in one of them because of your ethnic groups' reputation.

The Russians, however, have displayed great ingenuity in exploiting ethnic discord. One of the few units considered important to state security where you find Central Asians are those associated with internal security. Under these circumstances, the authorities are seeking to capitalize on the Churkas' hatred for Russians. One of the primary missions of MVD (Ministry of Internal Affairs) units is to guard penal institutions, and the Central Asians have a reputation for being cruel overseers, especially hostile to Russians.

Soviet soldiers stationed abroad are usually Russians, preferably from peasant backgrounds. The rationale for this policy is that "the Russian peasants are very much attached to their villages and families, and would rarely think of running away. Also, they are not Western oriented. Indeed they are afraid of the West because it is something they don't know. For them, Russia and their relations back in the Motherland are everything."[41]

Although non-Russians frequently serve as noncommissioned officers, "the Soviet officer corps is ethnically Slavic with an overwhelming Russian majority."[42] About 80% of the officers are Russian, and 10 to 15% are Ukrainians and Byelorussians, so only 5 to 10% of the officer corps is comprised of non-Slavs. Among the reasons for this situation is that officer recruitment tests are conducted in Russian, but the single most important one is that non-Slavs are simply discouraged from pursuing a military career.

According to official propaganda, the military provides the means to create a "new Soviet man" out of the disparate ethnic groups in the USSR. But while conceding their findings are based on limited evidence, the authors' conclude:

> The clear consensus to emerge from these interviews is that in the Soviet peacetime armed forces, ethnic conflict is frequent, perhaps prevalent, and

occasionally severe. In most cases, we believe that the Soviet armed forces fail to bring about a homogenization of interest and a leveling of ethnic consciousness. To the contrary, national distinctions in many cases, probably a majority, appear to be enhanced by military experience. Thus, one can conclude that, at best, service in the Soviet military does little to bring the diverse nationalities of the USSR together; at worse, it has the completely opposite effect, stimulating ethnic animosities that are not evident before military service.[43]

Since 1917 the Russians have adopted myriad strategies to destroy values and loyalties to which the USSR's ethnic minorities cling. They have failed. If anything, the non-Russians in the USSR have become even bolder in resisting both attempts on the part of their "elder brothers" to inculcate them with a Soviet (read "Russian") consciousness and a massive KGB campaign to crush ethnic civil rights activists. At times the KGB will enjoy victories, but the nationality question will continue to be a divisive force in Soviet society. In the face of austerity, relations between the Russians and the ethnic minorities will get worse.

Notes

1. For example, Andrew Greeley, *Ethnicity in the United States: a Preliminary Reconnaissance* (New York: John Wiley and Sons, 1974). In the case of the Soviet Union, many prominent scholars of that society have slighted the importance of ethnicity in the USSR. See, for example, Stephen F. Cohen, *Rethinking the Soviet Experience: Politics and History Since 1917* (New York: Oxford University Press, 1985).
2. Karl Marx and Friedrich Engels, *The Communist Manifesto* (New York: Washington Square Press, 1964).
3. Engels, in acknowledging the divisiveness of ethnicity, told a friend, "The bourgeoisie need only wait, passively, and the dissimlar elements of the working class fall apart again." Maurice Zeitlein, *Revolutionary Politics and the Cuban Working Class* (New York: Harper and Row, Torchbooks, 1970), p. 67.
4. Cynthia H. Enloe, *Ethnic Conflict and Political Development* (Boston: Little, Brown and Co., 1973), p. 42.
5. V. I. Lenin, "On the Rights of National Self-Determination," in *Selected Works* (New York: International Publishers, 1943), p. 267.
6. Hélène Carrère d' Encaussé, *Decline of an Empire* (New York: Newsweek Books, 1979), p. 15.
7. Robert Conquest, *Soviet Nationalities Policy and Practice* (New York: Praeger Books, 1967), p. 59.
8. Nikita Khrushchev, *Khrushchev Remembers* (Boston: Little, Brown and Co., 1970), p. 85.
9. d'Encaussé, *Decline of an Empire*, p. 34.
10. d'Encaussé, *Decline of an Empire*, p. 215.
11. d'Encaussé, *Decline of an Empire*, p. 217.
12. d'Encaussé, *Decline of an Empire*, p. 215.
13. Interview with Jonas and Ausra Jurasas conducted in the spring of 1979.
14. Richard J. Krickus, "Hostages in Their Homeland," *Commonweal*, 15 February, 1980, pp. 75–80.

15. Richard J. Krickus, "To the Finland Border," *Commonweal*, 25 September, 1981, pp. 523–26.
16. Harold Isaacs, *Idols of the Tribe* (New York: Harper and Row, 1975).
17. d'Encaussé, *Decline of an Empire*, pp. 69, 89.
18. d'Encaussé, *Decline of an Empire*, p. 101.
19. d'Encaussé, *Decline of an Empire*, p. 169.
20. d'Encaussé, *Decline of an Empire*, p. 173.
21. Alexandre Bennigsen, "Muslims," *Religion in Communist Lands* 6 (Autumn 1978): 32.
22. Bennigsen, "Muslims," p. 33.
23. Bennigsen, "Muslims," p. 40.
24. Bennigsen, "Muslims," p. 42.
25. d'Encaussé, *Decline of an Empire*, p. 229.
26. Jerry F. Hough and Merle Fainsod, *How the Soviet Union is Governed* (Cambridge, MA: Harvard University Press, 1979), p. 570.
27. Seweryn Bialer, *Stalin's Successors* (New York: Cambridge University Press, 1981), p. 27.
28. S. Enders Wimbush, "The Russian Nationalist Backlash," *Survey* 24 (Summer 1979): 40–41.
29. Igor Shafarevich, "Separation or Reconciliation? The Nationalities Question in the USSR," Alexandr Solzhenitsyn et al., *From Under the Rubble* (New York: Bantham Books, 1976), p. 87.
30. Wimbush, "The Russian Nationalist," p. 45.
31. Alexander Yanov, *Détente After Brezhnev* (Berkeley, CA: Institute of International Studies, 1977).
32. Alexandre Bennigsen, "Soviet Muslims and the World of Islam," *Problems of Communism* 33 (March–April 1980): 49.
33. Bennigsen, "Muslims," p. 50.
34. Bennigsen, "Muslims," p. 50.
35. Bennigsen, "Muslims," p. 47.
36. Bennigsen, "Muslims," p. 48.
37. Bennigsen, "Muslims," p. 49.
38. S. Enders Wimbush and Alex Alexiev, "The Ethnic Factor in the Soviet Armed Forces," *Conflict: All Warfare Short of War* 4 (Numbers 2/3/5, 1983): 105.
39. Wimbush and Alexiev, "The Ethnic Factor," p. 111.
40. Wimbush and Alexiev, "The Ethnic Factor," p. 111.
41. Wimbush and Alexiev, "The Ethnic Factor," p. 112.
42. Wimbush and Alexiev, "The Ethnic Factor," p. 127.
43. Wimbush and Alexiev, "The Ethnic Factor," p. 152.

CHAPTER THREE

Eastern Europe: Asset or Liability?

Don't talk to me about "socialism." What we have we hold!—Leonid Brezhnev
to Alexander Dubček prior to the 1968 occupation of Czechoslovakia

The Satellite States: An Asset

Russia has been invaded from the West twice in this century alone—the tsar's Russia in 1914 and Stalin's USSR in 1941. In both cases, the Germans easily brushed aside weak neighbors or acquired their help in assaulting the colossus to the east. Moscow's primary postwar security objective, therefore, was to secure a buffer zone in Eastern Europe, comprised of communist regimes loyal to the USSR. With the Kremlin-backed coup in Czechoslovakia in 1948, Stalin consolidated his control over a region that today is populated by over 100 million people.

Currently the Soviets and their allies have numerous divisions deployed in Eastern Europe, armed with conventional and nuclear weapons, poised to deal a crushing blow to a Western invader. When Ronald Reagan entered the White House it was estimated that the Warsaw Pact had 4 million men under arms in 173 divisions, in contrast to 2.6 million for NATO in 84 divisions. It had an advantage in tanks of 42,500 to 13,000, in antitank guided weapon launchers by a margin of 24,300 to 8,100. In addition, whereas the pact had 78,000 armored personnel carriers and infantry fighting vehicles, NATO had 30,000. The pact's numerical edge extended to aircraft too. For example, NATO had 1,950 fighter bombers to the pact's 1,920 but the pact had 4,370 interceptors versus 740 for NATO and 2,500 planes capable of carrying nuclear munitions to NATO's 800.[1] Since then, NATO's conventional capability has improved markedly but the Pentagon claims that the Soviet bloc has greater military "assets" than the Western alliance.[2]

To assess the comparative strengths and weaknesses of the blocs is a complicated task, but it is apparent that the Soviet Union does not have to fear a Western conventional attack. In the unlikely event that one took place, the invaders would meet stiff resistance in Eastern Europe, allowing the Soviets to mobilize forces in western Russia to deal with them should they ever get that far. On the contrary, in spite of efforts to upgrade NATO's conventional forces, it is the West that has reason to fear attack, and it is unlikely that a Pact attack with conventional forces would be stopped without NATO employment of nuclear weapons.

The Warsaw Treaty Organization (WTO) was formed in 1955 as a response to West Germany's entry into NATO. An additional, equally important incentive in integrating the WTO forces into a military alliance was to deny Eastern Europeans a territorial defensive capability, such as that built by Josip Broz Tito in Yugoslavia and Enver Hoxha in Albania. Neither the Yugoslavs nor the Albanians had taken these measures thinking they could defeat the Red Army in an all-out war, but they had hoped a territorial defense would guarantee that a Soviet invasion would prove costly to Moscow. In Yugoslavia's case, a Soviet attack could precipitate an East–West clash.

Soviet military planners concluded, therefore, that none of their client states in Eastern Europe should be allowed to adopt their own military plans, lest they develop a territorial capability. So when Romania adopted a more independent posture in the late 1950s and appeared to be developing a territorial defense force—made possible by the withdrawal of Soviet troops in 1958 and diplomatic and logistical support to Bucharest from Yugoslavia, China, and the West—the Soviet high command redoubled its efforts to consolidate control over the other satellite armed forces:

> In the early 1960s the Soviet Commander of the Warsaw Pact, Marshall A. A. Grechko, activated the military agencies of the WTO in order to try to halt Romania's movement toward adoption of a strategy of territorial defense and to preempt the possibility that rebellious Communists in the parties of other Pact members might try to imitate the Albanian and Romanian examples. The device Marshal Grechko used to restore Soviet domination over the armed forces of the WTO was the system of multilateral military exercises, which he introduced in 1961–62.[3]

Grechko stated publicly that one of the Pact's missions was to deal with "counterrevolutionaries" in Eastern Europe. "By drawing the Eastern European armies into frequent joint exercises with the Soviet forces in Eastern Europe and the western military districts of the USSR, Grechko forestalled the development of territorial defense capabilities by the Eastern European ministries. . . ."[4] The "Muscovite," or pro-Soviet, factions in the disparate parties approved of this development because they depended upon Moscow to keep them in power and a territorial defensive capability would strengthen the hand of their adversaries who sought to become independent of the USSR.

There are other factors denying satellite armies the capability to resist a Soviet invasion. These forces rely solely on Soviet munitions and equipment; they cannot undertake prolonged massive military operations without the cooperation of allied units; and ambitious officers must attend military training centers and academies in the USSR in order to further their careers. During their time in the Soviet Union their mentors can determine their loyalty, and they, in turn, acquire pro-Soviet attitudes reinforced by the knowledge that should Moscow's influence dwindle in their homelands, so will their own.

In addition to being a military asset to Moscow, the satellites have provided the Soviets with economic advantages. After the German defeat, the Soviets acquired the industrial capacity of East Germany and Czechoslovakia, Poland's coal and shipbuilding complexes, and Bulgaria's, Romania's, and Hungary's agricultural products and light manufacturing output. Stalin blatantly exploited the Eastern Europeans by extracting billions in raw materials, assets, and manufacturing production from their economies. In 1949, the Council for Mutual Economic Assistance (CMEA) was formed to give Moscow control over the economic development of the region. Henceforth, the Soviets exchanged shoddy goods it could not sell abroad for Eastern European products that helped restore the Soviet economy.

In the 1960s, when the USSR had limited access to Western markets, the satellite countries provided a more or less captive market for Soviet products. The bloc countries subsidized Soviet economic development by providing low-interest loans enabling Moscow to exploit and ship its oil and gas. They also contributed to Soviet economic growth through involvement in "bloc ventures" that were disproportionately located in the USSR.

The satellites have reduced the Soviet defense burden by providing manpower and money to field WTO forces. Their contribution to the bloc's logistical infrastructure—roads, railways, airfields, and pipelines—have served Soviet economic activities, too, often at great cost to their own economies. Recently the satellites have had to share in the burden of assisting the communist LDCs associated with CMEA, such as Cuba, Ethiopia, and Vietnam.

Soviet hegemony in Eastern Europe is a political and ideological asset to the Kremlin. Moscow's domination of the Eastern European communist parties has played a vital role in containing the influence of anti-communist and anti-Soviet elements in the region. Soviet hegemony in the region also gives credence to Moscow's claim that it is the ideological center of world communism and supports Andrei Gromyko's frequently quoted assertion that there is no "international question of significance which can be decided without the Soviet Union or in opposition to it." Obviously, without domination of Eastern Europe, the Soviets would wield less influence in Western Europe.

In the 1920s membership in the comintern required that all communists be subservient to the CPSU, and in the 1930s Stalin purged leading Eastern European comrades to tighten his hold over their parties. He even dissolved the Polish Communist Party to improve relations with Hitler. Stalin could not tolerate independent communist parties in the region because independence in one country could spread to other ones. "This process, once begun, might have inspired factions within the Soviet party to reconsider the proper relationship of national communist parties to each other, including the mutual relationships of the national party organizations of the Soviet republics."[5]

It was with this fear in mind that Stalin sought to depose Tito. Although he failed in Yugoslavia, he purged the parties elsewhere in the region. His primary target was the "home communists" who had remained in their countries during the war. "Stalin reserved the leading positions in the Eastern European parties for the 'Muscovites'—the Communists who had spent their war years in the USSR and were largely dependent on Stalin for their position in the national parties."[6] Stalin's death gave rise to greater independence in the satellite countries and an outpouring of discontent on the part of their people. This caused Khrushchev to adopt a "new course" (initiated by Georgy Malenkov) that encouraged the leadership in the region to strive for legitimacy on its own—without, however, becoming independent of Moscow.

But in the aftermath of the Prague Spring, the Kremlin took measures to tighten its grip. Sergei Kovalev, writing in *Pravda* after Dubček's demise, outlined the Brezhnev doctrine, which circumscribed Eastern European independence:

> There is no doubt that the people of the socialist countries and the Communist Parties have and must have freedom to determine their country's path of development. However, any decision of their's must damage neither socialism in their own country nor the fundamental interests of the other socialist countries nor the worldwide workers' movement, which is waging a struggle for socialism. This means that every Communist Party is responsible not only to its own people but also to all the socialist countries and to the entire Communist movement. Whoever forgets this in placing sole emphasis on the autonomy and independence of Communist Parties lapses into one-sidedness, shirking his international obligations. . . .[7]

The looming threat of the Red Army did not prevent the rise of Solidarity in Poland, but its demise underscores what the Kremlin must deem to be one of its primary political assets in the region: the tens of thousands of functionaries in Eastern Europe whose careers are endangered by "anti-Soviet" elements in their countries. Because these "Muscovites" cannot acquire popular support through their actions, they depend upon the Soviets to keep them in power.

To a significant degree, "Soviet influence in Eastern Europe depends on Soviet control over appointments to the upper echelons of the East European party leadership and on the preservation of a Soviet capability for military intervention to prevent either the capture of the local party hierarchy by communists with domestic bases of support or the destruction of the party control system by local anti-communist forces."[8]

This explains why, contrary to wishful thinking in the West, the Polish army was able to crush Solidarity without direct intervention by the Red Army. This unpleasant fact has prompted Walter Lacquer to conclude that "the only successful revolutions in the Communist bloc are those carried out from above, not from below, and the revolutions from above are not usually democratic in character."[9]

The Satellite States: A Liability

Although many Western commentators lament that there is little hope for liberalization in Eastern Europe, the Soviets are also unhappy about developments there. From the Soviets' vantage point, their clients are becoming military, economic, and political liabilities—not assets.

The proposition that the satellites are a strategic liability is supported by Moscow's doubts about their reliability in a war and fears that the very troops the Soviets have armed and trained may one day turn their weapons against their mentors.

In comparing the military capabilities of NATO and the WTO, the reliability and effectiveness of the satellite forces must be given considerable weight. If attacked, most satellite units probably would resist, but if the WTO initiated hostilities, many would be reluctant to fight or would do so ineptly. Soviet units would have to lead the attack, while all but the most trusted satellite units would be used in support operations well behind the lines of combat. Because of doubts about their loyalty and effectiveness, Soviet strategists must discount them in making war plans. Indeed, uncertainties about the performance of Eastern European units must be deemed a major deterrent to a WTO *coup de main* against NATO's armies.

Simultaneously the Russians know that partisans in Poland and other parts of Eastern Europe would destroy WTO communications and transportation systems, oil and gas pipelines, and pumping stations. Having used partisan units to good effect against the Germans in the last war, the Russians appreciate how troublesome they can be even to a large, well-trained, well-led, and well-equipped army. In the event of war, Soviet units would be diverted to suppress partisans and saboteurs operating behind their lines.

The Soviets have never faced large numbers of satellite troops in combat, but in October 1956, General Bela Kiraly and other anti-Soviet officers in the Hungarian Army sought to mobilize troops, police, and civilians into a unified fighting force to oppose the WTO forces invading their country. Kiraly later claimed that if the "Revolutionary Committee of the Armed Forces which he formed had more time, it would have eventually wrested control of the regular armed forces from the pro-Soviet commanders in the Hungarian officer corps. . . ."[10]

Czechoslovakian military units did not resist the Pact invasion in 1968, so a clash with Russian troops was avoided. On several occasions beginning in the 1950s, however, the Soviets were prepared to crush "anti-socialist" uprisings in Poland but decided against this move because they feared units of the Polish Army would resist.[11]

Soviet fears about clashes with bloc troops or armed civilians are well founded. Economic and political problems in Eastern Europe promise to get worse, and these liabilities may precipitate open resistance to communist regimes in the region, forcing the Red Army to intervene.

Today, as has been true for many years, living standards in Eastern Europe are higher than they are in the USSR. In the decades following World War II, economic growth rates in the region were among the highest in the world. Living standards were well below those in the West, but economic prosperity helped ameliorate widespread discontent with unpopular regimes. By the late 1970s, however, the satellite economies began to feel the impact of the worldwide recession. In Poland the annual rate of industrial production from 1971 to 1975 was an impressive 10.4%, and the planned growth rate for 1976 to 1980 was 8.5%, but in 1979 the economy only grew 2.8%. Although not as dramatically, output in other satellite countries declined during the last five-year plan of the decade. Czechoslovakia, for example, had a growth rate of 6.7% from 1971 to 1975, but it slipped to 3.7% in 1979.[12]

If there is a strong and protracted global recovery, the economic futures of the bloc countries may brighten. But over the long haul, the economic news will be bad, principally because the satellite economies are inhibited by the same forces restricting Soviet economic activity. Heinrich Machowski observes that the communists in Eastern Europe and the USSR "created . . . war economies, which proved very effective in mobilizing resources for a limited number of priorities . . ." but that "in the long run, the Stalinist economic model has proved disastrous for Eastern Europe, which is much more dependent than the Soviet Union on trade with the West."[13] After the Prague Spring, many regimes in Eastern Europe sought to protect themselves against a similar crisis by improving the lot of the consumer. The most painless way to do this was to borrow from the West. With their vaults full of "petrodollars," capitalist lenders were happy to comply. In 1968 the Soviet bloc owed the West several million dollars; by 1982 their combined debt amounted to $80 billion. But as Rezso Nyers, a former Hungarian Politburo member, has written:

> The strategy of relying on Western credits without economic reform failed. Experience has shown that credits are not well used in a centralized economy because there is no efficient mechanism for alloting resources.[14]

It was assumed that technology—increasing productivity, reducing energy use, and improving the quality of output—would solve the bloc's problems; however, "in order to produce progress, technology must be accompanied by greater democracy and managerial decentralization."

Poland illustrates this point. The government of Edward Gierek constructed new enterprises with Western loans, but because of mismanagement, the products flowing from them have been inferior and cannot compete with Western goods. The dead hand of the command economies in the region has contributed to a decline in East–West trade, which accounted for 6% of world trade in 1975 but slipped to 4% in 1982.[15]

The Western media have publicized the Soviet bloc's debt obligations but have ignored a problem of deep and growing concern to Moscow. The Soviets for many years have been subsidizing the economies of Eastern Europe; by 1980 Soviet trade subsidies to the bloc countries amounted to $21 billion. As Michael Dobbs has observed, "The Soviet Union is one of the rare historical examples of an 'imperial metropolis' that exports cheap raw materials to its 'colonies'—and is used by them in return as a dumping ground for shoddy industrial goods."[16]

For years the most important commodities provided by the Soviets to the satellites were oil and gas. By 1978 Poland was the only country in the region producing more energy than it was using. The other satellites were dependent on foreign oil, primarily from the Soviet Union. Moscow also sold them gas and petroleum at prices below those prevailing on the international market. By 1979 90% of the oil imported by Bulgaria, East Germany, and Hungary came from the USSR, and the figure for Czechoslovakia was 85%.[17] Valerie Bunce writes that Soviet assistance to Eastern Europe in all forms from 1971 to 1981 amounted to $133 billion. This burden and a large defense budget resulted in a Soviet economic plan in 1982 which, for the first time, did not call for an increase in living standards.[18]

Such Soviet generosity reflects legitimate concerns in the Kremlin about political discontent in bloc countries rising as living standards decline. Soviet sensitivity along these lines persists because the USSR's relationship with its clients is not marked by fraternal cooperation but outright imperialism. Also, Soviet leaders realize that the ability of pro-Soviet regional leaders to maintain social order is linked to economic prosperity. It is with such considerations in mind that Gorbachev sees the satellites more as liabilities than as assets. The Polish crisis of 1980–81 is the most vivid reminder of this.

The Polish Experience

It has been assumed for over a hundred years, by both supporters and detractors of Marxism, that a Marxist revolution represented the most serious threat to capitalism. But the Marxist revolution that erupted in Poland in 1980 revealed that an uprising led by and for workers is a major threat to rulers of communist, not capitalist, countries. To label the Polish revolution Marxist may strike some observers as hyperbole, but Marx and his followers assumed that a proletarian revolution would be comprised of the following ingredients:

- After years of exploitation, the workers acquire a new political consciousness and, overcoming fear of their oppressors, rise up in a spontaneous display of solidarity to try to topple them from power.
- Their major weapon is the strike, and their principal instrument of revolution (according to some Marxists) is the labor union.
- The most progressive elements of the intelligentsia join the workers to facilitate the destruction of the old order.
- The ruling oligarchy, in violation of the "democratic principles" it claims to uphold, uses brute force to crush the revolution.

All of these ingredients were at work in Poland. Abraham Brumberg, a leading U.S. student of contemporary Poland, has cited seven factors that contributed to the rise of Solidarity. If the observations of other commentators are included, we can report the following with confidence.

1.   The shipyard workers in Gdansk who initiated the strike action— which spread across the country to steel mills, mines, factories, and eventually to schools, offices, and farms—were not cowed by memories of state oppression. Ten years earlier, the government had used force to crush a strike in this city on the Baltic, and a number of workers were killed. But that did not dissuade the shipyard workers from challenging the authorities in 1980. It is noteworthy that most of the leaders and militants were relatively young people, such as Lech Walesa, who was in his late thirties. Their actions testified to the failure of the regime, which dominated the schools, the media, and other vital areas, to win the support of young people. Moreover, most commentators attribute Solidarity's success to the Polish workers being better educated and more sophisticated in 1980 than they were a decade earlier.

2.   Efforts on the part of organized dissident groups—led primarily by intellectuals such as those associated with the Self-Defense Committee (KOR)—proved successful in educating the workers about the regime's shortcomings and devising strategies to publicize them. This assistance was an important factor in Solidarity's rapid ascendancy. Contrary to the claims of U.S. scholars, who have reported a gap between intellectuals and workers in

Eastern Europe, both groups collaborated effectively throughout the life of the union.

3.   The intellectuals did not have to work hard to convince the workers, peasants, and students that the regime was oppressive, corrupt, and incompetent. Even loyal members of the Polish Communist Party were appalled by the corrupt practices of their superiors.

4.   In addition to rising levels of education, urbanization also had a profound impact on the militancy and sophistication that the workers displayed in 1980 and 1981. Over the past 20 years, millions of Poles have left the countryside for the city. Marx predicted in the 19th century that this transformation would give rise to revolutionary consciousness on the part of the uprooted peasantry. Ironically, in the 20th century, a ruling class governing in his name suffered the consequences of this process.

5.   Gierek, who replaced Wladyslaw Gomulka after the 1970 outbreaks, sought to win the support of his people through an ambitious economic development program, which relied heavily on Western loans to modernize the economy. For a while, real economic progress was made, fueling popular expectations; these were dashed in the late 1970s by the failure of the economy to sustain the living standards to which the Polish people aspire.

6.   Brumberg reminds us that Polish trade unionism has a long history. This heritage proved to be vital to the success of Solidarity. By 1981, the organization had ten million members, representing a cross section of Polish society, including many men and women who belonged to the Polish Communist Party. For about a year, the only truly independent labor movement in the Communist world thrived in Poland. The unions in Moscow, Peking, Havana, and Hanoi are sham organizations, associated with reactionary regimes as hostile to worker's organizations as were the far-right regimes of the 19th century.

7.   The failure of the Communist government to destroy the Catholic church—the only organization in Poland that has the support of the Polish masses—clearly was vital to the rise of Solidarity. Without the church, it is doubtful whether Solidarity would ever have materialized.[19]

Today, Solidarity is no longer a viable labor organization; it has, for all intents and purposes been demolished. But the men in the Kremlin and their counterparts in Warsaw, Prague, and other Eastern European capitals know that while "the Polish disease" may be in remission, it will one day manifest itself again. The next time, if the rebellion spreads, the Red Army may have to intervene in more than one country.

After Poland?

Western analysts agree that the Soviets must prepare for another uprising in Eastern Europe. They disagree only about the timing—will it be in the near or long term?—and the impact—will Moscow be able to handle it without much difficulty? Or, will it mean the use of troops, precipitating a host of new problems for the Soviets both inside and outside their empire?

Bruno Kreisky, the former Austrian chancellor, predicted in late 1982 that there would be another outbreak in Eastern Europe in about ten years: "It takes at least 10 years for another generation to arise which has not had the experience of defeat. Ten years after Hungary—Czechoslovakia. Ten years after Czechoslovakia—Poland. In the next 10 or 12 years you will see it again."[20]

Some scholars, such as Walter Lacquer, believe the Soviets will not have much trouble dealing with outbreaks in the region, but others disagree. Bialer, for example, has written:

> Until now, fortune has favored the Soviet Union in its dealings with the empire. Revolts, rebellions, unrest, and reform movements have almost always erupted in one satellite country at a time. The coming decade may well bring the coincidence of outbursts among increasingly restive elites and populations in several East European countries at the same time.[21]

If this should come to pass, or if the outbreak is less widespread but compels the Red Army to intervene, this action could have fateful consequences for the Soviet Union at home and abroad. The Soviet invasion of Czechoslovakia gave impetus to the dissident movement in the USSR, and one of Moscow's gravest concerns about Solidarity in Poland was that developments there would stir up discontent on the part of non-Russians in the USSR. The Soviets can expect that another Hungary, Czechoslovakia, or Poland will have potentially significant implications for dissent within their own country.

At the same time, the Red Army's crushing the revolt could have a dramatic impact upon the West. There is no question that one thing that deterred Moscow from using its troops in Poland was the detrimental impact it would have had on the campaign to convince the Western Europeans that they have no reason to fear Soviet military might, that Stalinism is dead, and that social order in the Soviet empire can be maintained without resorting to terror. The Soviets know that "another Hungary" could undermine Moscow's campaign to convince the West that it is needlessly spending money on weapons to deter an attack from the East that will never come. It could bolster those "revanchists" in West Germany who are intent upon unifying Germany under an "anti-Soviet" regime and help the Reaganites in their quest for a space-based defense, the Strategic Defence Initiative (SDI).

Simultaneously, Moscow's image among leftists abroad would be further tarnished. The demise of Solidarity prompted the late Enrico Berlinguer, leader of the Italian Communist Party, to openly chastise the Soviets for the role they played in the Jaruzelski coup. Solidarity's suppression was the last straw for Soviet apologists in Paris, who had resisted the campaign among French intellectuals to distance themselves from left-wing orthodoxy. In the United States, Susan Sontag caused an uproar when she shared her thoughts about the coup with an audience of leftist intellectuals in New York City:

> What the recent Polish events illustrate is something more than that fascist rule is possible within the framework of a communist society.... What they illustrate is a truth that we should have understood a very long time ago: that communism is fascism.... Not only is fascism the probable destiny of all communist societies ... but communism is in itself a variant ... of fascism. Fascism with a human face.[22]

The governments in Eastern Europe can avoid insurrectionary situations or prevent them from undermining pro-Soviet rule if they occur. Economic growth is essential here; most of their citizens will endure political autocracy if their living conditions improve. But can the Communists sustain high growth rates and not jeopardize their political base? Most observers believe they cannot. Philip Windsor, however, among others, contends that the satellites can adopt reforms to improve output without political liberalization, and that close economic contact with the West need not compromise the integrity of Communist regimes. Hungary, for example, has gone further in experimenting with free-market mechanisms than any bloc country, but this has not led to political liberalization or anti-Soviet policies. Hungary has had extensive economic contact with the West as well, but this has not resulted in the Hungarian government embracing bourgeois democracy.[23]

If enterprising leaders demonstrate to Gorbachev that "liberalization" does not mean the destruction of communism in the region or the rise of anti-Soviet regimes, he might give the Eastern Europeans his blessing. If the satellite regimes secure popular support through economic growth, instead of political intimidation, the Soviets are likely to spend less time worrying about the satellites and devote more energy and resources to resolving their own predicament.

Unfortunately for Gorbachev, there is little likelihood that this will happen. He is prepared to allow the Hungarians to continue experimenting with free market mechanisms, but if not expanded, they will be incapable of resolving Budapest's economic problems more fully. Moreover, they need to be accompanied by political reforms. Andras Hegedus, a former Hungarian prime minister, has said that if the Eastern European countries are going to resolve their economic problems, Moscow must permit "constructive opposition" to communist rule. The conservative Communist Party leaders in Hungary must acknowledge that "in order for economic reform to be meaningful, there has to be greater political democracy too."[24]

Of course, this linkage between economic and political liberalization explains why Soviet-bloc leaders are fearful of experimenting with economic policies that rest on the dilution of party domination of the economy. Even Windsor concedes that tight party control of economic affairs vitiates "all necessary features of a complex modern economy." Among the "features" he mentions are "the flow of rapid and effective information, the ability to devolve decisions to a level where they could be guided by such information, the flexibility of arbitration between competing groups . . . ," etc.[25]

It is not clear, also, how deeply Moscow will let the bloc countries become entangled with capitalist economic interests. The Soviets delight in the fact that Western banks are bailing out bungling communist planners in Eastern Europe, thereby sparing them the honor of doing so. But whereas Communist governments may today be in a position to manipulate their creditors, history instructs us that creditors usually wind up dominating the relationship. It is not fanciful, then, to perceive the satellites' dependency upon Western capital as the first in a series of steps that will result in the Finlandization of Eastern Europe.

It is on the basis of such reasoning, bolstered by the economic determinism of Marxism, that observers in Moscow must be uneasy about extensive and enduring economic relations between their clients and their capitalist adversaries. In the summer of 1985, while the fortieth session of the CMEA council was being conducted in Warsaw, Gorbachev gave a speech in the USSR. He urged CMEA members to deepen "economic cooperative and economic integration," in order to "nullify the policy of economic pressure that is actively pursued by the West toward the socialist countries."[26]

Another consideration, unnerving to the conservative leadership in Eastern Europe, is the thought that once you give way to reformers' economic demands, they will not stop until they make a bid for political power, too. Given such fears, Eastern European leaders may choose the tried-and-true policy of repression, of digging in in the face of adversity, of not running the risk that reformist medicine may be more harmful than the ailment it is calculated to treat.

Repression, after all, has worked. The Poles, like the Hungarians and Czechs before them, have backed down in the face of military force and police-state terror. And even though it may be only a temporary solution in Warsaw, it may have greater longevity in Budapest, East Berlin, Sofia, Prague, and Bucharest. To lump the Eastern European countries together is a mistake because they are not culturally, politically, or economically homogeneous. To interpret developments in one bloc country as foretelling the future in other ones is to ignore these distinctions.

To hardliners in the Soviet bloc, the bottom line is political power. They can tolerate sluggish economic growth and popular discontent, as long as they can maintain their positions of influence. If need be, they will invite Soviet units into their countries to crush mavericks in the party, or dissidents outside of it, to remain in control. Many Western commentators, therefore, have concluded that analysts who foresee economic stagnation in Eastern Europe leading to the demise of communism are engaging in wishful thinking.

The "Finlandization" of Eastern Europe?

The notion that Soviet domination of Eastern Europe—and the existence of communist governments there—is a permanent condition is founded on three interrelated propositions. First, the "Muscovites" will rule the satellite countries for the rest of this century. Second, economic setbacks may foment popular discontent, but the "Muscovites" will squelch it. Third, if they are incapable of suppressing "anti-socialist" elements, the Soviets will intervene and do it themselves.

All of these propositions are plausible, but there is another scenario which may accurately presage the future: some elements in the bloc parties will initiate reforms that ultimately change the character of the regimes in Eastern Europe and reduce Moscow's influence over them.

Charles Gati has written that a "mini-coalition within the Warsaw Pact" has emerged, setting "both an economic and political agenda" that is "out of phase with Moscow's words and deeds." The people involved are not dissidents or communist mavericks—they are the existing leaders. The West began to take note of their independence in the early 1980s, when the Soviets sought to prevent the deployment of "Euromissiles" scheduled for December 1983. The Kremlin warned the Western Europeans of "dire consequences" should Pershing IIs be deployed in West Germany and Tomahawk missiles in England, Italy, Belgium, and Holland. Soviet propagandists did not declare détente defunct, but they were icy in their relations with the Europeans and urged their clients in the bloc to adopt a similar posture.[27]

To the surprise of many observers, however, the governments of Hungary, East Germany, Romania, and even Jaruzelski's regime in Poland challenged Moscow's position. Mátyás Szürös, the Hungarian party secretary in charge of foreign affairs, wrote an article in a Hungarian journal claiming that Moscow could not formulate a "common strategy" for the Soviet bloc. According to Gati, Szürös "affirmed the desirability of détente between the small and medium-sized countries of Eastern and Western Europe, suggesting that 'contacts between particular socialist and capitalist countries can flourish at a time when the general trend is one of deterioration in East–West relations.'" Other writers remarked that the Hungarians were no longer clearing high appointments with Moscow, as had been customary.[28]

The East Germans, who had always sought to please the Soviets, have recently rankled them by maintaining close relations with their brethren in the Federal Republic of Germany. In the summer of 1984, the German Democratic Republic negotiated a large loan with West Germany. In return, the East Germans guaranteed that more people would be allowed to emigrate from the GDR to the FRG. It was originally surmised that this exchange of cash for freedom was a cynical deal, consistent with earlier obnoxious behavior of the East Germans. However, the East German leader, Erich Honecker, had more than monetary considerations in mind. He had discovered that his popularity blossomed with each arrangement that brought the divided Germanies into close contact. Honecker's cordial relations with the FRG had given his government legitimacy in the eyes of his people, a goal that had previously eluded him and his predecessors. He was not about to sever relations with the West Germans, even if such ties displeased the Soviets.

Meanwhile, Romania enhanced its reputation for being a recalcitrant member of the "socialist community" when it refused to comply with Moscow's dictate that the "fraternal socialist countries" not attend the 1984 Summer Olympics in Los Angeles. The fact that Nicolae Ceauşescu's athletes did well at the games, and were subject to special attention and praise, was an added affront to the Russians. Moscow's reluctance or inability to punish the Romanians did not go unnoticed by other bloc countries either.

The Soviets lashed out at such displays of "nationalism" and "separatism." Following a common practice, they voiced their displeasure through surrogates—for example, the Czech party newspaper, *Rude Pravo*, which attacked the East Germans, Hungarians, and Romanians for seeking favors from the West. They made pointed criticisms of their own too. Oleg B. Rakhmanin, an official in the Soviet Central Committee, scolded the wayward Eastern Europeans for defining "the role of large and small countries outside the concept of the class struggle and the fundamental contradiction between socialism and capitalism." The United States, he warned, was seeking to exploit discord within the Warsaw Pact, a fear reinforced by reports from the White House that Reagan was thinking about inviting Eastern European leaders to Washington.[29]

There were several reasons for these displays of bravado on the part of the bloc leaders. First, with the collapse of the Polish Communist regime, Moscow had sent a disconcerting message to the Eastern European Communist governments. The Soviets would not stand behind bloc leaders who were incapable of keeping their people in line but would find others who would. To some satellite leaders, this was an open invitation to ambitious underlings to attempt to topple them by exploiting popular discontent. Consequently, if popular support was a litmus test for staying in power, even the "Muscovites" had nothing to lose by adopting reforms repugnant to the Russians but popular with their own people. This, of course, was a risky game, because in the past the Soviets had punished bloc officials who exceeded what the Russians deem to be "tolerable reforms."

During the period of de-Stalinization in the mid-1950s, several Eastern European governments sought to attract popular support by allowing greater dissent and providing their people more consumer goods. At first, the Russians encouraged these reforms, but their permissive attitude changed dramatically after the 1956 Hungarian revolution. Reformers were purged and dissidents silenced throughout the Soviet bloc. Henceforth, communist leaders in the region had greater reason to fear Moscow's wrath than their people's anger.

In 1968, Alexander Dubček wrested power from Stalinists in Czechoslovakia. He told Brezhnev that, unlike Imre Nagy in Hungary, he intended to keep his country in the Soviet camp. He would allow greater dissent and embrace new economic policies, but he would not turn his back on communism. Brezhnev was unimpressed, and he replaced the leaders of the Prague Spring with hardliners whose rigid rule has since hampered the country's economic performance.

But there is a second reason why the Soviets may allow the Eastern Europeans to entertain previously proscribed reforms: if the bloc economies slump further, popular discontent could reach explosive proportions, giving rise to one or more "Polands." Third, at a time when the Soviets are preoccupied with serious problems of their own, they would be disinclined to closely follow developments in Eastern Europe.

Soviet foreign policy priorities represent a fourth reason why bloc leaders feel they could entertain reforms the Soviets had deemed dangerous, political liberalization, or undesirable: greater independence from Moscow. Since NATO's inception the Soviets have tried to drive a wedge between the Americans and the Europeans; in the early years after World War II, they relied primarily upon fear and intimidation. Recently they have been more subtle. Rather than directly threaten the Western Europeans, for example, they have sought to exacerbate fissures in the alliance, such as differences over trade, policy toward revolutionary movements in Central America, and SDI.

It appears that the satellite leaders now realize that this Soviet campaign can work to their advantage. By coming down hard on the bloc countries, the Soviets know that they are aiding and abetting hardliners in the West, who cite their hegemony in Eastern Europe as evidence that the USSR is an imperialist power and argue on that basis for heavy defense spending. Moscow's campaign to woo Western opinion, therefore, may give the bloc leaders greater license to embark on reforms that may be displeasing to the Soviets.

Finally, the Soviets have indicated that the satellites will get less economic support from Moscow. In 1984 Moscow conducted the first Soviet bloc economic summit in 15 years. "The Russians offered no remedies" to the satellites' economic problems "and no alternatives that the East Europeans could adopt."[30] To make matters worse, the Soviets informed them they would have to pay more for Soviet gas and oil, and that Moscow would only accept quality goods in return—goods the Eastern Europeans could sell for hard cash elsewhere. But that was not all: the Soviets informed their clients that they would have to provide more capital to help the USSR modernize its economy.

This last set of observations is particularly important because it lends substance to the observation that the Finlandization of Eastern Europe is a more palpable threat to the USSR than the Finlandization of Western Europe is to the United States. The basis for this conclusion is that the bloc countries cannot comply with economic demands that the Soviets made in 1984 without greater, not reduced, commercial relations with the West. Indeed, in the aftermath of the summit, Hungary received a $450 million loan from the World Bank—an organization that Moscow characterizes, with justification, as a tool of U.S. economic hegemony. This was just one of several moves the Hungarians made to achieve closer economic harmony with the West—in the face of Soviet advice to the contrary.

Several months later (July 21, 1984), the Polish legislature, the *Sejm*, announced sweeping amnesty for political prisoners. Top Solidarity leaders were released from prison, those underground were told that they could come out of hiding without fear of persecution, and even intellectuals associated with the KOR—such as Adam Michnik and Jacek Kuron—were freed. The government took these measures to seek a resumption of economic relations with the United States that had been discontinued with Solidarity's demise.

Future Prospects

Will Gorbachev tolerate displays of independence in Eastern Europe, now that he is in firm control? It is noteworthy that the Western press saw his ascendancy as good news for the Eastern Europeans. Soon after taking power, a headline in the *Los Angeles Times* read, "Gorbachev May Be Eastern Europe's Best Hope for Evolution," while one in the *Washington Post* proclaimed, "Soviet Allies Optimistic on Modernization." Scholars, meanwhile, recalled that in the past a leadership change in Moscow frequently involved a housecleaning in satellite capitals. Rather than receiving understanding and support from Moscow, the bloc leaders might once again be slapped down with the mailed fist.

Thus far Gorbachev has proceeded cautiously, neither upholding optimistic nor pessimistic forecasts. In 1985, the Warsaw Pact was renewed for thirty more years. Some of the satellites, such as Romania, only wanted a 10-year extension, while East German officials indicated their displeasure with heavy defense outlays at a time when their economy needed capital for economic expansion. But the Soviets cited the U.S. defense surge, among other things, as justification for continued "vigilance."

Like their counterparts in Western Europe, the Eastern Europeans want to reduce their heavy defense budgets, which they have had to live with for forty years, but the Soviets, like the Americans with NATO, have maintained steady pressure on their allies to sustain them. This pressure will not subside until their is a significant reduction in NATO and WTO conventional forces. Consequently this is one of many reasons why the satellites would like to see détente resurrected.

On the economic front, Gorbachev has cautioned the bloc leaders against becoming too entangled with the West: He has urged them to more closely coordinate their policies within the framework of CMEA and has told them that Moscow expects to receive quality goods from them in trade. Gorbachev has derided experiments with free market mechanisms, but he has not pressed the Hungarians, who have been most partial to such experiments, to desist. The truth is that the experts in Moscow have no answers to their clients' economic problems. Thus, rhetoric aside, Gorbachev will allow the Hungarians and East Germans (who, like their comrades in Budapest, have demonstrated economic acumen) to adopt economic policies that would be characterized as "anti-socialist" were they to appear in the USSR.

Politically *Pravda* has taken the satellites to task for making too much of national attributes in arguing that there are many roads to socialism, and it has attacked those leaders who "claim that small countries can mediate between the great powers." But other Soviet organs, such as the CPSU journal *Kommunist*, have conceded "that national interests among socialist countries need not be identical and that to ignore such interests would do more harm than good."[31]

The Soviets have made it clear, however, that they do not want the East Germans to move too fast in expanding political relations with West Germany. Gorbachev will stick to this position as long as U.S.–Soviet arms control negotiations fail to produce results pleasing to Moscow. For the Eastern Europeans, then, an overall improvement in U.S.–Soviet relations, along with progress on arms control, is essential to the resolution of their growing internal problems. Gorbachev may prohibit the adoption of far-reaching reforms under any circumstances, but he is more likely to allow reforms if his concerns about the U.S. military threat subside along with East–West tensions.[32]

Notes

1. Carnegie Panel on U.S. Security and the Future of Arms Control, *Challenges for U.S. National Security: A Preliminary Report Part II* (Washington: Carnegie Endowment for International Peace, 1981), pp. 53–94.
2. The U.S. Department of Defense, *Soviet Military Power 1985* (Washington: Government Printing Office, 1985), p. 133.
3. Christopher D. Jones, *Political Autonomy in Eastern Europe*, (New York: Praeger Publishing, 1981), pp. 228–29.
4. Jones, *Autonomy in Eastern Europe*, p. 229.
5. Ernst Kux, "Growing Tensions in Eastern Europe," *Problems of Communism* 29 (March–April 1980): 27.

6. Kux, "Growing Tensions," p. 6.
7. Charles Gati, "From Cold War Origins to Détente," in Charles Gati, ed., *The International Politics of Eastern Europe* (New York: Praeger Publishing, 1976), p. 16.
8. Jones, *Autonomy in Eastern Europe*, p. 78.
9. Walter Lacquer, "What Poland Means?," *Commentary* (March, 1982): 27.
10. Jones, *Autonomy in Eastern Europe*, p. 78.
11. Jones, *Autonomy in Eastern Europe*, p. 78.
12. Kux, "Growing Tensions," p. 28.
13. *Washington Post*, 14 December 1982.
14. *Washington Post*, 14 December 1982.
15. *Washington Post*, 14 December 1982.
16. *Washington Post*, 14 December 1982.
17. Jack Kramer, "Soviet–CMEA Energy Ties," *Problems of Communism* 34 (July–August 1985): 32–47.
18. Valerie Bunce, "The Empire Strikes Back: The Evolution of the Eastern Bloc From a Soviet Asset to a Soviet Liability," *International Organization* 39 (Winter 1985): 18–20.
19. Abraham Brumberg, "Solidarity Forever," *The New Republic*, 21 March, 1981, p. 16.
20. *Washington Post*, 14 December, 1982.
21. Seweryn Bialer, "The Harsh Decade: Soviet Politics in the 1980s," *Foreign Affairs* 59 (Summer 1981): 1019.
22. *Newsweek*, 22 February 1982, p. 28.
23. Philip Windsor, "Stability and Instability in Eastern Europe," in Karen Dawisha and Philip Hanse, eds., *Soviet–Eastern European Dilemmas* (New York: Holmes and Meier, 1981), p. 199.
24. *Washington Post*, 14 December, 1982.
25. Windsor, "Stability and Instability," p. 197.
26. Vladimir V. Kusin, "Gorbachev and Eastern Europe," *Problems of Communism* (January–February 1986): 42–43.
27. *Washington Post*, 8 July 1984.
28. *Washington Post*, 8 July 1984.
29. *Washington Post*, 8 July 1984.
30. *Washington Post*, 8 July 1984.
31. Kusin, "Gorbachev," pp. 43–44.
32. Kusin, "Gorbachev," pp. 43–44.

CHAPTER FOUR

What is to be Done?
Three Alternative Futures

Generally speaking, the most perilous moment for a bad government is when it seeks to mend its ways. — Alexis de Tocqueville

Legitimacy in the Soviet System

Since 1964 political power in the Soviet Union has been transferred smoothly from one leader to another. In Gorbachev's case, something unprecedented occurred: he was chosen to replace Chernenko before the old man died, and he functioned as the power behind the throne until that time. But while the Soviets have had a peaceful changing of the guard, the accumulation of crises in the USSR may precipitate a power struggle akin to the one that occurred after Lenin's death.

There are two reasons for this forecast. First, when the Soviet predicament was in its early stages in the 1970s, the geriatric leadership had no stomach to change things drastically, and they ignored the accumulation of crises discussed in the preceding three chapters. From now on, however, the Soviet predicament will get worse, and the new generation of leaders will be unable to stand pat—unlike their predecessors, they will be around for a long time, and if they do nothing *they* will suffer the consequences.

Second, although the younger people replacing the old guard realize they must act, it is unclear whether they have agreed upon a common course of action. Confusion in the Kremlin may produce political gridlock, and bold new reforms may not occur. Conversely, if Gorbachev transfers his tough rhetoric into structural changes that threaten the prerogatives of the elite and the vast body of lower-level bureaucrats, a power struggle is likely to occur. Figurative, and perhaps literal, bloodletting will disrupt the consensus in Soviet ruling circles.

In this connection, the major thrust of this chapter is to discuss three futures that conceivably can produce solutions to the Soviet crisis. First, however, let us briefly discuss how Soviet regimes have acquired the mantle of legitimacy since 1917, because Gorbachev's principal challenge is to maintain the regime's legitimacy, in the face of an accumulation of crises compelling him to adopt policies that would alienate a large cross section of Soviet society.

Lenin's intellect, Stalin's ruthlessness, Khrushchev's guile, and Brezhnev's steadfastness contributed to their ability to rule the USSR. But the Soviet system has survived serious internal and external threats because most of the people deem it legitimate, responsive to their needs, and capable of maintaining order at home while protecting them against external threats. Reduced to a simple dichotomy, political order in any society rests on one of two foundations: political power or political authority. In the first instance, people obey their political leaders because they are fearful of the consequences if they do not—imprisonment, economic deprivation, or even death. In the second one, people obey because they believe their rulers have the right to make them do so—by virtue of tradition, merit, or other criteria. Social order, then, is achieved in the first case through coercion, in the second one through consensus. In most societies, one can find both political power and political authority at work, but in democratic societies, the latter is more evident, while in autocratic societies the former is. But autocrats can gain legitimacy if they deter foreign adversaries, foster economic growth at home, and do other things deemed to be in the people's welfare.

From the outset, the Bolsheviks sought to secure social order through political authority, promising to adopt policies that favored the many and not the few. Yet even prior to Lenin's death in 1924, they had applied force to eliminate real and imagined opponents and to intimidate the masses. After Stalin emerged as Lenin's successor in late 1929, he resorted to a policy of systematic terror that prevailed until his death. Nevertheless, during the war Stalin's popularity soared with the perception that he was the strong leader, the motherland needed to rebuff the hated Germans.

Stalin's successors scrapped the draconian policies associated with his rule. Khrushchev's famous speech at the Twentieth Party Congress in 1956, which delineated "Stalin's crimes," was calculated not only to undermine the influence of the Stalinists who were Khrushchev's competitors but also to pave the way for a liberalization drive that survived for several years after his removal in 1964. By the late 1960s Brezhnev had reimposed tighter controls over the population, and with Andropov's assistance begun crushing the dissident movement.

Notwithstanding Brezhnev's reliance on political power to achieve social order, he preferred to govern by political authority. Rule via political power alone is expensive, necessitating a vast police apparatus that has access to all corners of Soviet life. It fosters a climate of fear and suspicion that even affects the leadership because, under such circumstances, "no one is safe." Brezhnev enhanced the regime's image by transforming the Soviet Union from a major regional power to a superpower. By the mid-1970s, the USSR achieved nuclear parity with the United States and developed an air and sea-lift capability that enabled Moscow to project its military power throughout the world. Later in the decade, therefore, when the economy began to falter, the Soviet people could take pride in their country's global status, and thus justify to themselves the sacrifices they were making. After Ronald Reagan's election, the Kremlin exploited the new president's anti-Soviet rhetoric, and his vows to "rearm America," resurrecting the Soviet people's fear of war.

The support of ordinary Soviet citizens is vital to the regime, but of special importance is the loyalty of party functionaries, government officials, technocrats, and managers, who are appointed to their posts through the *nomenklatura* system. The Kremlin leaders can take comfort in the fact that the *nomenklatura* and the Soviet middle class are likely to support them, should the masses dare to challenge the regime. According to journalist Robert Kaiser, who lived and worked in the USSR in the early 1970s:

> The cardinal domestic achievement of the Brezhnev era was to broaden the Soviet regime's base of active support. When the Brezhnev group took over in 1964, a relatively small elite benefitted personally from the system. Under Brezhnev the system of privileges and special rewards for the members of the elite grew dramatically, as did the size of the elite that was eligible for them. By enhancing the living standards of these people, Brezhnev enhanced the stability of the Soviet regime.[1]

The steadfastness demonstrated by many of the party cadres, law enforcement officials, and professional soldiers in Poland has given credence to this observation. They believed—with some justification—that were Solidarity to gain control of Poland, they, along with their superiors, would be punished. Undoubtedly their counterparts in the USSR today believe that were the regime's enemies to turn the tables, they would fill the prisons, labor camps, and psychiatric hospitals occupied currently by democrats and ethnic activists.

Although the Soviet leadership can take comfort in the people's support (and passivity) and that of the middle class, it has cause to worry about disunity in its own ranks. After all, authoritarian regimes often fall because of bitter infighting on the part of the ruling oligarchy, not because of grassroots discontent. Such fissures have not significantly afflicted the Soviet leadership;

they share common beliefs, values, and interests that are a source of unity. Bialer states that the major features of this consensus are as follows:

> Opposition to a liberal-democratic political organization of society;
> The commitment to a one-party state and to the leading role of the party within the state;
> A deep-seated fear and mistrust of spontaneity in political and social behavior, which induce an interventionist psychology and stress the need of strong central government, of organization, of hierarchy, and of order;
> The cult of national unity and the condemnation of individuals and groups who threaten to impair that unity;
> Deep-seated nationalism and a great-power orientation which provides the major effective durable bond among the elites and between the elite and the masses;
> The commitment to a Soviet East European empire;
> The radical decline of the impulse to reshape society and a commitment to the basic structure which Soviet society has attained;
> The withering away of utopianism and a commitment to the rationalization of the system;
> The belief in and commitment to progress understood particularly in a highly material and technical way and combined with a technological and scientific ethos.[2]

Many observers concede that the regime must grapple with the problems scrutinized in the last three chapters but believe it can make necessary adjustments by operating within existing political and economic frameworks. Others, however, claim it will either have to liberalize or re-Stalinize Soviet society to survive. All of these viewpoints are discussed in the three scenarios below—"Welfare State Authoritarianism," "Liberal Reform," and "Russian Fascism."

Three Futures: Welfare State Authoritarianism

Several years after replacing Chernenko, Mikhail Gorbachev has consolidated his power in the CPSU, filling key slots with "his" people and removing possible competitors from positions of influence.

Although he is free to act boldly, Gorbachev has been cautious in adopting economic changes. His performance sits well with the *nomenklatura*, who are ill-disposed toward dramatic policy shifts because they fear losing the prerogatives of power. Besides, the younger among them have waited patiently for their superiors to retire, and they are not about to change the rules now that they are filling top slots they long coveted in the party, government, and military.

Satiric commentators in Moscow have characterized Gorbachev as the leader of a "Mexican-style revolution." Like the long line of presidents who have ruled Mexico, Gorbachev is fond of making "revolutionary" pronouncements but clings tightly to the status quo. For several years after ascending to power, it appeared as if he would shake up the Soviet bureaucracy and take on colleagues in the party hierarchy who opposed reform. But his political instincts told him that if he did so he would trade places with comrade Grigory Romanov (whom Gorbachev removed from office soon after taking power) or perhaps share the fate of another Romanov, named Nicholas. When discrepancies between his forceful rhetoric and his frail actions are brought to his attention, he gets indignant and reminds his inquisitors that "anti-Soviet" elements would love him to move prematurely in solving the country's problems.

The stresses that the USSR is experiencing, he says, are a natural part of "socialist development." The workers and peasants have suffered most from slow economic growth, but they understand they must make sacrifices if the Soviet armed forces are to maintain their capacity to keep the "capitalist warmongers" at bay. In conversation with a delegation of Italian communists, Gorbachev cites an article published in a "progressive" Italian newspaper, quoting a Russian steelworker who said he was glad to sacrifice "to keep the motherland strong." A female street sweeper told the same journalist that "everybody is experiencing hard times, people here and in the West, too, but in our country everyone who wants one has a job, and no one is thrown out into the street to fend for themselves like unemployed are in capitalist countries."

A reporter for *Time* magazine reveals that conditions in the countryside are more grim than in urban areas, but that the peasants—isolated incidents aside—have demonstrated that the fatalism of the Russian masses persists. The peasants' silence is also attributed to the fact that those with small private plots have been consuming food they grow or have bartered it with city folk for consumer items scarce in small villages.

The military, as expected, has remained vigilant in opposing efforts to "bribe" the people by plying them with consumer goods at the expense of the defense budget. They are supported by civilian hard-liners who argue that, in the face of the massive Western campaign to gain military superiority, defense cuts are unwarranted.

Economic belt-tightening, however, has prompted ethnic minorities in many places to take to the streets protesting living conditions. The authorities take comfort in the fact that such demonstrations are ad hoc, not premeditated, and the perpetrators do not offer much resistance when the police confront them. Moreover, the Ukrainian, Baltic, and Central Asian leaders fear political upheavel with the same grim foreboding that their Russian counterparts do, and the vast majority of the people they represent have little stomach for confronting the state.

In Eastern Europe, the "Muscovites," emboldened by the Soviets' hard line, have conducted campaigns to deal with "troublemakers" and to pacify the people. According to Western sources, dissidents in the satellite countries have been "lying low"; they are convinced Moscow would welcome the opportunity to deploy WTO forces to protect fraternal socialist countries from "counterrevolutionaries."

The general secretary's position is bolstered by the shared consensus of values and interests unifying the Soviet elite: liberalization of Soviet society is dangerous; the Party must remain strong and dominate the country in the same fashion that it has in the past; control over the satellites must be firm; and the Soviet Union must do whatever is necessary to maintain its military preparedness.

Three Futures: Liberal Reform

It is 1990. For the third consecutive year, the Soviet economy has grown by less than 2%. Economic hard times have reduced living standards; no one is starving, but the average family is surviving on a "wartime" diet of cabbage, potatoes, and little meat. The housing shortage has worsened, and families lucky enough to get apartments cannot fill them with appliances and furniture because there is a two-year waiting list for such items. At first, like previous generations, the people complain, drink more vodka, continue to display a casual attitude toward work, expropriate more government property but take no steps to convert their economic discontent into organized political protest. However, when industrial managers convince the Kremlin not to purchase more foreign grain, but instead to use the hard cash to expand industrial production, the food situation deteriorates. This incites riots in many cities; in other places, workers put down their tools, refusing to resume work until the government makes more food available. These outbreaks shock the general secretary, but he concludes that they involve a small number of "hooligans" and that to kowtow to their demands is to invite even more widespread protest.

His prognosis is wrong, and atempts to squelch the protest backfire. In towns small and large, housewives break into food stores, cleaning the shelves of stock. In factories, workers led by militants demanding free trade unions put down their tools and refuse to pick them up until union representatives of their own choosing are recognized by the authorities. Public transportation employees in Leningrad, Moscow, and Kiev refuse to operate their vehicles until their wage demands are met. Perhaps tempers would have cooled after these initial outbreaks, had the government not ordered militia and KGB units to crush the rioters and strikers in a brutal display of force, resulting in hundreds killed and thousands wounded.

Henceforth there are numerous reports of militiamen refusing to use force against protesters, and in some places they join them in a demonstration of solidarity. In other areas, KGB zealots are astounded when, upon entering factories, workers confront them and then beat them senseless. On at least two occasions, weapons taken from the KGB agents are used against the second wave of security forces that attack the workers' sanctuaries. As news of such courageous acts spread, workers become even bolder and rush to fill the ranks of newly independent unions. Following the course of Solidarity's growth, peasants, students, and office workers request their own charters.

Party neo-Stalinists are shaken after meeting with members of the Soviet general staff. The generals assert that it would be foolhardy to use Red Army units to crush the protests. This is not the time to use force but to negotiate with the strikers. There is reason to suspect that many enlisted men would turn their weapons on the KGB and perhaps even their officers if ordered to fire upon the people. The generals are alarmed that they no longer can play one ethnic group off against another—for example, in Kiev, a unit of Uzbeks refused to attack street demonstrators. "Obviously, provocateurs had infiltrated these units, and there is evidence that they have succeeded in other units, too."

The role of non-Russian activists in the unfolding drama is underscored by party and government officials from outside the Russian Republic offering to throw their weight behind liberals in the Politburo and Central Committee in return for greater autonomy. They are adamant in demanding that Russians holding high positions in their areas be sent home to be replaced with indigenous people. They remind their Russian comrades that students in the Baltic republics, the Ukraine, Armenia, and Central Asia are displaying displeasure with Moscow's Russification campaign by refusing to use Russian in their classrooms. What started as an ad hoc coalition of non-Russian university students now is developing into a well-organized student organization with branches throughout the USSR.

Meanwhile, intelligence sources warn that "Muscovites" in the satellite parties are in danger of losing control if demands for liberalization are not met. They can prevail, but only with the help of the Red Army to pacify people emboldened by mass protest in the USSR.

Cable traffic from Soviet diplomats outside the empire is almost as ominous. Several client states are now conducting secret talks with the Americans about improving relations with Washington and have sent Cuban troops and Russian advisers packing. In other LDCs, governments friendly to the West are making preparations to even scores with Libya, Ethiopia, and South Yemen by supporting "counterrevolutionary" movements in these countries and perhaps even by invading them. These "reactionary American puppets" are convinced that Moscow, preoccupied with turmoil within its empire, is not about to lend a helping hand to its allies.

It is against this backdrop that Gorbachev is replaced by a troika of liberals after a marathon weekend session of the Politburo. They move quickly to implement a range of economic and political reforms to placate the Soviet people. They fill stores with as much meat as they can requisition from government warehouses, agree to negotiate with the new trade unions, invite leaders from the non-Russian republics to Moscow to discuss their grievances, and take steps to give policymakers at the republic level and below a greater voice in economic planning.

In return for pledging to provide more consumer goods, however, the new leaders introduce policies to enforce greater discipline and output in the labor force; they warn workers who arrive at work drunk, take time off without permission, or do sloppy work that they will lose their jobs or be reassigned to less pleasant, lower-paying positions. Their bosses are given the same warning, and to their surprise many managers are demoted, changing coat and tie for work clothes.

In the countryside, steps are taken to shift a larger proportion of agricultural output from collective to private farms, and the peasants are guaranteed that if they increase productivity, their living conditions will improve. To demonstrate the government's good will, roads and public utilities are constructed or expanded in remote areas of the USSR that had changed little since the revolution.

The troika receives enthusiastic support in the non-Russian republics when it allows local people a greater voice in party and government affairs; decisions previously made by Russians are now made by Armenians, Lithuanians, Kazakhs, etc. In the Russian republic itself, regional and local government officials welcome the opportunity to play a more significant role in decisions once monopolized by remote bureaucrats in Moscow.

Hardline "Muscovites" in Eastern Europe are informed by their Soviet mentors that if they cannot live with reforms long advocated by "liberals" in their countries, they should step aside. Bloc leaders are advised that they can count on more help, especially in the critical area of energy, but they are warned not to interpret Moscow's new permissiveness as an indication that they can leave the Warsaw Pact.

Several days after taking over, the liberals send a top-level delegation to Geneva to resume arms control negotiations with the Americans. (Talks had been abandoned when the superpowers could not reach an agreement on SDI.) They instruct their ambassador in Washington to begin inquiries about a summit conference to discuss ways East–West tensions can be reduced. The United States, Japanese, and Western European governments, meanwhile, promise to expand trade and technological transfers with Moscow and its allies in Eastern Euirope.

Three Futures: Russian Fascism

After Gorbachev is killed in a plane crash, there is a bitter struggle for power in the Kremlin between reformers and neo-Stalinists. This precipitates protests by dissidents, disgruntled workers, anxious party officials, and angry functionaries who previously had been cowed into silence. In many cities, workers battle with security forces attempting to break strikes and street demonstrations. Students clash with KGB agents purging students and faculty from the country's universities. And Russian troops, attempting to arrest mullahs accused of "anti-Soviet" actions, are fired upon in Central Asia by members of the Sufi brotherhood. In Eastern Europe, several governments are taken over by reformers demanding the installation of social democratic parties, free elections, independent trade unions, and the expulsion of Soviet troops from their homelands.

In many parts of the Russian republic, and in areas where ethnic Russians live in large numbers, counterdemonstrations are led by neo-Stalinists. Proclaiming "Russia for the Russians," they break strikes; attack Jews, Central Asians, and other "aliens;" and enter schools, factories, and research centers, carrying away "liberals" and other "traitors." At first, some members of the Central Committee, neutrals in the struggle, urge that the leaders of these mobs be arrested. But upon learning that powerful members of the party, KGB, and military are controlling the "fascists"—as their enemies call them—they join the neo-Stalinists and tip the scales against the "liberals". Outspoken opponents of the fascists are rounded up and sent to labor camps; several of the "most dangerous" are killed "resisting arrest," and many others "commit suicide."

The fascists and their allies in the Central Committee conclude that the only way to save the regime from anti-socialist elements is to exploit Russian nationalism. The Russian people are courted by promises to deal harshly with those ethnic minorities that are stabbing their "elder brothers" in the back by collaborating with "bourgeois chauvinists." Leaders in the Ukraine, the Baltic countries, the Caucasus, and Central Asia, who were so designated by their Russian comrades, are purged from high party and government posts.

Turning to the gathering storm in Eastern Europe, the Soviet armed forces invade Poland by land, sea, and air to crush a resurgent Solidarity. Many units of the Polish army join the civilians who have taken up arms to defend their country. They fight bravely for two months, but are ultimately beaten by a larger and better-armed adversary. Casualties on both sides are heavy, and the fascists in Moscow exploit the anger of Russian families who have lost their loved ones, by adopting even more widespread draconian policies within the USSR. With Russian help, neo-Stalinists in other satellite countries return to power, and thousands of their opponents are jailed and liquidated in the most massive terror campaign since Stalin's days.

The Soviet media proclaim that "American imperialists" and "German revanchists," in collusion with "Chinese revisionists," are responsible for unrest in the Warsaw Pact countries. Red Army officers display captured U.S. weapons via TV clips from "the front" in Poland. A battered Lithuanian "terrorist" admits before the cameras that the group he commanded had received supplies from West German agents. Captured "Chinese cadres" who led Uzbek "counterrevolutionaries" are shown marching down a mountain road to POW camps.

The U.S. State Department announces that the new Soviet government has abrogated all existing East–West treaties, and Washington calls its ambassador home for consultation. War rumors spread when it is learned that a third wave of reservists are being called up in the USSR, even though WTO forces are now only encountering isolated pockets of resistance. Reports from China are even more alarming. Radio Beijing announces that Soviet forces have destroyed Chinese airfields, communication systems, rail lines, and munitions depots located close to the Sino–Soviet border. Diplomats in China report the Soviets' warning that if the PRC does not pull its troops back from areas near the Soviet Union, the Soviets, "in self defense," will destroy them by "applying any means necessary."

Worried leaders in the Third World report that regimes aligned with Moscow have been receiving massive supplies of arms and equipment accompanied by Russian advisers. Diplomats in Iran claim the Red Army has crossed that country's border, and it is believed the Soviets are bent on toppling the government in Teheran and may be planning to drive south toward the Persian Gulf.

The president of the United States places U.S. forces on a worldwide alert. His national security adviser informs him that the neo-Stalinists in the Kremlin are using the "foreign threat", out of desperation, to mobilize the Russian people behind them, to consolidate their power at home, and to justify the use of Soviet troops in Eastern Europe and China. The NSC adviser reports that the Soviets are not moving into Iran to gain control of the Gulf but concedes they have occupied the northern area of Iran, and that they plan to stay there indefinitely.

CIA sources claim that resistance throughout the Soviet empire to the fascist coup has been crushed and that the United States must be prepared to deal with the neo-Stalinists who are in firm control of the party, state, military, and KGB. Prospects of a more moderate leadership returning to power any time soon are remote.

Analysis: Why Sovietologists Favor the Welfare State Scenario

Most Sovietologists believe that the Welfare State Authoritarianism scenario best describes the likely course of events to take place as Gorbachev grapples with his crisis.[3] In a moment we shall provide reasons why this is the case, but first let us briefly explain why the "liberal" and "fascist" scenarios are not deemed credible by close observers of the Kremlin.

The Liberal Reform scenario is based on many implausible assumptions; we need mention only three of them. First, there is little evidence that the

Central Committee of the CPSU and the Politburo harbors "liberals," people who, in the face of a crisis, will adopt reforms and not resort to repression to safeguard the regime. Second, what we know about the military's role since Brezhnev's death indicates that it will throw its weight behind leaders who prefer the mailed fist to the velvet glove in dealing with disgruntled subjects. Third, few scholars believe that the Soviet people will act like Poles and offer organized resistance to the regime, demanding free trade unions and so forth. Some may be so inclined, but they would not be a significant proportion of the population. The same goes for the non-Russians; many ethnic activists have courageously resisted Russian imperialism, but the vast majority of their brethren have remained silent.

The Russian Fascism scenario is flawed because, in addition to the same criticisms that apply to the liberal scenario—for example, liberals in the Soviet oligarchy and widespread demonstrations on the part of ethnic minorities—the leadership appreciates that manipulating Russian chauvinism could backfire.[4] Neo-Stalinists are prepared to use the Russians' prejudices to scapegoat the regime's mistakes, but few analysts believe they would undertake the kind of massive nationalist crusade depicted in the scenario. On the contrary, the Kremlin has sought to placate the non-Russians, and many ethnic minority comrades have demonstrated loyalty to the regime because their careers are linked to its success.

The case for the Welfare State Authoritarianism scenario is stronger. The USSR is clearly in for some hard times economically, but the Soviet people have modest material expectations, and most will endure economic setbacks in silence. The regime knows it cannot allow living standards to slip precipitously, and it will protect the Soviet masses from real hardship. Food will be ample, even though the quality may leave a great deal to be desired. Consumer goods will be scarce, but workers will be mollified by job security and free medical care.

Both the liberal and fascist scenarios postulate that the regime will be incapable of or unwilling to make adaptations and will doggedly resist change. But as Jerry Hough and other prominent U.S. scholars have pointed out, the regime has demonstrated on numerous occasions that it will reverse its course if necessary. The changes, however, will be implemented within the institutional and power arrangements of Soviet political and economic life.[5]

It is worth stressing, moreover, that Hough and many of his colleagues no longer describe the Soviet Union as "totalitarian"; they prefer, instead, the designation "authoritarian." George Breslauer, for example, says the totalitarian label does not accurately describe power relationships in the USSR today. The difference beween a totalitarian and an authoritarian society is that in the former there are no independent centers of power—the state controls all sectors of society. But Breslauer writes that the Soviet Union "has moved in the direction of institutional or 'corporate pluralism' at the top" of

Soviet society. Under these circumstances, several layers of technocrats, party workers, and government officials who work below the gaze of the ruling elite "have a voice in major decisions," and the Kremlin "in its social policies has abandoned the use of terror as an instrument of mass policy."[6] The words "welfare state" are appropriate because the government's policies include "a basic commitment to minimal and rising levels of material security, public health, education, and welfare for the masses." In addition, "its commitment to welfare includes an egalitarian commitment to job security and low prices for basic commodities—even at a cost of considerable economic inefficiency and a decline in entrepreneurial initiatives."[7]

The 1980s may mean economic hard times for the growing Soviet middle class, but little trouble is likely to be forthcoming from this source, because the millions of technocrats, scientists, managers, and other men and women critical to the system's viability have a stake in the region's legitimacy. They are unlikely to support anti-Soviet change. As their counterparts in Poland demonstrated in helping to crush Solidarity, fundamental changes are deemed a grave threat to themselves and their families.

Breslauer, in acknowledging the importance of the Soviet middle class, however, concedes the possibility of what he calls "elitist liberalism" replacing "welfare state authoritarianism." He writes of the former as "middle-class liberalism providing autonomy for the managerial class, but without according similar concessions to the masses."[8] Under these circumstances social equality will be played down and economic efficiency stressed, reinforcing wage differentiation and job insecurity to stimulate productivity. More people will share privileges presently restricted to the most prominent Soviet citizens, but in absolute terms they will only constitute a minority of the population.

Turning to ethnic discontent, many Sovietologists grant that non-Russian restiveness will cause problems for the Kremlin in the years ahead. But apart from scholars of the nationality question and Soviet émigrés, most seem to believe that ethnic minority discontent has been exaggerated. Russians hold the key posts in the party, the government, and the military, but they have allowed members of other ethnic groups to prosper economically, to achieve educational progress, and to enter the professions and positions of influence in all areas of Soviet life. In 1982, an Azerbaidzhani, Grydar Aliyev, was appointed a full member of the Politburo. Before Gorbachev was selected, Aliyev was frequently mentioned as the future general secretary of the CPSU. In 1985 Eduard Shevardnadze, a Georgian, replaced Andrei Gromyko. Furthermore, data suggests that some of the non-Russian republics have received proportionately more capital investments than the Russian republic. Living standards in the Baltic republics and several other areas of the USSR are higher than those enjoyed by the average Russian.

The Central Asians may make greater political, economic, and cultural demands, but the prospect that they will become an organized force in opposition to the regime is unlikely. If one compares the material and educational advantages of the Central Asians with the plight of their brethren in many Muslim countries, it is clear that they are much better off. Even analysts claiming that ethnic self-consciousness is on the rise acknowledge that the Central Asians have not demonstrated organized political opposition to the Russian-dominated regime. As regards ethnic minority leaders who enjoy positions of importance in the USSR, declining Russian influence is not likely to work in their best interests. Also, leading U.S. Sovietologists, such as Brian Silver, contend that the Russification program is working: the younger and better educated ethnic minorities living in urban areas are most inclined to speak Russian and to associate their material advancement with the adoption of "universalistic" Soviet, and not "particularistic" ethnic values.[9]

Discontent within Eastern Europe will cause problems for the "Muscovites" and thereby be a source of concern for the Kremlin, but the Soviets and their clients will continue to handle it as they have done in the past. The proximity of the USSR to Eastern Europe and the Kremlin's capacity to project its military power there provide little hope that people hostile to the Kremlin will be permitted to gain positions of influence in the satellite countries.

In the aftermath of the Jaruzelski coup, Walter Lacquer wrote that we have to face the harsh truth that significant changes in the Eastern European regimes will not occur as a result of internal developments.[10] He contends that the liberalization of communist regimes will only take place as a consequence of changes within the USSR which would give legitimacy to similar reforms in Eastern Europe. The USSR in the 1980s, therefore, will not be affected to any significant degree by developments in Eastern Europe. On the contrary, it can only occur the other way around.

Finally, economic difficulties, turmoil in Eastern Europe, and ethnic discord will cause problems for the Kremlin, to be sure, but there is no reason to believe they will destroy the Soviet regime. Should they prove to be more serious than they have been in the past, the "Soviet crisis" will serve as an incentive for the neo-Stalinists to unify, crush their opponents in the ruling oligarchy, and pacify the general population.

A More Pessimistic Assessment

The ability of the Soviets to grapple with past crises accounts for the popularity of the Welfare State Authoritarianism scenario. But the Soviet crisis can be viewed in a more ominous light without engaging in the kind of fantasizing that prevails among some elements of the far right. The Soviet Union faces a pre-revolutionary situation that, at the very least, will foment an acute crisis of legitimacy in the USSR; at worst, it could precipitate internal warfare reminiscent of the civil war years.

Economic Upheaval

> There can be no grounds whatever for the Kremlin hoping that the present economic crunch will prove to be transitory and that developments a few years hence will ring in a period of new and easy prosperity.[11]

This view of Timothy Colton, a Canadian scholar, is by no means a minority one. Indeed, a majority of commentators knowledgeable about the Soviet economy agree that far-reaching macro- and microeconomic reforms must be adopted, to close the gap between East and West and improve living standards. Even casual observers of the USSR are aware of the measures most often mentioned to achieve these objectives.

The system of centralized planning must be scrapped, in favor of one that allows decision-makers at the local level greater authority. To reduce corruption and increase the delivery of vital goods and services to consumers, private entrepreneurs should be allowed to operate more openly. To improve housing and increase the output of consumer durables, money must be shifted from the military–industrial complex to light manufacturing. Since the Chinese have allowed their peasants greater leeway in private farming, the output of food in the People's Republic of China has increased dramatically. If the Soviets were to permit more of their farmers to work private plots, the output of fruits, vegetables, poultry, and meat would improve markedly. In the USSR today, privately operated acreage occupies about "only about 4 percent of arable land but produce[s] 60 percent of the country's potatoes, over 40 percent of its eggs and fruits, and about 30 percent of its meats, milk and vegetables."[12]

In light of the pervasive dissatisfaction with the economy's performance, one would think that the leaders and the people alike would endorse economic reforms. But there are a number of reasons why this is not the case, although since Gorbachev's ascendancy many observers curiously have forgotten them.

The ruling elite is wary of economic reforms because there is merit to the Marxist contention that changes in a society's substructure, or economy, will inevitably affect institutions in the superstructure, such as government. Fundamental economic reforms, therefore, entail corresponding political changes; in short, economic liberalism and political pluralism go hand in hand. In addition to the Polish example, the Soviets are convinced that the Prague Spring had its origins in economic reforms adopted in 1966.

Bureaucrats with cushy jobs are wary of reforms, too. Many industry managers and government ministers obtained their jobs through the "old boy" network in the party, not through merit. Andropov spoke about revising the *nomenklatura* system, which permits this network to endure, but backed off before he died, presumably because of resistance on the part of the bureaucracy.

Finally, the workers are unhappy with their economic situation but they, too, are wary of efforts to increase productivity contingent upon changes in their working conditions, pay scales, etc. For example, if the government is going to improve productivity through incentives, it must scrap an egalitarian salary system adopted in the 1950s. Reportedly, Soviet workers want to keep this system, because it provides them with an economic security they cherish more than high salaries.

The Soviets' economic problem is a serious one, and it is likely to get worse, not better, over time. But rather than taking measures to resolve it, the Soviets will attempt to treat its symptoms and ignore its structural sources. If so, many analysts believe this will create serious political problems for the regime. Alexander Yanov writes: "If a further drop in the growth rate or economic stagnation is allowed to occur, the aristocracy may be swept away by a massive cataclysm."[13] Few Western commentators believe the backlash will take on such dramatic forms, but they concede that the regime's inability to meet the people's material expectations could cause it serious political problems. Improved living conditions have helped the Soviet population endure rigid bureaucratic controls, hours spent waiting in long lines for milk and soap, declining opportunities to attend universities, and blatant inequities—such as the privileges enjoyed by the party elite in a "classless society."

If the economy continues to falter, will economic discontent be transformed into political protest? Here the distinction between "low" and "high" politics becomes relevant. It has been assumed that if economic disgruntlement produces political discontent, it will take on the aspects of low politics—complaints about insufficient meat, appliances, and apartments. Mass discontent will not involve issues associated with high politics—the rule of law, human rights, and the like. This has been the case in the past, but why is it that pundits who have made a great deal of Gorbachev's youth and imply that he will do things differently have not done the same thing in their assessments of how the people will respond to a protracted period of hard times?

Given the Soviet masses' traditional patience in the face of adversity, it is difficult to envisage their taking to the streets in hostile displays of protest. It is even more difficult to imagine their engaging in such behavior in a calculated, organized fashion. Yet it is not inconceivable that the younger generation will respond to slipping living conditions and economic opportunities in a more militant fashion than their parents.

Kaiser says, "A generation gap has emerged in the Soviet Union" and "the Russians may be about to have their version of the '60s."[14] Economic austerity will feed feelings of alienation on the part of young people, whose expectations exceed those of their parents and have been heightened by government propaganda. They will not be happy either that a seat in a university will be unavailable to them, unlike the experience of their older brothers and sisters. In "the early 1960s, 57 percent of all secondary-school graduates were being admitted to higher education, but a decade later . . . only 22 percent were making it in."[15] Colton argues that the discontent of young people denied access to universities can be assuaged by increasing their ability to purchase consumer goods with the salaries they earn, but if such goods are unobtainable, they will have additional reason to be angry with the government.

Enduring economic austerity will foster alienation not only among the young but also among the middle class, the workers, and the peasants — that is among all segments of Soviet society whose dreams about improved living conditions will be dashed. In a collectivist, totalitarian society, the state monopolizes the economy and, therefore, must take responsibility for its performance. At some point the people will direct their anger at the political elites. Even if mass discontent is ad hoc, leaderless, and diffuse, it will exacerbate many problems responsible for the economy's ills in the first place — low productivity, corruption, absenteeism, and the like. A protracted economic crisis will, in turn, make it exceedingly difficult for the regime to deal with other crises threatening it.

Rising Ethnic Discord

Since 1917 the Russians have adopted myriad strategies to destroy the group values and loyalties of the USSR's ethnic minorities. They have failed. If anything, the non-Russians have become bolder in resisting efforts by their "elder brothers" to inculcate them with a Soviet consciousness. A massive campaign, launched by the KGB in the late 1970s, to crush organized ethnic civil rights organizations has been successful: Their members have been exiled, imprisoned, intimidated into silence, or killed. But the Kremlin's victory is a temporary one similar to those the government of South Africa has been achieving for years: in the wake of each "successful" campaign, the blacks soon reaffirm their protest and display even greater determination to fight their white masters.

A phenomenon is at work in South Africa that is also occurring in the USSR: as people enter the modern world, they become more, not less, conscious of their ethnicity. In December 1982 Yuri Andropov acknowledged the relationship when he said that economic and social developments among the ethnic communities are "inevitably accompanied by the growth of their national self-consciousness," not its decline.[16] The nationality question will continue to be a divisive force in Soviet society and, in the face of austerity relations between the Russians and the ethnic minorities, will get worse.

The impact of rising ethnic discord upon the regime can be assessed by addressing two vital questions: how long can the USSR remain "a prison of nations," and what bearing will a growing sense of Central Asian identity have upon Soviet society?

The collapse of Western colonialism, liberating over a billion people in Asia and Africa, was a significant outcome of World War II. It signified a victory for human rights and was a cause for rejoicing among people who believe that one day democracy will be a worldwide phenomenon. It is perplexing, therefore, that so little attention has been devoted to the existence of the world's last colonial empire—that dominated by the Russians.

Conservatives have lashed out at Russian imperialism, but their outrage has been held suspect because of their indifference to human rights violations in authoritarian countries associated with the "free world." Many leftists cite the right's hypocrisy to explain why they do not target the Russian empire for criticism. Some liberals justify their silence on the grounds that there is nothing we can do about it—unless we are prepared to resort to nuclear war. In addition to these explanations, there is a fourth one, a psychological coping mechanism called denial, to which people of various political hues adhere. That is, if Russian imperialism is acknowledged, then East–West discord must be seen in a truly ominous light. The East–West competition is not merely the product of post-World War II blunders and fears associated with the military buildup spawned by the Cold War, but a rivalry that involves profound differences and unreconcilable worldviews. What is at stake are conflicting views of political liberty, the sanctity of life, and the rule of law. To acknowledge Russian imperialism is to concede that the East–West struggle cannot be resolved through technological quick fixes, as some overly optimistic advocates of arms control or nuclear superiority would have us believe.

We shall return to this matter later; it is mentioned here to underscore the dilemma facing the Soviet ruling elite. How can leaders who celebrate the Enlightenment and claim to be enemies of oppression believe that Russian imperialism can endure for many more decades? Denial is at work here, too. The awesome power of the Soviet state cannot be ignored, but how can the Russians expect to subjugate millions of people and not ultimately pay a heavy price in return—a price that precipitates violent clashes between them and the ethnic minorities?

Because of their size, strategic location, and growing sense of peoplehood, the Turco–Iranian peoples of Central Asia represent an especially serious threat to the Russian empire. This threat has its roots in internal and external developments.

Within the USSR the linkage between Islam and nationalism, the existence of clandestine organizations, and the growing interest in Islam among young people are all responsible for fears about the Central Asians' loyalty. It is inevitable that they will demand greater political, cultural, and economic autonomy from the Russians than they have had up to now. Demands that indigenous people replace Russian party and government officials and industrial managers will undeniably mount. As the Muslims become bolder in making such demands, relations between them and the Russians will deteriorate, especially if Russian nationalist demands that the "Churkas" be put in their place are honored. Wimbush has observed:

> It is difficult to imagine a more powerful catalyst for an open and militant Russian nationalism than the self-assertion of Soviet minorities. Opportunities for minorities to assert themselves increase in step with the growth in the relative size of their populations, with the expansion of their economies, and with the enhanced political sophistication of their elites. Daily strife between Russians and non-Russians will become more intense, especially in the cities of the national republics where social distinctions depend largely on ethnic affiliation, where, for the most part, Russians and non-Russians are highly segregated, where competition between them for jobs and elite positions is potentially at its most fierce, and where instances of ethnically inspired violence . . . will continue to multiply as other conditions become less palatable for both sides.[17]

The Russian leadership has avoided concerted efforts to play off their people against ethnic monorities (in most instances), but if history is a guide, they *will* resort to such measures, as Stalin did, if they believe the Central Asians represent a serious political threat to them. This approach, and the adoption of oppressive measures, may prove to be effective in the short run, but over the long pull they will foster even greater hatred of the Russians and alienate Muslims beyond the borders of the USSR.

The Soviets are presently concerned about foreign "provocateurs" attempting to turn the Central Asians against the Russians. Until several years ago, agents of "Western imperialism" and "Zionism" were accused of such crimes, but now Middle Eastern influences are cited as the culprits. In the 1980s the volume of material published in the Central Asian media "devoted to the 'Islamic problem' has grown enormously, strongly suggesting a stimulus provided by occurrences in Afghanistan and Iran."[18] Modern technology guarantees that the Soviet Muslims will become more susceptible to the flow of information from Islamic sources outside of the USSR. One reason the Soviets invaded Afghanistan was to prevent Islamic fundamentalism from spilling over into Soviet Central Asia. But even if they defeat the Afghans, Moscow will be incapable of checking the spread of Islamic influences among the Central Asians.

There are reports that Afghan mujahideen have developed networks in Soviet Central Asia. They "have made a concerted effort to reawaken awareness of the historicalities and a sense of common purpose among the Tajiks and Uzbeks in northern Afghanistan and their brethren directly across the border on the Soviet side."[19] For their part, the Turco–Iranian peoples in the USSR would like Afghanistan to be incorporated into the Soviet empire. The Islamic community in the Soviet Union would thus grow by many millions, enhancing the Muslims' influence there.

The Russians are in a very difficult position. They may muddle through the 1980s, but the Central Asians will not endure Russian imperialism for many more years without protest. The December 1986 riots in Alma Ata, which erupted when the Kazakh Communist Party leader, Dinmukhamed Nunaev, was replaced by a Russian, Gennadi Kolbin, are indicative of the stormy days ahead for the Russian rulers.

Other non-Russian ethnic groups will also become less passive in the face of Russian hegemony. It is uncertain what development(s) will precipitate open and widespread violent opposition to Russian chauvinism, but the Kremlin can be certain it will occur, just as the whites in South Africa can be sure that blacks there will one day rise up in massive opposition to their fascist rule.

Turmoil in Eastern Europe and Finlandization

Soviet concerns about Eastern Europe take two forms: an outbreak as serious as the one that occurred in Hungary in 1956 and the Finlandization of Eastern Europe.

It is inevitable that the Soviet Union will encounter armed resistance to its rule in Eastern Europe. In the fall of 1984, when dissident priest Jerzy Popieluszko was murdered by the secret police, many observers feared people would take to the streets to topple the government. Had they been urged to do so by church or Solidarity leaders, they would have complied even in the face of certain defeat.

Western analysts are convinced that one or more of the satellite regimes will be openly challenged in the near future. They are less certain whether a modest application of force can crush the revolution or whether a massive invasion akin to that of Hungary will be necessary.

The rise of a movement like Solidarity leaps to mind when one considers the origins of a future anti-Soviet upheaval in Eastern Europe. One can envisage another scenario, however—one that may be more likely in light of recent displays of independence on the part of "pro-Soviet" leaders: A "Muscovite" regime adopts relatively liberal economic and political reforms in an attempt to win the hearts and minds of the people. It skillfully manipulates the Kremlin's fears about popular discontent to secure Moscow's approval for these "bold" moves. The regime does so believing it can channel reform in favorable directions, but over time "things get out of hand." Intellectuals and students demand the end of censorship, workers form independent unions, and some members of the party and government attack their superiors for clinging to "outmoded" Stalinist policies.

Horrified by this turn of events, the Soviets threaten to intervene after the government admits it cannot keep the people in line. Intoxicated by their victories, the people have become emboldened and some of the "Moscovite" functionaries join liberal dissidents in an alliance for "full reform." Fearful that "anti-Soviet" forces have taken over the country, the Red Army intervenes and crushes the "counterrevolutionaries," who, with the assistance of their own army, resist the Russians for months.

One can hypothesize a number of other plausible scenarios of this kind, but all include the assumption that armed resistance to Soviet imperialism is very likely to take place in the next ten years.

The spectre of the Finlandization of Eastern Europe is a second prospect that must cause sleepless nights for Soviet leaders. Prior to the deployment of the cruise and Pershing II missiles, neoconservatives warned about the Finlandization of Western Europe. Massive street demonstrations opposing the deployment of the Euromissiles, and the accusations of some Europeans that the Americans were a greater threat to peace than the Russians, were cited as evidence that the Finlandization of Western Europe was a real prospect. As predicted by the American right, U.S. allies had become intimidated by Moscow's nuclear edge over the United States. If the protesters were successful in their campaign, this would be the first step in a series that would transform NATO into a hollow alliance. Eventually the Western Europeans would become Soviet vassals. While the Soviets would not be ensconced in Paris, London, Bonn, or Rome, the leaders there would allow Moscow a virtual veto over their foreign and defense policies.

One hears less talk about Finlandization in right-wing circles today, but the topic probably will resurface the next time the United States and its NATO partners disagree over defense matters. Presently, it is the Soviets who have reason to fear that their control over the Eastern Europeans is slipping. Although commercial ties between Moscow and Eastern Europe have expanded, the satellites continue to look outside the communist bloc for economic opportunities. The Soviets have warned them about getting too closely entangled with the West, but to no avail. In the early 1980s the total hard currency indebtedness of the Eastern Europeans to the West was about $60 billion. Efforts to secure Western trade, technology, and capital will continue to foster closer relations between the satellites and capitalist governments and firms. Consequently the Eastern Europeans will become more susceptible to capitalist efforts to drive a wedge between them and the Soviets, and less able to prevent the democracies from influencing their internal affairs.

The Soviets are deeply worried about this set of circumstances, but they cannot do much about it. The satellite communist governments lean more heavily on economic prosperity for legitimacy than does the USSR. The Jaruzelski coup has intimidated "troublemakers" throughout the Eastern bloc, but it is only a matter of time before regimes lacking popular support are faced with widespread political unrest, because they cannot meet their people's economic demands. Under these circumstances, they will have to declare martial law and/or request the intervention of the Red Army to control their people.

Moscow, therefore, may have to accept one of two unappealing prospects: allow the satellites to adopt more far-reaching economic reforms and permit them to become more entangled with the West economically, or keep discredited pro-Soviet governments in power by employing the Red Army in a more direct manner, thereby running the risk of a massive uprising.

What we are observing may be depicted as the third stage in the development of modern capitalism. Marx devoted his genius to delineating the first stage of early capitalism—its growth at the expense of feudalism and the conditions that would eventually lead to its demise. Lenin outlined the second stage of capitalism, imperialism—the highest stage of capitalist development. He conceded that Marx had been wrong, in part, about the destructive course capitalism would take: Marx did not foresee that the capitalists, through imperialism, would avoid revolution at home by exporting their "contradictions" to the Third World. In the process, however, revolutionary conditions would spread worldwide. Henceforth the entire globe would become ripe for socialist revolutions.

Soviet writers depict the third stage in terms of a worldwide economic crisis that will finally bring down the imperialist system. But they have blithely ignored the fact that capitalism can avoid this calamity, through the welfare state and multilateral policies that stabilize the international economy. Furthermore, what may be one of the most significant features of capitalism in its third stage is the capacity to innovate and adapt to change and to entangle socialist societies in a web of economic relationships dominated by the capitalists. Should the world economy collapse, the socialist economies would collapse with it. Should it endure, the socialist economies would ultimately be destroyed by capitalism's economic prowess.

Revolutionary Upheaval

Soviet theorists reject the notion that their predicament could spawn revolutionary upheaval in the USSR. They contend that a revolutionary situation develops when the ruling class cannot resolve crises within the existing institutional framework. This observation, however, is relevant to capitalist societies, not socialist ones. To understand why this is the case, Soviet writers employ their theory of "contradictions," an integral part of Marxist dialectics. Contradictions exist in socialist societies, but they are "nonantagonistic"; that is, they involve differences between the authorities and the people that are reconcilable and, therefore, cannot produce revolution. "Antagonistic contradictions," found in capitalist societies, involve conflict between the rulers and the ruled; they are irreconcilable and capable of producing revolution.[20]

Lenin said that objective conditions provide the basis for revolution— "impoverishment of the countryside, depression in industry, a general feeling that there is no way out of the present political situation. . ." but revolution will not occur if subjective conditions do not also exist.[21] A critical subjective element is the presence of a revolutionary cadre capable of mobilizing the masses into an insurrectionary force. Without one even a corrupt, oppressive, bourgeois regime can muddle through for decades.

For all intents and purposes, this is the conclusion of Western observers who adhere to the "Welfare State Authoritarianism" scenario. The Soviet leaders will make modest changes and not have to worry about popular discontent because the subjective conditions necessary to transform it into organized protest simply do not exist in the USSR.

Not all Western Sovietologists agree, however. The German writer, Ernst Kux, rejects the "nonantagonistic/antagonistic" dichotomy the Soviets cite in disclaiming that a socialist society can be stricken by revolution. He supports his case with empirical evidence: "Most of the existing 'socialist states' have gone through crises and experienced 'revolutionary situations' in which the workers rose against communist rule, beginning with the Kronstadt Uprising of 1921 in Soviet Russia."[22] More recent examples include Hungary in 1956, Czechoslovakia in 1968, and Poland in 1980–81. Since the Jaruzelski coup of 1981, Soviet leaders have warned about the Party losing touch with the people, thereby fomenting a crisis—although they stop short of predicting a revolutionary outcome. There is then no theoretical barrier to revolution in a socialist society and certainly no reason why one should not occur in a reactionary one like the USSR.

Ideology and the existence of concrete problems aside, however, Gorbachev's ascendancy has caused Kremlinologists to reassess Moscow's ability to cope with its crisis. Unlike the frail old men who preceded him, Gorbachev is healthy, young, energetic, and appears to have a first-rate mind. Only weeks after replacing Chernenko, he demonstrated that he recognized the serious nature of the Soviet crisis and was prepared to deal with it quickly and boldly. To the surprise of Western observers, he moved immediately to consolidate his position and with positive results. He appointed people loyal to him to important party and government posts. Like him, they are relatively young men, not wedded to the status quo but ready and able to deal with their society's problems. He shocked many Kremlinologists when he removed Grigory Romanov from the Politburo—the man said to be his most formidable rival in the Kremlin. He astounded them further when he replaced Andrei Gromyko, who had served as foreign minister for twenty-seven years, with Eduard Shevardnadze, the Georgian party chief who had conducted an effective anti-corruption campaign in his home republic.

Here was further proof of Gorbachev's political clout. Prior to this move, conventional wisdom was that he would be too preoccupied with domestic affairs to devote his precious time and goodwill to foreign policy. But since Shevardnadze had no international experience, his appointment indicated that

Gorbachev planned to make his imprint on Soviet foreign policy immediately and not merely follow the path paved by Gromyko, one Gorbachev believed was too fixed on relations with the United States.

Gorbachev's anti-corruption campaign has alienated many influential elements of Soviet society, and his anti-alcoholism policy does not sit well with ordinary citizens. Nonetheless, the fact that he has not backed down on these drives demonstrates that he means business. And rather than relying on the power of his office alone, he has courted the people in an effort to enlist their support for his reforms. Like a Russian Lyndon Johnson, he has "pressed the flesh" of citizens on the street, in factories, and on farms. Western diplomats report his American-style campaigning is being favorably received, that the people are expressing confidence in their country's future and their young leader's capacity to deal with its problems. Here is a man in charge. To issue dire warnings about a Soviet empire in decline does not make sense under these circumstances.

To jump to the conclusion that the Soviet crisis will destroy the Leninist regime and the Russian empire any time soon is foolhardy, but to state categorically that the Soviets will resolve their crisis without experiencing grave damage is no less foolhardy. It will be years before it can be determined what impact Gorbachev's leadership and policies will have upon the Soviet crisis and how the people, the *nomenklatura*, and the top leadership will respond to them. Gorbachev may have second thoughts about dramatic changes after discovering the fears of the old-timers were not groundless— that is, economic liberalism is linked to freer political and intellectual expression. And even after taking what Gorbachev believes are bold steps, nothing of great significance may happen. Indeed, the economic situation may get worse.

Failure to address the Soviet crisis will create divisions within the ruling elite, exacerbate ethnic discord, and alienate the people. Eventually the confluence of these phenomena will precipitate internal upheaval of monumental proportions. The regime may withstand the trauma for years, perhaps decades, but like a patient weakened by a grave illness, it will become susceptible to other lethal diseases: a Bonapartist solution to the crisis, a coup d'état, or perhaps even a civil war. One cannot state categorically that outcomes this grave will materialize, but to dismiss them as well nigh impossible because of the regime's past ability to resolve its problems is to engage in a mechanistic view of history.

One can state with greater confidence that Soviet hegemony is on the decline in Eastern Europe. Gorbachev's strong stewardship may lead the Kremlin to believe it can reassert influence over the region, but over time it will be more difficult to control developments there. The Soviet empire may not come crashing down like a house of cards but like a diabetic, slowly disintegrate and eventually lose control of its extremities.

Proponents of the muddle-through thesis dismiss the possibility of disintegration, thinking somehow or other the Soviet Union is immune to the dynamics of historical change. This belief is so widespread that many Western commentators refuse to follow the logic of their own observations that the USSR is in deep trouble and may be approaching, or already experiencing, a societal crisis.

Others, however, concede this possibility. For example, after telling us why he thinks the regime will overcome its difficulties without major adjustments, Timothy Colton writes:

> If conservatives or reactionaries gain the upper hand in the 1980s, or if bungled reforms come to naught, none of these things will be achieved and pressing problems will go unrectified. The likelihood would be high that the 1990s would bring a crisis of legitimacy and far more searching dilemmas for the regime, with its core structures and values open to question and under attack as never before.[23]

In other words, the Soviet Union may be afflicted by antagonistic contradictions leading to the demise of the Soviet regime and the disintegration of the Russian empire.

Notes

1. *Washington Post*, 14 November 1982.
2. Seweryn Bialer, *Stalin's Successors* (New York: Cambridge University Press, 1981), p. 196.
3. For a comprehensive discussion of several possible Soviet futures, see George W. Breslauer, *Five Images of the Soviet Future: A Critical Review and Synthesis* (Berkeley, CA: Institute of International Studies, University of California, 1978).
4. Alexander Yanov is one of the leading exponents of the idea that a fascist scenario is credible. See his *The Russian New Right* (Berkeley, CA: Institute of International Studies, University of California, 1978).
5. Jerry F. Hough, from a speech at the National Defense University, Washington, D.C., on November 7, 1985.
6. Breslauer, *Five Images*, p. 12.
7. Breslauer, *Five Images*, p. 12.
8. Breslauer, *Five Images*, p. 12.
9. Brian Silver, "Social Mobilization and the Russification of Soviet Nationalities," *American Political Science Review* 68 (March 1974), pp. 87–94.
10. Walter Lacquer, "What Poland Means?," *Commentary* (March 1982): 27.
11. Timothy J. Colton, *The Dilemma of Reform in the Soviet Union* (New York: Council on Foreign Relations, 1984), p. 31.
12. Colton, *The Dilemma of Reform*, p. 67.
13. Alexander Yanov, *Détente After Brezhnev* (Berkeley, CA: Institute of International Studies, University of California, 1977), p. 78.
14. *Washington Post*, 14 December 1982.
15. Colton, *The Dilemma of Reform*, p. 21.
16. Colton, *The Dilemma of Reform*, p. 19.
17. S. Enders Wimbush, "The Russian Nationalist Backlash," *Survey* 24 (Summer 1979): 49–50.

18. Alexandre Bennigsen, "Mullahs, Mujahidin & Soviet Muslims," *Problems of Communism* 38 (November–December 1984), p. 29.
19. Bennigsen, "Mullahs," p. 37.
20. Ernst Kux, "Contradictions in Soviet Socialism," *Problems of Communism* 33 (November–December 1984): 14.
21. Kux, "Contradictions," p. 5.
22. Kux, "Contradictions," p. 7.
23. Colton, *The Dilemma of Reform*, p. 21.

PART TWO

The American Predicament

CHAPTER FIVE

American Liberalism: From the Founding Fathers to Jimmy Carter

"Winning's not everything. It's the only thing."—Vince Lombardi

American Liberalism and the American Dream

The day that Gerald Ford was sworn into office to replace his disgraced predecessor, the Senate minority leader composed a memo:

> August 9, 1974
>
> The Honorable James Madison
>
> Sir:
> It worked.
>
> Sincerely,
> Hugh Scott
> United States Senator

Later that day, as Richard Nixon departed Washington for his San Clemente sanctuary, television commentators were heaping praise on the founding fathers, too. They and their colleagues in the print media would continue to do so for two years until the cacophony of applause reached a crescendo on July 4, 1976.

The bicentennial celebration was an enthralling experience for most

Americans, including some of the nation's most cynical souls. From early morning to late in the evening, television treated them to a frenzy of patriotic activity from Atlantic to Pacific, from the Gulf of Mexico to the Canadian border. The spectacle of the "tall ships" moving gracefully under the Verrazano Narrows Bridge into New York harbor captured the eyes and uplifted the spirits of millions of television viewers. Everywhere, men, women, and children wearing Puritan, colonial, and frontier garb mingled with marching bands, majorettes, and local national guard units in festive parades. Even a honky-tonk celebration in New Orleans's French Quarter, marked by Dixieland jazz, seemed to fit the mood of pride, fellowship, and joy that enveloped the nation. Happy birthday, America!

For weeks afterwards, many people from all walks of life spoke about the Fourth of July, 1976, with special reverence. Members of the older generation remarked that the last time they had experienced such a tangible feeling of national unity and purpose was during World War II. Youngsters whose capacity for wonder had been numbed by protracted exposure to television and hard rock revealed, if only momentarily, that it was still within their capacity to "get off on" an event that met their parents' approval.

Foreign observers who witnessed the bicentennial were impressed, too. They had good reason to be. During most of the 1960s, they had been treated to television footage depicting the assassination of three American leaders, urban rioting, campus violence, and numerous other incidents strongly suggesting that the United States was on the brink of revolution. Things did not improve a great deal for Americans in the 1970s either. After more than ten years of fighting, the United States retired from Vietnam; soon afterwards, the corrupt Thieu government, which it had supported with American blood and treasure, collapsed. The news at home was also disheartening: Vice President Spiro Agnew was forced to resign, and President Richard M. Nixon followed when it was learned he had subverted the same Constitution for which 55,000 American servicemen had purportedly sacrificed their lives in Southeast Asia.

By 1976, however, the mood in America had changed dramatically. Black militants and white radicals spoke favorably about working for change within the system; some of them, such as Bobby Seale and Tom Hayden, ran for public office. On college campuses, fraternities, formal dances, and good grades preoccupied most students; unconventional behavior, strident anti-establishment rhetoric, and displays of intensity about social issues had become passé. Charles Colson, who gained notoriety for declaring that he would run over his grandmother to reelect Richard Nixon, and Eldridge Cleaver, who fled the United States to avoid serious criminal charges, found Christ and the Republican Party. After two years of soul-searching over the "Watergate horrors," the American people regained their composure and spoke proudly about the nation's capacity to grapple with a grave constitutional crisis without resorting to violence or wrenching political upheaval.

Admirers abroad were generous in their praise, too. Prior to the Watergate crisis, Jean-François Revel had written in *Without Marx or Jesus*: "The revolution of the twentieth century will take place in the United States. It is only there that it can happen and it has already begun. Whether or not that revolution spreads to the rest of the world depends on whether or not it succeeds first in America." The book outraged French leftists and radicals in America who reviled the "revolutionary" institutions that Revel had celebrated—bourgeois democracy and capitalism. Watergate, they claimed, proved that America was on the brink of disaster, but Revel responded that the peaceful resolution of the crisis only proved that he had been right all along.[1]

Revel perhaps suffers from hyperbole, an affliction which is a hallmark of the Gallic left. But when one considers the plight of other countries in the world, it is not farfetched to speak of the United States as "exceptional," if not revolutionary.

In most pluralistic societies, racial, religious, and ethnic divisions have produced violence, coups d'état, and civil wars—not a common psychological bond. In many other countries, the vast majority of people endure grinding poverty while the ruling oligarchy lives in luxury. In still other places, champions of modernization and advocates of traditionalism are locked in bitter combat. Although in different ways, the foregoing applies to developed countries like Spain, Canada, and the USSR, as well as to developing ones like Pakistan, Vietnam, and Iran.

The United States is one of a handful of countries where social order has been achieved through consensus—political authority, and not coercion—political power. If pressed, most Americans would argue that the adhesive binding their society together is the belief in a trinity of convictions—popularly characterized as the American dream—that are political, economic, and cultural in nature. For generations of our people, the American dream has meant political liberty; economic abundance; and a culture marked by the sometimes paradoxical values of religious piety, egalitarianism, and individualism.

Some scholars refer to these same phenomena as the basis for the American political culture. Others choose to speak of them as vital components of Lockean liberalism, the public philosophy that has prevailed in the United States ever since the founding fathers transformed John Locke's ideas into a program for governance. Whatever term one employs, the political, economic, and cultural factors involved account for an anomaly of our society. Elements of Lockean liberalism that contributed to our country's past achievements presently are the source of the American predicament. To understand this anomaly, we must assess the major components of Lockean liberalism and the social forces that have a bearing on the "American experience," and chart them as they have evolved since the founding of the United States.

Political Foundations

After the British surrendered at Yorktown, the first generation of U.S. leaders were confronted with two awesome problems. First, how could they forge a national identity—an "American identity"—out of a diverse population that in many places did not share a common linguistic, religious, or cultural heritage? The Revolutionary War had promoted a common bond of nationalism as leaders and simple folk alike fought for their independence. Still, they lived in a vast land where economic, social, and cultural differences threatened to foster regional, not national, loyalties.

This first problem was compounded by the second one, which involved superseding the political authority of the thirteen states with a single, national political order. The Articles of Confederation failed to accomplish this objective: they gave the states vast powers and greatly restricted those of the central government. The new Constitution, drafted at the Grand Convention of 1787, was designed to reverse this relationship, and it was achieved through a conspiracy of sorts. Many opponents of a strong central government were misled into believing that the Philadelphia gathering had been called merely to "revise" the Articles of Confederation. Some, such as Patrick Henry, did not attend, and those who did were outsmarted by men like James Madison and Alexander Hamilton, who were bent on scrapping the basic law in favor of a new one giving the central government vast powers and dramatically reducing those of the states. Had the framers of the 1789 Constitution failed in this endeavor, it is quite possible that the country would have fragmented into three parts—New England, the Mid-Atlantic states, and the South—each of which would eventually have become an independent political system.

The leading figures of the new republic were exceptional men, intellectually gifted and politically adroit. Most of them, Thomas Jefferson, James Madison, and John Adams in particular, were schooled in Western politics and philosophy. They had read the great thinkers of Greek and Roman antiquity. Products of the Enlightenment, they were especially influenced by the ideas of 17th and 18th century thinkers who justifed, forthrightly or by indirection, the ascendancy of men like themselves to political prominence at the expense of the monarchy and titled aristocracy—Thomas Hobbes, John Locke, and Baron de Montesquieu.

The thinker who had the greatest impact on them was John Locke who, in defending the Glorious Revolution of 1688, justified the gentry's sharing power with the crown. Locke had faith in the capacity of free men to conduct their affairs and rejected the Hobbesian rationale for an absolute monarchy, that without power monopolized by the Leviathan, "the life of man" would be "solitary, poor, nasty, brutish, and short." Locke claimed that all men were endowed with natural rights, that sovereignty was not a divine gift to the king but resided in the hands of the people, and that the basis for civil society was a compact the people negotiated with their political representatives. If the political authorities violated the contract by denying the people their right to life, liberty, and property, the people could tear it up and negotiate another one with a different set of representatives. Essentially that is what our ancestors did when they severed relations with King George in 1776.

Locke's emphasis on the importance of private property was also pleasing to the enterprising Americans. Generations of thinkers preceding him had seen a discrepancy between the public good and private interests, but Locke proposed that the public interest would be best served in a society where private interests were secure. The most likely outcome of a constitutional arrangement that allowed men to maximize their material advantages was social harmony, not anarchy.[2]

Although confident about the capacity of men to govern themselves, the founding fathers feared the centralization of political authority even in the hands of their freedom-loving compatriots. There were two reasons they felt this way. First, they could not forget the mistreatment they had suffered at the hands of the British monarchy and parliament, which abused political authority at the expense of the colonies. After independence, this fear did not quickly subside: witness the Articles of Confederation, which diffused power among the 13 states. And even though the framers of the 1789 Constitution acknowledged the necessity for a stronger central government, they expressed concern about the usurpation of political authority during and after the Philadelphia convention.

The second spectre that haunted them was the abuse of power on the part of a majority—the ordinary people of the new republic. John Adams was forthright in expressing his conceren on this matter:

> We may appeal to every page of history we have hitherto turned over, for proofs irrefragable, that the people, when they have been unchecked, have been as unjust, tyrannical, brutal, barbarous and cruel as any king or senate possessed of uncontrollable power. The majority has eternally and without one exception usurped over the rights of the minority.[3]

Beyond these fears, the founding fathers recognized that one of their principal and most difficult tasks was to strike a balance between public authority and individual liberty, between the power of government to ensure social order and the right of the people to enjoy their inalienable rights. This meant diffusing power; for, as Madison wrote, tyranny involved "the accumulation of power, legislative, executive, and judicial, in the same hands, whether of one, a few, or many, and whether hereditary, self-appointed or elective. . . ."[4] By adopting a tripartite form of government, the framers sought to diffuse power along functional lines. By selecting a federal system, they sought to disperse it geographically.

The intellectual prowess of the founding fathers aside, ideas do not grow and flourish unless they are planted in fertile soil. As Louis Hartz observed over a quarter century ago, conditions unique to the United States were essential in the transformation of liberal political and economic ideas into a practical framework for government. The absence of feudalism to bestow power, wealth, and status upon those born into the ruling class was one of the most important conditions contributing to the rise of liberalism in America. To no small degree, the deep-seated ideological cleavages that persist to this day in Europe can be traced to a feudal past when the line between the rulers and the ruled was well defined.[5]

The refusal of Europe's elite in the 19th and 20th centuries to make room for either the working class or the middle class led to internal warfare, exemplified by the Russian Revolution, Fascism in Italy, and Nazism in Germany. Although reluctantly, the rich and powerful in America acceded to demands from below for a voice in the political process; slaves and women aside, ordinary people in the United States were the first in history to wield real influence in government decision making. By the mid-19th century, property restrictions on white male enfranchisement were eliminated. Although the Eastern and Southern Europeans who entered the country by the millions—over a 40-year stretch, beginning in the late 1880s—encountered resistance, they also gained access to the political system at a time when their relatives at home remained disenfranchised.

The dramatic transformation of the U.S. economy that occurred in the aftermath of the Civil War, however, catapulted industrialists, financiers, and the people who served them into political prominence. Unlike the leaders who had preceded them, who adhered to the notion of noblesse oblige, they were advocates of Social Darwinism. Only the fittest survived in society; inequalities in income were a natural part of a healthy social system; and people who attempted to tamper with this natural order were enemies of progress. Social Darwinism provided the captains of industry with the rationale to employ political authority against the disgruntled farmers, angry urban workers, and military socialists who were demanding a larger share of the wealth that the new industrial system was producing.

But the new elite used its domination of the polity to violate the constitutional principles celebrated in the Bill of Rights and subsequent amendments to the Constitution. In the fifty years preceding the New Deal, the civil liberties of political "radicals" and labor "agitators" were systematically violated. Socialists and pacifists were imprisoned on trumped-up charges, and law enforcement agencies were frequently employed to break strikes and oppress those who sought to empower workers in the nation's mines, mills, and factories. The due process clause of the Fourteenth Amendment, which was drafted to protect free blacks against states violating their civil liberties, was employed to protect business enterprises from government regulation. The Supreme Court made this possible by interpreting the word "person" in the amendment to include "corporations."

Populist parties mushroomed with rural discontent, but they were largely single-issue, regional movements that flourished briefly and then vanished from the political arena. The Socialist Party of America, under the charismatic Eugene Debs, looked as if it were about to become a significant political force on the eve of World War II. However, the war, ethnic divisions, and ideological differences split the party, and the fear of violence and arrest compelled many socialists to tear up their cards. The Democratic party, which attracted millions of urban workers and their rural counterparts, had the potential to mobilize the nation's disgruntled masses into a truly effective force for change; but a cultural chasm kept the small-town Protestant and urban immigrant voter from locking arms in political solidarity. The nativist harangue of Democratic fundamentalists such as William Jennings Bryan was not likely to win the votes of immigrant Catholics and Jews.

The upheaval generated by industrial capitalism, culminating in the Great Depression, paved the way for progressive reform in the 1930s. Henceforth workers, liberals, Catholics, Jews, blacks, and Southern populists were mobilized by Franklin D. Roosevelt into a countervailing force to big business and interests that had dominated the political process since the 1860s. After World War II the influence of these groups would grow, spawning new social welfare programs and stripping away discriminatory laws that denied blacks political equality. As the Civil Rights movement reached its peak in the 1960s, sex-related discrimination came under assault. In the next decade, traditional forms of racial and sexual discrimination declined in all areas of American life.

The above represents conventional wisdom about the achievements of our political system and why, though it is imperfect, the vast majority of our people support it. It is worth noting, moreover, that unlike James Madison, political scientists today portray interest groups—what Madison called factions—in a more positive light. Prior to World War II, interest groups were still deemed detrimental to democratic government, but after the war a rationale was established for the existence of interest groups in democratic societies. There was nothing wrong with people who shared a common economic or social bond joining together to press their claims on government. On the contrary, in a pluralistic society one had to expect a diversity of political views and demands. How could the public interest be harmed by those very groups and interests that together represented the public?[6] What political scientists call "interest group" or "Lockean" liberalism works as follows:

1. All of us belong to one or more interest group—e.g., the United Auto

Workers, the National Farm Bureau, the Chamber of Commerce, the National Association for the Advancement of Colored People, the National Organization for Women, and so forth—and it is through such groups that we affect the political process.

2. Powerful economic interests may enjoy certain advantages, but other groups influence the political process because they are numerically large, well organized, have adroit leaders, or possess other non-economic resources that explain why even the nation's largest corporations often discover that "you can't win them all." Because just about every segment of society possesses one or more of these resources, all groups can participate in the great game of politics.

3. Given the multiplicity of organized interests, the complexity of our society, and the size and diversity of our people, it is unlikely that a single source will dominate any policy area for long.

4. For all the preceding reasons, a dogmatic right–left approach to the study of U.S. politics simply does not square with the facts; that is, public policy is not a matter of businessmen always lining up on one side and labor on the other. Due to the pluralistic nature of our society, many interests usually at odds with one another may, at times, find themselves "sharing the same bed."

5. Although some groups in the United States are more powerful than others, even the weakest know that they can expect a piece of the pie. This phenomenon is based primarily on Yankee pragmatism, not noblesse oblige, on the part of the U.S. elite: to ignore the needs of the weaker interests is socially disruptive and, therefore, detrimental to the privileges the most powerful groups enjoy.

Here, then, is a partial answer to the question: How has the United States created a unity out of racial, ethnic, and religious diversity—sources of social discord and political upheaval in most of the world's multiethnic societies? It also explains why most Americans accept the primacy of national political authority and do not persist in their advocacy of state sovereignty. Americans, whatever their background, believe that they have a voice in political decisions affecting them. Even those who contend that the system favors the rich and influential concede that it is not unresponsive to the concerns of ordinary citizens and that the most privileged groups often have to compromise in the face of popular pressure. Though not perfect, our system of government is one of the fairest in the world and that is why public order in the United States is founded primarily upon consent and not coercion.

Adam Smith's "Invisible Hand"

In countries where there is little economic mobility, the effects of accumulated poverty, ignorance, and discrimination divide the "haves" and "have nots." Consequently, even in ethnically homogeneous countries, economic inequality produces serious political cleavages setting Right against Left. This explains why the communists in both Italy and France continue to be a force to be reckoned with. It is also the basis for political upheaval throughout much of the Third World.

Conversely, economic prosperity in the United States has contributed to civil order, has denied both right- and left-wing extremists political legitimacy, and accounts for the fact that the vast majority of Americans believe in the free enterprise system, which is an integral part of American liberalism. It is noteworthy that the first and most comprehensive defense of the capitalism system ever put to pen occurred in 1776.

In the very year that the Americans flung the Declaration of Independence in King George's face, Adam Smith, a professor of moral philosophy at the University of Glasgow, published his influential book, *The Wealth of Nations*. It would provide the rationale for releasing the economy from the bear hug of government, which the mercantilists believed was essential to a nation's economic development. Smith contended that natural economic laws regulated production and consumption, wages and profits, booms and busts, and he spoke of this market mechanism in terms of an "invisible hand," which, if left alone, worked as deftly as a Swiss watch. Government's role was the limited one of providing for matters the private sector could not handle — the construction of roads and canals, overseeing public health, and other critical enterprises not the proper function of the market. Smith warned against government tampering with the process, for it could seriously short-circuit the free market and wreak havoc in society. Those misguided souls who sought to employ government power to spare the poor and the needy pain and anxiety would only complicate matters and prolong their suffering.

The laws governing the economy were harsh, but they also were benign. Periodically the solemnity of the market would be shattered by recessions hurting worker and employer alike, but such dislocations were a necessary part of the inevitable movement toward equilibrium. Soon, after a period of decline, economic activity would begin to hum once again. In contrast with other 18th century practitioners of the gloomy science, Smith was optimistic about the future and felt that, if left alone, the free market would afford every member of society, the highest and the lowest, the opportunity to prosper.[7]

Contrary to what some conservatives would have us believe, however, the founding fathers did not follow Smith's counsel in making economic policy. They read him, and his ideas were deemed gospel by succeeding generations of Americans, but they were not always acted upon. Indeed, the most influential members of Washington's administration, such as Alexander Hamilton, the first secrety of the treasury, and other business-minded leaders thought it incumbent upon government to establish the framework for economic development. They argued that it was precisely because the Articles of Confederation retarded economic growth that a new constitutional arrangement was needed; not long after Washington was sworn in as the first president of the United States, the "Hamiltonians" successfully lobbied for the adoption of policies that expanded government's outreach into the economy. The national debt was refunded at face value, a national bank was created, and tariffs were imposed upon the importation of foreign goods to protect infant American enterprises.

Government measures of this nature were important in the economic development of the United States, but public involvement in the economy was modest. Economic activity that occurred within the context of the market was modest, too. Well into the early 19th century, the dominant form of economic activity was the "domestic household," the largely self-sufficient yeoman farm. Moreover, most businesses belonging to the market economy were small local enterprises.

The market system would grow on the eve of the Civil War and expand dramatically after the conflagration, as the self-sufficient yeoman farmer faded from the scene and new business enterprises—agricultural and industrial—which were an integral part of the market economy, flourished. Farmers in many parts of the country were cruelly hurt by the high rates charged by the railroads to ship their goods and by the banks to finance their small enterprises. This disenchantment produced organized resistance to corporate capitalism in the form of the populist movement. But although the Populists at times employed radical rhetoric (and some advocated socialist reforms such as nationalizing the railroads), most were not opponents of capitalism per se. Rather, they were disgruntled small entrepreneurs, angry that they were not getting a large enough slice of the pie. Later, in part because of government assistance, but largely because of economic enterprise and natural market readjustments—the mechanization of agriculture and the transfer of surplus labor to urban employment—farm income rose dramatically.

As the populist movement faded, socialist-minded political and labor activists sought to mobilize middle-class radicals, urban workers, and former Populists to destroy capitalism, which they claimed as the source of economic injustice in the United States. But they searched in vain for a class-conscious working class that would provide the mass base responsible for the success of their brethren in Europe.

In addition to the ethnic, religious, racial, and regional divisions already mentioned, the American workers did not display class solidarity because in America one could improve one's living standards. Werner Sombart, the

German author of *Why There is no Socialism in the United States*, wrote, almost 100 years ago, "On the reefs of roast beef and apple pie, socialist Utopians of every sort are sent to their doom."[8] There are few historians, even Marxists, who would deny that economic growth in the aftermath of the Civil War helped integrate succeeding waves of immigrants into U.S. society. During the tumultuous years from the late 1880s to World War I, when millions of immigrants from Eastern and Southern Europe arrived, they did not prosper as rapidly as our history books allege, but there is no doubt that they accepted the core values other Americans cherished—equality, the work ethic, individualism, etc.—because they did improve their economic position. They did not discard their Old World values and traditions altogether, but this union of an American value consensus with economic prosperity minimized the impact of class and other divisions, which later would give rise to communism in Russia and fascism in Italy and Germany.

The Great Depression caused millions of Americans to lose faith in the economy's capacity to maintain, much less improve, their living standards, but a steadfast belief in the nation's political institutions and core values helped mollify the discontent that gave rise to political extremism in Europe. The New Deal, of course, helped alleviate the people's plight and assuaged their fears about the future, thereby negating the prospect that more radical changes would be adopted. The resurrection of the American Federation of Labor (AFL) and the formation of the Congress of Industrial Organizations (CIO) also enabled workers to strive for better working conditions and wages within the system's existing institutional framework and henceforth helped harmonize labor–management relations.

World War II ended the Depression, but there were those who feared it would resume after the war. Although high rates of unemployment and inflation in the postwar years were cause for alarm, they soon declined. "The years from 1950 to the early 1970s were the longest period of growth that capitalism had ever experienced, almost a quarter century of nearly uninterrupted expansion."[9] From 1947 to 1965 the buying power of the average worker in the United States rose by more than 36%.[10] With postwar prosperity, more working people than ever before could purchase new cars, labor-saving appliances, television sets, phonographs, and even a dream house in one of the mushrooming suburbs. Millions of youngsters—whose parents had, at best, secured a high school diploma—entered college, with the knowledge that in four years they could look forward to the amenities of the burgeoning middle class. To these people, the American dream was not an illusion but a reality. Their good fortune, in turn, contributed to the decline of the left as a significant force in the political system. The New Deal, the rise of the labor movement, and the capacity of the economy to improve the worker's living standards demonstrated that capitalism could be reformed peacefully.

By the late 1960s, the percentage of black and Hispanic Americans who previously had been denied the fruits of prosperity had reason to be reassured. Millions of them, whose parents had struggled a lifetime in poorly paid jobs as sharecroppers, maids, janitors, and day laborers, were entering the nation's colleges, earning middle-class incomes and filling professional and executive positions. During the 1960s the average American's standard of living rose, denying radical elements mass-based support for change. At the same time, conservatives began to look upon Keynesian economics in a more positive light. The "new economics" had produced prosperity and provided an alternative to the radical left's claims that poverty could be eliminated only through a revolution and a drastic redistribution of wealth. Economic inequities could be handled by far less draconian measures within the system. By enlarging the pie, every segment of society could move up the ladder simultaneously.

Adam Smith, perhaps, would disapprove of the pivotal role that government played in the "mixed economy," but he could take comfort in the free market's tenacity in the face of a swelling public sector. It continued to account for most economic activity in the world's leading capitalist society; economic decisions were still made largely on the basis of supply, demand, and competition. Two hundred years after he wrote *The Wealth of Nations*, the success of capitalist economies vindicated the Scottish philosopher. American capitalism included hard times, but no objective commentator could dispute that it was the most productive economic system in history.

A Culture of Progress, Individualism and Piety

The sparks that ignited the Englightenment flashed across Europe at a time when a few thousand hardy souls were establishing settlements in the New World. The genius of Galileo, Newton, and Bacon would thrust a new and enthralling vision before mankind, one based upon reason and scientific discovery. It was now possible to break the shackles of ignorance and superstition that had blighted the Middle Ages. Society did not have to stagnate; conditions that had denigrated and cowed man for centuries could be changed. Henceforth nature could serve him.

Although the Enlightenment originated in Europe, it was in America where the new vision first captured the imagination of an entire people. As it was translated into human action, we saw the ascendancy of modern culture. There has been a storehouse of books written about "modernity," but perhaps the best way to distinguish the modern from the premodern world is to cite three social facts unique to the United States. First, by the late 18th century, Americans were preoccupied with living, while most of the world's inhabitants were still dwelling upon death. In most places poverty, ignorance, despotism, and an early death were accepted as unalterable facts. The prospect that there was an alternative to destitution was unthinkable. Like their ancestors, the vast majority of the world's people believed that the only escape from the harsh conditions of life was death.

A second feature of American culture, which appeared prior to the onset of modernity in other areas of the Occident, was the celebration of the individual. Long before people broke free of the bonds of communal life in Europe, the individual in America was given license to embark upon what he deemed to be his proper course of development. He did not first have to seek permission of the community.

The celebration of the individual was associated with a third social fact unique to the New World: a belief in progress. Foreign visitors were struck by the confidence that the Americans exuded, especially their cavalier attitude toward the dangers and hardships that were to be endured as they drove deeper into an untamed wilderness. The pioneers believed that they could manipulate the forces of nature to produce abundance and were convinced decades before their cousins in the old country that applied science could help them achieve a heaven on earth.

Why were Americans the first to display that confidence about the human condition that historians associate with modern culture? After all, in the late 18th and early 19th centuries, science was more advanced in Europe than it was in the United States; the industrial revolution first occurred in Great Britain, not America; the world's leading scholars were in Oxford, Paris, Heidelberg, and other European centers of learning, not in Williamsburg, Boston, Philadelphia, or New York. All the conditions associated with modernity appeared in the Old World before crossing the Atlantic to the new one, so how can we contend that ours was the first modern society?

The factors unique to the United States that support this claim are diverse: in addition to the political and economic elements previously discussed, the nation's geography, its abundance, an egalitarian social system, and a conviction, rooted in religion, that we are a chosen people, are all relevant.

On July 2, 1893, the American Historical Association gathered in Chicago to help celebrate the World's Columbian Exposition. A historian from the University of Wisconsin, Frederick Jackson Turner, presented a paper entitled "The Significance of the Frontier in American History," at the meeting, that captivated thoughtful people for many decades because it provided the "key" to American society. Turner contended that "the peculiarity of American institutions is the fact that they have been compelled to adapt themselves to the changes of an expanding people. . . ."[11] In grappling with the frontier, Americans acquired a national identity marked by the love of liberty, individualism, and innovation. The frontier also served as a safety valve, dissipating discontent that built up in the urban East.

Turner's thesis came under heavy fire in the 1930s for being simplistic, one-dimensional, and deterministic. But thirty years later, a new generation of historians reaffirmed the importance of the frontier as a vital element in our folklore as well as in fact. Turner's vision moved reformers like Teddy Roosevelt, Woodrow Wilson, and Franklin D. Roosevelt to produce a surrogate frontier in the form of government programs that would channel the people's energy into positive outlets. FDR saw the New Deal in such terms, and John F. Kennedy's New Frontier and Lyndon Johnson's Great Society were proffered with much the same purpose in mind.

Whatever one thinks of Turner's thesis, the nation's vast land mass, much of which contains millions of acres of the world's most fertile soil, bountiful timber, abundant water, and enormous amounts of fossil fuels and other precious raw materials, has made it possible for the United States to become history's richest society. The obvious economic ramifications of this phenomenon aside, the cornucopia of goods and services that Americans enjoy has made an indelible imprint upon our culture, and our abundance has captured the imagination of people everywhere.

American films are popular worldwide. They dazzle moviegoers with a spectacle of grand homes replete with labor-saving appliances, gadgets to entertain, big cars, stylish clothes, and bountiful food and drink. Intellectuals denigrate them for being vulgar and materialistic, but to the millions who relish them, life as depicted by Hollywood represents nirvana. Abundance, the reality of affluence, but even more so the expectation that one could obtain it, is one of the reasons why the United States is the only industrial society without a significant socialist movement.

The left has failed to attract working people because of another unique feature of the United States. While Sombart's "reefs of roast beef and apple pie" passage has been widely quoted, he provided this observation to explain why socialists found it hard to appeal to working Americans:

> Snobbery concerning one's social position is also probably less widespread in the United States than it is in Germany. The individual is not valued for what he is, still less for what his parents were: he is valued for what he accomplished.[12]

In Europe workers flocked to socialist parties because they sought social equality as well as economic justice. The promise of egalitarianism did not create much interest among American workers, however, because very early in their country's history an individual's self-worth was measured by the ability to achieve, principally the ability to make money, and not by accidents of birth, religion or one's formal education or speech patterns, as was true of Europe. The American dream promised that even those of humble origins would be judged on the basis of their performance, gaining status and wealth by the sweat of their labor, the creativity of their minds, and the dexterity of their hands.

Working Americans adopted the same value system that drove their affluent countrymen—materialism, the work ethic, and individualism—and the United States was spared serious class conflict to a large degree because of this attitudinal consensus. As Lipset wrote in *The First New Nation*, "the worship of the dollar, the drive to make a profit, the effort to get ahead through the accumulation of wealth, all have been credited to the egalitarian character of the society, that is, to the absence of aristocracy."[13]

These secular factors contributed to our culture of confidence, but the religious conviction that "we were among God's chosen people" was as important, or even more so, in shaping American culture. "The boundless energy," Robert Bellah has written, "that has always characterized this people undoubtedly stems in part from this feeling which is similar to that of a child who has been especially favored by its parents."[14] Before the Pilgrims touched upon the shores of America, they spoke of it in terms of "New Jerusalem." Centuries later, even after Americans adopted a more liberal view of religion and the deity, the idea that they were blessed by God did not disappear. A decade before the revolution, John Adams said: "I always consider the settlement of America as the opening of a grand scheme and design in Providence for the illumination of the ignorant and the emancipation of the slavish part of mankind all over the earth." Almost 100 years later, Herman Melville wrote: "And we Americans are peculiar, chosen people—the Israel of our time; we bear the ark of the liberties of the world."[15]

After the Civil War, when the forces of industrialization gained momentum, rapid economic change was perceived as part of a grand heavenly design, too. The rich enjoyed great wealth not only by dint of their ingenuity and labor but because they had been selected by God. That was a popular theme articulated in the nation's churches. In the words of William Lawrence, Episcopal bishop of Massachusetts, "In the long run, it is only to the man of morality that wealth comes."[16] Bellah reminds us that even Americans who opposed the capitalist system resorted to biblical terms to attract the proletariat to socialism. Eugene Debs, the most successful socialist in U.S. history, for example, spoke of "the workers" as "the saviors of society. . . ."[17]

In the 1970s the religious revival that swept the country was proof that while the religious impulse had waxed and waned, it remained deeply imbedded in American culture. The interconnection between religious piety and "liberal" political and economic notions, moreover, was exemplified by the fact that in those geographic areas where Protestant fundamentalism pulsated with the greatest strength, hostility toward "big government" and "socialism" was most widespread.

The American culture of confidence explains why Americans have almost always associated change with progress, and why they have set their sights on a measure of economic abundance no other people dreamed possible. To no small degree, the conviction that Americans can solve all manner of problems accounts for the facility with which they have traditionally struck out in new directions, confident that "things will turn out favorably." We are a nation of "winners" because we are innovative, pious, and tough.

The Malaise of the Late 1970s

Beliefs shape thought and action, but over time they die if there is no substance to them. The American dream has prevailed because for most Americans it has produced a real, not imaginary, harvest of political freedom, economic abundance, and social and cultural opportunities. In the wake of the twin evils of Vietnam and Watergate, Americans pondered such observations with pleasure, and the intoxicating effect of the bicentennial infused them with confidence about the future. When Jimmy Carter entered the White House in January 1977, pollsters reported that for the first time in years there was a rise in the number of people who professed optimism about the country's future.

Eighteen months later, however, Carter's stock had slipped badly in the polls. He was accused of being politically inept. He had run against Washington as a "citizens' candidate," and after entering office he proved that he was indeed an "amateur." Even with a Congress controlled by his own party, Carter was unable to pass legislation he deemed vital to the nation's welfare. He lost his first conflict with Congress, after attempting to eliminate expensive pork barrel projects that had little justification. Substantively, Carter was right, but he ignored political reality. The programs involved were bread and butter for the constituents of Democrats and Republicans alike, and few representatives or senators had the courage to oppose the practice of awarding unnecessary public works projects to the "folks back home."

Carter's leadership flaws aside, the major problem confronting the nation was stagflation—slow rates of economic growth on the one hand and high rates of inflation on the other. There were a number of reasons for this condition: Lyndon Johnson's refusal to raise taxes soon enough to pay for the Vietnam War, growing competition for U.S. markets from foreign firms, and rising prices for the commodity most vital to economic prosperity—oil.

In 1974, in the wake of the Yom Kippur War, oil-rich Arab countries had placed an embargo on buyers friendly to Israel. Later the Organization of Petroleum-Exporting Countries (OPEC) more than doubled its crude oil prices, causing consuming nations to engage in panic buying. The outcome was a fourfold increase in petroleum prices in 1974. Cheap oil had helped fuel the economic prosperity industrial democracies had enjoyed throughout the 1960s and early 1970s. This price hike caused the worse recession since the 1930s. In the United States "GNP fell by 6 percent from its peak at the end of 1973 to the beginning of 1975, while the unemployment rate jumped from 4.7 percent to 9 percent. . . . [M]easuring the price change from the third quarter of 1973 to the fourth quarter of 1974, the oil tax was $16.4 billion [1974 dollars], or 1.2 percent of our GNP."[18]

The United States produces considerable oil of its own and has large supplies of natural gas and massive coal resources. Nevertheless, like its allies in Europe and Japan, it was vulnerable to another energy shock. But it did not take sufficient measures to avoid the second one, which struck in 1979 after the shah of Iran was forced to step down. The subsequent 180% price hike checked what appeared to be an economic recovery in the making. The mood in the White House, therefore, was gloomy: polls informed Carter that his support was plunging. The president's aides pondered what would happen if the gas lines reached the proportions they had in 1974, or if the country were stricken by another exceptionally cold winter. Even if there were sufficient home heating fuel, the price would be high. Jimmy Carter, making preparations to run again in 1980, would be blamed.

In July, after returning from an economic summit in Tokyo, Carter skipped a scheduled vacation in Hawaii and returned to Washington to deal with the worsening energy crisis. He retreated to Camp David where for ten days he met with leaders from every major group and interest in the country—blacks, labor, business, etc. On July 15, he delivered a highly publicized prime-time television address, but he did not say much about the energy crisis:

> I want to talk to you right now about a fundamental threat to American democracy. . . . The threat is nearly invisible in ordinary ways. It is a crisis that strikes at the very heart and soul and spirit of our national will.

To support this assertion he said, "For the first time, a majority of our people believe that the next five years will be worse than the past five years." Here he was referring to polls indicating that a profound turnabout was underway in the attitudes of the American people. For the first time since the Great Depression, millions of them were expressing doubts about the capacity of the country to emerge from the existing economic crisis unscathed. Carter went on to say that the malaise contained both political and cultural components. "Two thirds of our people do not even vote," and "the willingness of Americans to save for the future had fallen below that of other people in the Western world."[19]

Ronald Reagan, the frontrunner for the GOP presidential nomination, accused Carter of blaming the American people for his ineptness. The instincts of the American people were as sound as the country's political and economic institutions, Reagan proclaimed. If provided proper leadership, the country's problems at home and abroad would be resolved. For example, Reagan asserted that if the liberals left the free market alone, it would bring forth a new era of prosperity in America, and if the country rearmed to countervail the Soviety military threat, things would look up for it abroad as well.

Perhaps Carter's "malaise speech" was politically motivated, but there were ominous signs that the American people had doubts about government, the economy, and the country's future. Polls showed that from 1958 to 1978, there was a sharp rise in the number of Americans who said:

> "Government is run for a few big interests"—from 18 to 74%. "Government cannot be regularly trusted to do what is right"—from 25 to 70%. "Government is run by people who don't know what they are doing"—from 28 to 56% (1964). "Government wastes a lot of tax dollars"—from 46 to 79%.

Other studies showed that a declining number of Americans were bothering to vote. In 1980 the turnout was the lowest since 1948. And still others indicated declining faith in Congress and the two major parties. In July 1979, when asked whether they believed there was a "crisis of confidence" in the political system, 86% said yes.[20]

The factor most often cited for their disenchantment was not Vietnam or Watergate, but the nation's economic troubles. They had reason for such concerns. On January 30, 1980, Jimmy Carter delivered his economic report to Congress, predicting a recession for the new year. This was the first time since the practice began that a president had forecast a recession. It also was the first time that a president had predicted the country would be afflicted by double-digit inflation for the next twelve months. Most economists had interpreted the first signs of economic troubles in the early 1970s as short-term dislocations, but by the late 1970s all but a few reported that the nation's economic difficulties were long-term, a product of stuctural forces, not cyclical ones. Among the specific symptoms of the nation's economic predicament, the following were underscored: declining growth in rates of productivity; growing foreign competition, such as Japanese penetration of U.S. automobile, television, stereo, and business machines markets; an aging industrial sector that was falling behind foreign competitors; a shortfall in capital desperately needed to modernize the industrial base, caused in part by government crowding out of the private sector in competition for capital; and the refusal of the American people to save.

While economists dwelt upon the macroeconomic problems afflicting the economy, ordinary Americans expressed alarm about declining living standards, rising unemployment, and outright poverty. Median family income adjusted for inflation rose 3% a year from 1960 to 1969, but from 1970 to 1978 it rose by a meager eight-tenths of 1%. In 1978 and 1979 the real purchasing power of workers declined: wages in 1978 rose by 7.7%, while consumer prices jumped 9%; in 1979, although wages increased by 8.7%, consumer prices grew by 13.3%.[21]

The recession would cause unemployment for millions of people who had never before been afflicted by joblessness. Blue-collar workers who had put in as much as twenty years in a factory lost their jobs. Many of them would not get their jobs back, while others would have to settle for lower-paying jobs in the service industry. Black Americans, of course, were hit hardest by the recession. In early 1979, while white adult male unemployment was 3.6%, white adult female unemployment 5%, and white teenager unemployment 13.7%, it was 7.8, 10.6, and 32.7%, respectively, for black men, women, and teenagers.[22]

Working women of all ages were hurt by the recession. In the 1970s there was a dramatic increase in the number of women who entered the labor force. Between 1973 and 1978, three-fifths of them were single, divorced, widowed, or separated, so a large number of them were primary breadwinners who could not rely upon their spouse's income to pay the bills.

Finally, the nation's war on poverty was suffering a setback. In 1973, 23.0 million persons lived in poverty, but in the next two years the recession caused 2.9 million more people to join the ranks of the poor. By 1976 economic activity had picked up, and 900,000 persons worked their way out of poverty, but by 1977 only 300,000 could do so, and by 1978 only 200,000 were so fortunate.[23] Perhaps the greatest tragedy of all was that the children of the poor were destined to become wards of the state for most, if not all, of their lives—robbing them of self-esteem and dignity, and guaranteeing society serious problems.

In the face of bad economic news, many pundits began to speculate about political repercussions. Dean Burnham, a prominent MIT political scientist, wrote: "It is hard to imagine how ... high unemployment, and persistent declines in the mass standard of living can be sustained indefinitely without producing a political explosion."[24]

There were no concrete signs that such an explosion was soon to occur, however. On the contrary, people appeared to respond to their problems by turning inward, away from the public arena. This was understandable given their dim view of government and the state's capacity to solve their problems. Declining faith in the polity's fairness and justified fears about the economy's capacity to maintain growth accounted for claims, now becoming widespread, that the American dream was unraveling. Indeed, the American predicament was not confined to the political and economic arenas—it manifested itself in doubts about the strengths of the cultural values that we and our forebearers had always cherished. People were worried about rising crime rates, the American family in disarray, our schools in turmoil, and a decline in the work ethic. They also had doubts about American know-how.

Crime rates in the United States were among the highest of any industrial society. The assassinations of President Kennedy, Martin Luther King, and Robert Kennedy, as well as the abortive attempt on George Wallace's life, all within a ten-year span testified to a deeply ingrained compulsion toward violence in America. By this time suburban crime had become a serious concern in most states, and the crimes included murder, assault, and rape—not just vandalism, car theft, and drug abuse. In spite of evidence that all of us were paying for the crime afflicting our society, many middle-class white Americans overlooked it because the poor and minorities were more inclined to be violent crime victims than they were.

People from all walks of life, however, had reason to be upset about the status of the family. From 1920 to 1975 there was a sixfold increase in the number of divorced women; between the mid-1950s and 1973 the divorce rate shot up by two-thirds. Significantly, whereas divorce was once associated with low-income groups, in the postwar years it had spread throughout all strata of society. A related problem was the growing number of single-parent families headed by women. "By 1975, 20% of all children were either living with a single parent or were being cared for by those not their parents."[25] A disproportionate number of youngsters living in such households were living below the poverty line.

Other examples of the family in decline included the plight of old folks whose children refused to care for them, the laissez-faire attitude parents took toward children, and the erosion of traditional values that accounted for an upsurge in teenage suicides, illegitimacy, and social diseases.

Studies of American education revealed that despite the fact that more money was being allocated to educate our children than ever before, many could not read, write, or calculate with the same facility as their older brothers and sisters, who had finished school in the 1960s. The failure of our schools was exemplified even more so by the revelation that in many parts of the country functional illiterates were earning high school diplomas. Teachers responded that they were being burdened with tasks the family and community had once performed, such as teaching preschool skills, providing after-school care, and dealing with a host of behavioral problems. In many schools teachers and students alike had little time for teaching or learning because they feared for their physical safety. In 1975, for example, over 66,000 attacks on teachers were recorded in U.S. public schools, including attacks with knives and guns. Violence in the schools exacerbated low teacher morale, which had been on the decline for years. The most pervasive source of discontent among teachers, of course, was low salaries. This factor, along with the others, explained why teachers were quitting their jobs in record numbers; one study revealed that 40% of teachers nationwide did not intend to remain in the profession.[26]

Turmoil in the schools explained why employers complained about the educational deficiencies of the young people entering the labor force. But their complaints were not limited to young workers. They also expressed concern about the negative work attitudes displayed by white- and blue-collar employees of all ages. Daniel Yankelovich and Bernard Lefkowitz conducted an exhaustive study indicating that there was substance to these concerns. Our society had become too preoccupied with work and making money, and we did not pay enough attention to fulfilling our human potential. Yankelovich and Lefkowitz found that three major impulses, first articulated in the 1960s, now were embraced by a majority of Americans, forming a new synthesis: "the pursuit of economic stability (even at the cost of reduced compensation), more modest material expectations, and the drive to establish maximum control over one's life and destiny."[27] If this was an accurate appraisal of the public mood, it strongly suggested that risk-taking, innovation, and the adoption of other measures traditionally accounting for high levels of economic activity were being rejected in favor of a risk-free environment and getting along with less.

Moreover, fears (fueled by the Three Mile Island incident in 1979) that nuclear power plants were more dangerous than the problem they were designed to solve, revelations about the misuse of pesticides, the dangers posed by lethal chemicals buried in shallow graves, and the threat of acid rains all indicated that we were mismanaging our technology and environment. Our inability to cope with technological problems was particularly annoying in light of world-renowned ingenuity in this area.

Finally, one of the most obvious examples of inability to cope with our problems was the terrible mess we had made of thousands of urban, suburban, and rural communities. After spending billions of dollars on community development programs, the condition of most of our cities was perilous. Suburban sprawl was looting the nation of scarce open space, poisoning the environment, and fostering skyrocketing housing and public utility costs throughout the country, thereby denying the average American the most compelling symbol of the American dream—home ownership.

Not long after the nation's 200th birthday, then, we suffered a hangover from the celebration. As a nation our belief in progress as a linear process had been shattered, our conviction that technology could be adroitly applied to solve our problems had turned sour, and the conceit that we were a chosen people destined to escape the pratfalls afflicting other societies was superseded by grave doubts about our ability to cope with the problems which afflicted us. Jimmy Carter had reason to talk about the nation's "malaise."

Notes

1. Jean-François Revel, *Without Marx or Jesus* (Garden City, NY: Doubleday, 1971).
2. Victor Ferkiss has observed that Lockean liberalism rests on the idea that social order is achieved through the unity of property holders. See his *Technological Society* (New York: George Braziller, 1974).
3. Robert Bellah, *The Broken Covenant* (New York: Seabury Press, 1975), p. 33.
4. James Madison, "Federalist No. 47," in James Madison, Alexander Hamilton, and John Jay, *The Federalist* (New York: Tudor Publishing Co., 1937), p. 329.
5. Louis Hartz, *The Liberal Tradition in America* (New York: Harcourt, Brace and World, 1955).

6. One of the first books to adapt a more positive view of interest groups was David Truman's *The Governmental Process* (New York: Alfred A. Knopf, 1951).
7. For a lucid analysis of Smith's work, see Robert L. Heilbroner's *The Wordly Philosophers*, 4th ed. (New York: A Touchstone Book, Harper & Row, 1972), pp. 40–72.
8. Werner Sombart, *Why There is No Socialism in the United States* (New York: International Arts and Sciences Press, 1976), p. 48.
9. Robert L. Heilbroner, *Beyond Boom and Crash* (New York: Norton, 1978), p. 12.
10. *Wall Street Journal*, 8 February, 1978.
11. Frederick Jackson Turner, "The Significance of the Frontier in American History," in Ray Allen Billington, ed., *The Frontier Thesis* (New York: Holt, Rinehart and Winston, 1966), p. 9.
12. Sombart, *Why There is No Socialism*, p. 115.
13. Seymour Martin Lipset, *The First New Nation* (Garden City, NY: Anchor Books, 1967), p. 193.
14. Bellah, *The Broken Covenant*, p. 23.
15. Bellah, *The Broken Covenant*, p. 57.
16. Bellah, *The Broken Covenant*, p. 75.
17. Bellah, *The Broken Covenant*, p. 128.
18. Robert Dohner, "The Bedeviled American Economy," in Dan Yergin and Martin Hillenbrand, eds., *Global Insecurity* (New York: Houghton Mifflin Co., 1982), p. 61.
19. *New York Times*, 16 July 1979.
20. *Public Opinion*, October/November 1979, p. 29.
21. *Washington Post*, 25 November 1979.
22. Richard J. Krickus, "Growth and American Pluralism," in U.S. Joint Economic Committee: *Special Studies on Economic Change*, Vol. 1 (May 1980): 260.
23. Bureau of the Census, Advanced Report: "Money Income and Poverty Status of Families and Persons in the United States: 1978," P–69 (120) 1979, p. 28.
24. Walter Dean Burnham, "American Politics in the 1980s," *Dissent* (Spring 1980): 158.
25. *New York Times*, 20 April 1978.
26. *Wall Street Journal*, 9 January 1978.
27. Daniel Yankelovich and Bernard Lefkowitz, "National Growth: The Question of the 80's," *Public Opinion*, December/January 1980, p. 56.

CHAPTER SIX

Ronald Reagan and the Conservative Counterreformation

*These United States are confronted with an economic affliction of great propor-
tions. The economic ills we suffer have come upon us over several decades. In this
present crisis, government is not the solution to our problem; government is the
problem.* — Ronald Reagan, *First Inaugural Address*

Ronald Reagan rejected Carter's inference that the American people had
lost faith in themselves, their country, and their cherished ideals. What Carter
called a national malaise was in fact a national reawakening. The American
people had finally acknowledged that forty years of liberal Democratic rule
had wrought a bitter harvest. It had prompted Reagan to embrace conservatism decades before his fellow countrymen came to their senses. The social
safety-net programs introduced by FDR, Reagan said, were necessary to
safeguard the people against hard times, but Lyndon Johnson's Second New
Deal had gone too far. The Great Society's statist policies had undermined our
republican political institutions, our free enterprise system, and our cherished
values.

Although not conceding that the nation was in a state of crisis, Reagan
admitted that the United States had problems. In 1975, before an audience of
bankers, Reagan said the country's problems "all stem from a single source,
the belief that government, particularly the federal government, has the
answer to all our ills and that the proper method of dealing with social
problems is to transfer power from the private to the public sector. . . ."[1] Yes,

America was grappling with problems, but the liberals who had offered collectivist cure-alls to treat them had to take the blame for exacerbating these problems with their "crackpot" bromides.

According to the conservatives, our society's troubles were linked to the liberals' domination of our intellectual life, their collectivist approach to our social and economic problems, and their celebration of (or at the very least their tolerance of) values that subverted traditional American ideals. The conservatives were leading a counterreformation to restore Lockean liberalism, and this time they had the people on their side. The victory occurred in 1980 with Ronald Reagan's election, but the battle had been a long one.

The Political Roots of the New Conservatism

On the eve of World War II, while Ronald Reagan the film star was still a liberal Democrat who idolized FDR, conservative intellectuals were issuing warnings about the spreading blight of collectivism. In 1940 an émigré Austrian economist, Frederick A. von Hayek, wrote in *The Road to Serfdom* that collectivism would pollute the wellspring of political liberty in the West, and that the poison would eventually destroy Western civilization.[2] The book created a stir among that small segment of the American intellectual community that had not lost faith in classical liberalism, in the ideas Adam Smith had espoused—and most commentators believed had been discredited by the Great Depression.

The Road to Serfdom, however, had little impact on the mainstream intellectual community, which was dominated by liberals. This held true for many years after the war was over. Periodically, throughout the 1950s and into the 1960s, a disciple of von Hayek would write a book warning that our political liberties were being eroded by the expansion of the welfare state. In 1962, for example, Milton Friedman, a University of Chicago economist, fired a salvo at collectivism in *Capitalism and Freedom*. He observed that economics and politics were not "unconnected," that economic freedom was "an indispensable means toward the achievement of political freedom."[3] But with the concentration of economic power in the hands of the state, our political liberties were in grave jeopardy. Democracy could not function without private money to support a free, independent press and opposition parties; citizens denied the resources monopolized by government bureaucrats would be defenseless. Where a free market flourished, consumers—not government planners—dominated economic decision making.

The book was considered a curiosity by most intellectuals, except for the handful of true believers on the right who deemed it gospel. It was used by many teachers to provide balance to a debate dominated by the Left. At that time, it was difficult to find books challenging liberal orthodoxy, therefore, even educators who did not think much of *Capitalism and Freedom* put it on their reading list to expose their students to conservative ideas.

The liberals' ability to shape public policy persisted after the GOP wrested control of the White House from the Democrats. Eisenhower expressed displeasure with the welfare state, but did not dismantle it as many right-wingers hoped he would. He knew that the American people had embraced FDR's reforms and the best that could be done was to prevent many of them from being expanded and to change the direction of other ones. So, Eisenhower recalibrated housing and transportation policy to better meet the needs of the suburbs and the business community. But his ability to provide Republican alternatives to New Deal programs was undercut in the 1954 and 1958 elections, when liberals made gains in both the House and Senate.

The liberal Democrats remained in Washington after Eisenhower's back-to-back victories and continued to influence policy via the federal agencies with which they were associated. While they fought to sustain the New Deal through the bureaucracies, the liberals' fortunes improved as the electorate punished politicians who stated that they opposed the programs FDR had first championed. Barry Goldwater demonstrated how dangerous it was for Republicans to attack the welfare state when he was trounced by LBJ in 1964.

This development and an inherent pragmatism explained why Richard Nixon did not wage an all-out assault on the welfare state, as many liberals had feared he would. Under the guise of New Federalism, he stroked conservatives by emasculating the poverty program, reducing funding for older (Democratic) cities, and impounding Department of Health, Education and Welfare (HEW) funds earmarked for society's neediest citizens. But he did not tamper with safety-net programs such as social security. Indeed, for a brief period, during which Daniel Patrick Moynihan mesmerized him with the prospect of becoming an American Disraeli, he toyed with a family assistance plan (FAP) to replace the existing welfare system and in the process was chastized by right-wing guru William F. Buckley, Jr.

A self-proclaimed, life-long opponent of New Deal economic doctrine, Nixon alienated conservatives when, faced with spiraling inflation threatening his relection, he imposed mandatory wage and price controls in 1971. A year later, he primed a sluggish economy with a spurt of government spending. It was about this time when Nixon asserted that he, too, was a "Keynesian."

After Nixon's reelection in 1972, however, ideas associated with the right began to capture the attention of opinion-molders who had previously ignored or disparaged them. By the end of the decade, views once restricted to the *National Review,* the *Wall Street Journal,* and *Human Events* now were found in syndicated columns written by liberals.

Ironically, the people primarily responsible for giving intellectual legitimacy to a host of right-wing ideas were former socialists, Trotskyites, and liberals—neoconservatives such as Seymour Martin Lipset, Irving Kristol, Norman Podhoretz, and Michael Novak. A number of explanations have been offered to account for their moving along the political spectrum from left to right. One holds that they were outraged by the excesses of the New Left, by people who were attempting to move the center to the far left. They just remained where they always had been, at a spot just slightly left of center. Another, less generous, contends that these offspring of immigrant Jewish and Catholic parents and grandparents had made it into the mainstream of American life and forgotten about the people they left behind. The conservatives whom they came to work with closely in a common struggle against the "radical left" said, "You were rather late in seeing the light, but welcome aboard." Whatever factors explain their passage, they brought to the conservative counterreformation powerful intellectual resources. Given their impressive credentials, literary talents, and extensive contacts in New York and Washington, their assault on remaining liberals could not be ignored by the mainstream media and pundits who shape American public opinion.

These pointmen for the conservative counterreformation played a vital role in encouraging thoughtful people to accept the "conservative critique" of what was wrong with America. They produced studies demonstrating that liberal social policy had in most cases made things worse, not better. Forced busing produced more, not less, racial segregation in many school systems; affirmative action programs promulgated reverse discrimination; community development programs destroyed more neighborhoods than they revitalized; and federal programs contributed to declining standards of excellence in our educational system.

Many neoconservatives—Michael Novak, Ben Wattenberg, and Seymour Martin Lipset, to name only a few—found positions in conservative think tanks such as the American Enterprise Institute and the Hoover Institution, which by the mid-1970s were competing with liberal ones such as the Brookings Institution in public policy research and analysis. They produced an impressive array of books, monographs, and papers stressing the nexus between the free market and democracy. So, approximately fifteen years after *Capitalism and Freedom* was published, Friedman's ideas came into vogue.

In the bicentennial year, the country was clearly moving toward the right, so how could Jimmy Carter's election in November be explained? The dead weight of Watergate and the albatross of stagflation aside, Carter's victory was linked to ethnicity in at least two ways. First, like John F. Kennedy in 1960, Carter in 1976 received many votes from his co-ethnics, white Southerners. White voters from the old Confederacy, who had become accustomed to voting for Republican presidential candidates, made an exception in 1976 and helped bring down the curtain on the Civil War.

Carter's geographic origin figured into his victory in another, perhaps even more important, way. A product of a political subculture in the United States where American liberalism (read "20th century conservatism") remained strong, Carter was one of the first Democrats to recognize that voters from all across the land were beginning to "think like the good ol' boys" from Dixie. Enmity toward Washington, which had been growing in New York, Chicago, and other cities in the Snowbelt, due in part to unpopular liberal social policies, had become a national phenomenon. Both Gerald Ford and Jimmy Carter were aware of this and attempted to turn this impulse against their adversary.

Ford's strategy was to ignore the electorate's discontent about Watergate and a faltering economy, and to convince the voters that his opponent was really a liberal masquerading as a moderate. Ford promised to return power to the people, "where it belonged," and to reduce the outreach of the federal Leviathan the Democrats had created. Jimmy Carter artfully dodged this attempt to portray him as a "Dr. Frankenstein" who had created the "Big Government" monster, by making much of the fact that in contrast to Ford—a former congressman, House minority leader, vice president, and incumbent president—he was a peanut farmer who, "like other folks," was disenchanted with Washington. Furthermore, while both "Rebel" and "Yankee" beat up on big government, many Americans, perhaps unconsciously, concluded that Carter was truly hostile to Washington because for years the harshest antigovernment rhetoric had emanated from Dixie.

In his inaugural address, "The Ever-Expanding American Dream," Carter sought to distance himself from what had been the hallmark of the Democratic party since the thirties—affirmative government. He said that he had no new dream to set forth that day, and although he urged a fresh faith in the old one, he indicated that there were limits to what government could do for those who had not tasted the fruits of that dream: "We must simply do our best."[4] Like the Reaganites, Carter was advocating that the country return to a brand of American liberalism that had existed prior to the New Deal. The answers to our problems were to be found in the private sector, not the public arena.

Reagan's victory in 1980 was ensured by Carter's image as an inept leader, by rising levels of unemployment and soaring inflation, and by U.S. setbacks abroad—such as the taking of American hostages by terrorists in Teheran and the ill-fated effort to free them. Reagan, however, who displayed a real talent for communicating with the people, adroitly associated Carter with unpopular liberal programs that he disparaged by sharing anecdotes with his audiences—the story about the welfare recipient who rode up to the welfare office in a chauffer-driven Cadillac to get her check, or the woman who bought vodka with food stamps rather than food for her children. Reagan had a devastating anecdote for every social and economic scheme the "liberal collectivists" ever proposed.

The conservative assault on the liberals went beyond their ill-fated domestic schemes. The right saw a link between America's problems at home and declining influence abroad. Federal funds earmarked for "wasteful" domestic programs were responsible for the sad state of our military preparedness. Money needed to match the massive Soviet buildup was being used for programs that often exacerbated the very problems they were supposed to resolve. In the late 1970s conservatives became bolder in making such claims. The Soviet invasion of Afghanistan in December 1979 allowed them to taunt Jimmy Carter, who had entered office proclaiming that the Soviet threat had been exaggerated by his predecessors, with cries of "we told you so."

Ronald Reagan was especially insistent upon reclaiming America's image in the world through the restoration of its military might. Reagan's perception of America's status at this time was exemplified by what became known as the "window of vulnerability" scenario. It dealt with the Soviet Union's international ambitions, the U.S.–Soviet nuclear balance, and policies Washington had to adopt to cope with the Soviet menace.

Reagan contended that Kissinger and Nixon's view of the USSR was flawed. The Soviet Union remained wedded to worldwide revolution, and had not become a status quo power as Kissinger had contended. The Soviets had spent enormous sums of money on conventional and nuclear weapon systems for offensive purposes, not defensive ones, as Nixon had contended. The strategy they both shared, that of manipulating carrots—Western trade and credits—and sticks—maintaining a strong defense—in order to arrange a "new structure of peace in the world," was based on wishful thinking. It was extremely dangerous, too, because it would lull many in the West into a false sense of security about the Soviet Union's truly evil intentions, and thereby deny us the opportunity to brandish our military might.

This confrontational view of the Soviets, which was a firm part of the conservative world view in the United States for years, however, was held in disrepute by opinion molders. The people who clung to them were deemed "isolationist Republicans" or "simple-minded cold warriors," who lacked a sophisticated grasp of world affairs.

Here again, the neoconservatives lent vital support to the right's critique of U.S. foreign policy. Since most of them were Democrats, former Democrats, or people who had served Democratic administrations, and they believed America had a special mission to play in the world, they could not be accused of being partisan isolationists. Because they had impressive intellectual credentials, and were prolific writers and skilled polemicists, they could not be accused of being Neanderthals.

Podhoretz's *Commentary* provided a forum in which Eugene Rostow,

Theodore Draper, Edward Luttwak, Walter Lacquer, Richard Pipes, and Jeane Kirkpatrick lashed out against SALT II, détente, arms control in general, the Finlandization of Europe, U.S. nuclear strategy, and Jimmy Carter's human rights policy. In light of Soviet support of the Arabs in the 1973 Yom Kippur War, how could one possibly argue that Moscow wanted good relations with the West? Given Soviet-backed incursions into Angola, Mozambique, South Yemen, and finally their invasion of Afghanistan, how could anybody dispute that the Soviets' deemed détente a one-way street?— they grabbed territory in exchange for more liberal trade, technological transfers, and credits from the West. Reagan acknowledged his debt to Eugene Rostow, Paul Nitze, Richard Pipes, Richard Perle, and Jeane Kirkpatrick by appointing them to important posts in his administration.

The Soviets' international ambitions, of course, were not cause for concern as long as they lacked the military muscle to achieve such global objectives. But planners in the Pentagon stress a simple axiom: when measuring the threat posed by an enemy, do not dwell upon his intentions but his capabilities. Intentions can be changed quickly, but capabilities cannot. What worried many defense analysts in the 1970s was that the Soviets had caught up to, and soon would pass, the United States in strategic nuclear might.

From the late 1940s to the early 1970s, the United States was the world's premier nuclear power. Thus it was safe from Soviet attack. The Warsaw Pact had a conventional edge, but if we failed to halt the communists with conventional weapons in Europe, we would stop them with "nukes." America's edge was underscored in the fall of 1962 with the Cuban missile crisis, when Khrushchev sought to change the balance of power on the cheap—costing him his job in 1964. But in the aftermath of that setback, his successors vowed never again to allow the Americans to bully them. So they went about building a massive strategic nuclear arsenal with larger missiles, such as the SS-18, than we had in ours. And they did so at a time when the United States was preoccupied with the Vietnam War and led by men who believed that the best way to meet the Soviet buildup was through the negotiating process which resulted in the limits of SALT I.

In 1977 Richard Pipes warned in *Commentary* that Soviet military strategists did not accept the doctrine of Mutual Assured Destruction (MAD) but believed a nuclear war could be fought and won.[5] Later that year the Soviets conducted tests demonstrating that they had perfected MIRV (multiple independently-targeted reentry vehicle) technology, which would allow them to place several warheads on a single missile. The advantage we had enjoyed in this technology was no more. An analyst at the Defense Department, James Wade, worked up figures indicating that beginning in 1981 or 1982, the Soviets would have the capability to destroy approximately 80 to 90% of our Minuteman force in a first strike, and that this curve of vulnerability would continue a downward course until the late 1980s, when our new MX missile would be deployed. He called this dip in the graph the "bucket of vulnerability," but it later was replaced by the now commonly known term "window of vulnerability."[6]

When Reagan entered the White House, he persisted in claiming that in the 1980s the United States would be vulnerable to a Soviet first strike—that is, they would have the ability to destroy our ICBMs and thereby leave us no other prospect but to strike back against their cities. Such a response, of course, was MAD, and in rearming America he would close the window of vulnerability and adopt a new, more responsible nuclear doctrine.

The centerpiece of the U.S. response to the Soviet threat, therefore, was military. When Reagan pledged to rearm America, he meant that his administration would not stop deploying new strategic systems until the United States achieved nuclear superiority. Among other things this meant:

- Replacing our Minuteman and Titan II ICBMs with hydra-headed MX missiles.
- Replacing our aging B-52 bombers with newer B-1 bombers.
- Deploying our Trident II missiles, armed with D-5 warheads, with our nuclear submarine force.
- Upgrading our C^3I capability (command, control, communications, and intelligence).

Deploying these systems, however, did not make much sense unless we replaced our mutual assured destruction doctrine with a war-fighting capability. This was not a new idea. It had been espoused first by James Schlesinger, when he was Nixon's secretary of defense in January 1974, but remained in a state of limbo for several years until Jimmy Carter's defense advisers urged him to embrace a war-fighting capability later in the decade.

President Reagan and his secretaries of defense and state, Weinberger and Haig, stopped making statements about the prospects of acquiring a "war-fighting capability," of fighting a "limited nuclear war," and the like when such remarks facilitated the reappearance of the peace movement in Western Europe and the United States. Their silence did not, however, mean that they had scrapped plans to accomplish these objectives.

The Conservative Economic Critique

In 1980, when the nation was being wracked by stagflation, the right noted that, like the mercantilists of the 18th century, liberals in the 20th century had made the fatal error of looking to government to promote and sustain economic growth. Any fair-minded observer who compared the performance of state-controlled economies with capitalist ones had to conclude that the free enterprise systems were outdistancing their socialist counterparts in per capita income, rates of productivity, and quality of output. Also, contrary to Marx's claims, the ranks of the Western proletariat had not become swollen and impoverished, and the middle class had not disintegrated.

By contrast, the economies of the USSR, Cuba, and Vietnam were in absolutely terrible shape. The Soviet economy was sluggish, and growth rates were modest. Cuba, which had considerable economic potential, had failed to actualize it under the rule of its communist leaders, and it was costing the Soviets about $7 million a day to keep Castro's economy running. Vietnam, which at one time was the rice bowl of Asia, was not producing enough food to feed its people and had to rely upon outside assistance to maintain a subsistence standard of living.

Significantly, the developing countries with the most impressive rates of growth—Hong Kong, South Korea, Taiwan, and Singapore—had embraced the capitalist road to development. This explained why they were now giving the developed countries a run for their money in many areas previously dominated by the Western Europeans, North Americans, and even the Japanese.

The inflation raging in America was the root cause of declining economic activity. This inflation, in turn, was a product of excessive government spending and over-regulation of business. Lyndon Johnson's profligate spending on Great Society programs had overheated the economy, and his refusal to cut back on those programs to pay for the country's escalating involvement in Vietnam had set the economy on an enduring course of inflation. To make matters worse, the Republican Nixon and Ford administrations, which succeeded Johnson, resorted to the misguided liberal solution of higher taxes, instead of providing business with incentives to expand their activities—activities that, in turn, could enlarge national output and expand the tax base. Under these circumstances, and exacerbated by excessive wage demands, U.S. goods could not compete with those made abroad, and as profits slid, unemployment escalated.

Ill-conceived liberal policies adopted in Washington established a pattern of excessive spending by state and local governments as well. Encouraged by federal grants-in-aid, they developed an array of programs for the needy and expanded existing programs for the disadvantaged. Under these circumstances, the public work force naturally swelled. This enabled municipal unions to organize government employees, and cowardly politicians caved in to their demands for hefty wage increases and generous fringe benefits. The Great Society programs forged an alliance between bureaucrats at all three levels of government, and they worked closely with the "poverty warriors" who allegedly represented the people at the grass roots.

Conservatives watched from the sidelines, horrified by the mess the liberals were making of the economy. They remarked in despair that if the billions of dollars the collectivists had squandered over the past forty years had been placed in the hands of competent, enterprising entrepreneurs, the economy would be flourishing, not foundering.

Government overregulation of business was the second major source of stagflation. Conservatives professed that there was no such thing as the "public interest," only a collection of countless private interests in competition for society's resources. In the words of former Treasury Secretary William Simon, "There is no such thing as the People; it is a collectivist myth. There are only individual citizens with individual wills and individual purposes. There is only one social system that reflects this sovereignty of the individual; the free-market, or capitalist system, which means the sovereignty of the individual 'vote' in the market-place. . . ."[7]

To regulate business to enhance the "people's welfare," therefore, was senseless, and it was not cost free. Murray Weidenbaum, an economist at Washington University at St. Louis (who later became chairman of Ronald Reagan's Council of Economic Advisers), conducted research revealing that the price tag ran up to billions of dollars annually. Due to regulation, $2,000 was added to the cost of a new house; federal safety and environmental requirements added $666 to the average cost of a new car; and the paperwork involved in keeping pace with government red tape cost society a staggering $25 billion to $32 billion a year.[8]

In the 1970s no fewer than twenty major federal agencies were created, such as the Occupational Safety and Health Administration (OHSA) and the Environmental Protection Agency (EPA), to mention the two with which the business community was most unhappy. Altogether in 1980 the federal government spent about $6 billion to operate 56 agencies involved in regulating industry in some capacity. These agencies abused their mandate. Zealots from OSHA, for example, harassed businessmen for committing minor violations; this increased the cost of doing business and disrupted the workplace. According to one account, "some slight changes in EPA water pollution standards" would have saved "industry $200 million with no loss in water quality."[9]

In the long run, rising productivity was the only answer to stagflation, and this meant government regulation and spending had to be dramatically reduced while taxes were curtailed to spur capital investment in American enterprises. The new supply-side economists, such as Arthur Laffer, disagreed with old guard conservatives, such as Herbert Stein, about many economic issues—the danger of deficits, for example—but all conservatives and a growing number of liberals agreed that lower business taxes were essential to greater productivity.

Unlike the liberals, the conservatives knew what to do about our economic difficulties: leave private entrepreneurs alone to pursue profits through the discipline of the free market. Business interests would be served, but so would society's, for as Adam Smith said over two centuries ago, the mercantilists were wrong when they claimed that the secret to making a nation wealthy was state control of the economy. On the contrary, as our economic history had demonstrated, nations get rich when people are allowed to promote private gain through a free market unencumbered by state regulations. And, in turn, although unequally, the economic fortunes of every member of society are enhanced in the process.

The Conservative Cultural Critique

Insofar as conservatives conceded a cultural crisis in the United States, their analysis of it ran along two tracks—one secular, the other religious.

These preoccupied with the secular aspect were primarily concerned about the appeal of values that challenged a keystone to our culture, economic growth. The first real challenge to it occurred in 1972 with the publication of *The Limits to Growth*. This book was the product of a study conducted by the Club of Rome, an organization of businesspeople and environmentalists from the major industrial democracies. They had commissioned a team of Massachusetts Institute of Technology researchers to study the world's population problem, the impact economic growth would have on the earth's supply of natural resources, and its capacity to cope with ecological disruptions associated with development. Its findings were grim:

> If the present growth trends in world population, industrialization, pollution, food production, and resource depletion continue unchanged, the limits to growth on this planet will be reached sometime within the next one hundred years. The most probable result will be a rather sudden and uncontrollable decline in both population and industrial capacity.[10]

Although the book adopted a global perspective, it struck a particularly responsive chord among U.S. intellectuals, journalists, and environmentalists, who stressed that with a mere 6% of the world's population, the United States consumed 30% of its energy. Previously published books that warned about ecological destruction, overpopulation, and dependence on the Frankenstein monster of technology—Rachel Carson's *Silent Spring*, Paul Ehrlich's *The Population Bomb*, and Jacques Ellul's *The Technological Society*—had helped prime the pump for *The Limits to Growth*'s ominous message. But the energy crunch following the 1973 Yom Kippur War was cited as concrete evidence that the "New Malthusians" were right. They granted that the United States had neither the population problems afflicting most developing countries nor the resource limitations of other industrial societies; nevertheless, it could not escape a societal crisis promulgated by our insatiable quest for goods and services.

If we persisted in our bid for high rates of economic growth, we were fated to come to grips with two grim scenarios. First, either we dramatically curtailed our fervid economic activity, or at some point in the future—

perhaps even prior to the 21st century—we were bound to experience a cataclysmic economic collapse, fostering serious and widespread social unrest and political upheavel, culminating in a closed society. Second, even if we somehow avoided the first scenario, our profligate use of energy and chemicals would do irreversible damage to the environment, bequeathing to future generations poisoned air, polluted waters, and vast areas of ravaged landscape.

The New Malthusians lost influence when scholars scrutinized their findings and discovered serious flaws in their methodology. Consequently, their predictions about the limits to growth could be discarded, as could their prophecies of doom. Nonetheless, other analysts claimed that the energy and economic crises afflicting us justified claims that the United States was entering a period of austerity. This meant that we had to accept lower rates of economic growth and rein in expectations about our living standards. Conservatives were especially sensitive to these assertions, because they challenged the major underpinnings of our culture: our belief in progress, abundance, and American know-how. Most believed that this was a new ploy on the part of the radical left to undermine faith in our capitalist economy and bourgeois culture. The Marxists could no longer persist in the absurd idea that capitalism was doomed to destroy itself; through abundance, capitalism had avoided class warfare and fostered class cooperation instead. Therefore, the left was attempting to demonstrate that the very abundance capitalism produced was the source of our environmental crisis. It was merely a ploy to strike out at capitalism from another direction, an attempt to turn the American people against the free enterprise system.

To be more precise, leftists were proposing that economic growth would have to be checked to avoid grave damage to our ecosystem. Slow growth meant the average American would have to accept lower living standards, and the collectivists would then exploit the people's discontent and blame the rich for their plight. In other words, they hoped to resurrect class politics by manipulating the phony issue of economic inequality as they had done with considerable success in the 1930s.

The right concluded, therefore, that any attack on capitalism or progress was a direct assault on the American way of life. Robert Nisbet wrote:

> I can think of no intellectual change that has come over America in the latter part of the twentieth century that is more pregnant with institutional and material consequences than the almost complete disappearance—among intellectuals, not yet perhaps the majority of the people—of faith in progress.[11]

The naysayers represented a small proportion of the population, but they belonged to the "New Class" that wielded influence over most areas of American life. Their power stemmed from the important positions they held in the major institutions of our post-industrial society—the ones that collected and disseminated knowledge, processed information, and articulated cultural values and attitudes through a national network of like-minded people.

Even after they had wrested the reins of power from the liberals, the conservatives were outraged that their opponents dominated cultural life in the United States through the nation's colleges and universities, the mass media, the helping professions, and the entertainment industry. Their celebration of a self-indulgent, narcissistic life-style, as exemplified by the "laid back" values associated with California, influenced young people from all walks of life. College students and young workers alike were encouraged to spurn material success, to develop their human potential, and to seek instant gratification. Go for it!

Under these circumstances was it any wonder that productivity in America was declining or that savings were dramatically lower than in other industrial democracies? The liberal cultural clerisy, in short, was responsible for the new matrix of values that Yankelovich and Lefkowitz found in their studies.

The liberals also had distorted the traditional American concept of equality. The founding fathers' reference to equality in the Declaration of Independence was predicated on the notion of equality of opportunity, not equality of condition. Michael Novak drove home this point in a number of his works, warning that it was foolhardy to measure the performance of our society against what amounted to a "new religious doctrine" because it is impossible to bring about equality of condition. People possess different capacities, talents, and personalities; to employ state power to homogenize the population was to engage in a form of social alchemy which could produce only pervasive discontent. Those misguided souls who persisted were debasing one of our culture's most cherished values—the quest for excellence and enterprise. This, in turn, denied society the human resources needed to cope with a world that was becoming more uncertain and dangerous.[12]

The left's preoccupation with equality, moreover, was not genuine; it was a mask behind which left-wing intellectuals hoped to enhance their own position in society. And, according to Aaron Wildavsky, this New Class wanted to exploit its influence to reap crass monetary, not transcending intellectual, rewards for its efforts. The radicals did not have the money to "buy what they want; so their task, as they define it is to convince others to pay collectively for what they cannot obtain individually. Thus, government lies at the center of their aspirations and operations."[13] In other words, a liberal New Class favored collectivist policies to serve its self-interest, and this calculated attempt to rip off the taxpayer was another reason to oppose government programs allegedly designed to serve the "public interest."

While the neoconservatives assaulted the liberals' debasement of our culture largely along secular lines, the New Right, spearheaded by religious fundamentalists, waged a holy war against the "secular humanists." Barry Goldwater's abortive quest for the presidency in 1964 had attracted to the

Republican Party grassroots activists such as Paul Weyrich, Richard Viguerie, and Howard Phillips, who said they were more comfortable with the inhabitants of Main Street than the traditional Republican power elite on Wall Street. The New Right activists were appalled that the leaders of the GOP ignored grassroots support for their cause. Weyrich professed that to no small degree this condition prevailed because the Eastern establishment, which had long dominated Republican politics, was as elitist as its liberal adversaries.

In the wake of the Goldwater debacle, "movement conservatives"— Weyrich, Viguerie, Phillips, and others like them—sought to reach out to that vast body of "Silent Americans" the GOP had neglected. In many places the local leaders best positioned to accomplish this objective were fundamentalist ministers whose congregations were aroused by the publicity associated with the excesses of the counterculture in the stormy 1960s.

The people who flocked to Jerry Falwell's Moral Majority and similar organizations, which mushroomed in the 1970s, were the mass base for the country's fourth "great awakening." As William G. McLoughlin has observed, on several occasions in American history when the country was undergoing various forms of trauma, traditional values have been reaffirmed through religious revivals. The first "great awakening" preceded the American Revolution, occurring from roughly 1730 to 1760; the second, from 1800 to 1830, enfused Jacksonian Democracy and the Abolitionist movements with moral purpose; and the third appeared from 1890 to 1920 in response to the havoc wrought by the industrial revolution and the new migration from Eastern and Southern Europe.[14] As the third "great awakening" demonstrated, the thrust of these religious revivals could bolster political impulses at both ends of the political specrum—the progressivism of the Social Gospel activists and the religious bigotry of the reactionaries who gathered around the tent of Billy Sunday.

The fourth "great awakening," however, has been dominated by conservatives. The "religious right" is preoccupied with abortion, feminism, homosexuality, and other social issues as interpreted through the prism of born-again Christian doctrine. Many New Rightists were attracted to Jimmy Carter in 1976 because of his religious piety: He, like them, had rediscovered Christ. In 1980 they flocked to the banner of another candidate—Ronald Reagan—who claimed to be among their number, although his church attendance was questionable. The former film star's appeal suggested that right-wing politics was as important to them as fundamentalist religious doctrine.

This is not, however, to discount the importance of religion to the New Right. Mass movements tell us a great deal about a society's concerns and values. The fundamentalist revival, which represented the only viable mass movement in the 1970s, demonstrated that religion and old-fashioned American liberalism were alive and well in the United States. In 1979 the Gallup

Organization released a report that stated: "For the first time in nearly two decades, an upturn is recorded in church attendance, with 42 percent of adults attending church or synagogues in a typical week."[15] The fundamentalist churches, the southern Baptists, the Mormons, and the Seventh Day Adventists were growing rapidly, while the old-line Protestant churches—the Presbyterians, the Congregationalists, and the Episcopalians—were losing members. One out of every three adult Americans—nearly fifty million—claimed to be a "born again" Christian, most of whom were Protestants. While this was true of 61% of the Baptists, only 11% of the Episcopalians made this claim.

At this time, the evangelicals—who accepted Christ as their personal savior, held that the scriptures were the word of God, and felt called to spread that word—were clearly the most vocal of all religious groups in the country. They made their presence felt nationwide through the activities of dynamic preachers, who were skillful in their use of radio and TV to turn the multitudes toward Christ. Among the most successful Christian Right programs were Jerry Falwell's "Old Time Gospel Hour," Oral Roberts's "Oral Roberts Show," and Pat Robertson's "700 Club." At this time there were 1000 members of the National Religious Broadcasters Association, and many of their television programs reached two million people at a shot. An estimated fourteen million people regularly watched such shows, and their radio counterparts claimed one hundred fifty million regular listeners. These electronic preachers inspired listeners and viewers to donate $500 million annually, to support their ministries.

Furthermore, whereas outlets for mass paperback books—drug stores, supermarkets, etc.—once only carried detective thrillers, sexy novels, and how-to books, one now could find "religious-oriented" books authored by fundamentalists. The New York publishing houses, most of whom had previously ignored fundamentalist writers, henceforth actively sought them out. This was no surprise because Hal Lindsey, author of seven religious works including one of the all-time best sellers, *The Late Great Planet Earth*, had sold a combined total of twenty-one million books.

The fact that there was such a large reading audience for these works told us something about the fourth "great awakening." In the third, which had swept the country in the 1920s, those people attracted to the Elmer Gantrys of the period were poorly educated, primarily rural, and elderly. Gallup found in the 1970s that by contrast, the people flocking to the Jerry Falwells were young, middle-class, and lived in cities and suburbs as well as in rural areas.

The evangelicals linked up with other right-wing activists who blamed the liberal clerisy for all manner of social ills—pornography, family disintegration, etc. Phyllis Schlafly, a "pro-life," anti-Equal Rights Amendment (ERA) spokeswoman, for example, credited the women's movement for soaring divorce rates, promiscuity, and lesbianism. Groups like the National

Organization for Women were to blame for mothers entering the labor force in massive numbers, leaving the kids to fend for themselves at home. Mrs. Schlafly, a bright, articulate lawyer, claimed an essential part of "liberationist ideology" was that women could not fulfill themselves by performing traditional roles at home, but had to look beyond their families for self-actualization. Gloria Steinem and the *Ms.* "crowd" contended that marriage and motherhood were conditions akin to slavery, which men imposed upon women. Mrs. Schlafly noted that the "libbers'" solutions to the nation's social problems were collectivist—publicly funded day-care centers, displaced homemakers programs, battered wives' halfway houses, etc. Clearly, if such programs were adopted on a wholesale basis, the state's outreach would expand, and bureaucratic exponents of "the new morality" would rear American children, brainwashing them to believe that traditional male and female roles were outmoded and detrimental to their well-being.

By the late 1970s the evangelical preachers and the Schlaflyites began to expand their political concerns beyond social issues and the dangers of humanism. They warned against big government and big unions, and spoke about capitalism as the economic system most consistent with Christianity. During the 1980 presidential primaries, they worked hard to get their people elected as delegates to the convention in Detroit, where they helped nominate Ronald Reagan. During the general election, they raised an impressive campaign war chest for candidates, of either party, who espoused their issues. Many politicians who had formerly ignored or disparaged them as contemporary Elmer Gantrys now supported their legislative agenda.

Others who had refused to concede that the religious right was a potent political force could not persist in this notion after the 1980 election. Ronald Reagan was the most conservative president elected since Herbert Hoover, and Jerry Falwell and his brethren were justified in claiming that they had played a vital role in inflating his victory margin. The New Right deserved credit for helping the GOP secure a majority in the Senate, giving the Republicans domination over that body for the first time since the 1950s. The media publicized Terry Dolan's "hit list." As promised, the National Conservative Political Action Committee, which he headed, worked mightily to defeat liberal Democrats. Just how much NCPAC had to do with the elections' outcome is unclear, but prominent liberal senators such as Birch Bayh, George McGovern, Gaylord Nelson, John Culver, and Frank Church were defeated. The Democrats maintained control of the House, but two liberal stalwarts, Democratic Whip John Bradamas and House Ways and Means Chairman Al Ullman lost their seats.

In 1980 conservatives also were pleased by census and economic data demonstrating that the fastest growing region of the country, the Sunbelt, was populated by Americans conservative in their political, economic, and religious beliefs. Snowbelt districts would lose congressional representation, while conservative ones in the South and West would gain new seats in Washington. With such observations in mind, conservatives proclaimed the 1980s would be their decade, in much the same fashion that the 1960s had belonged to their enemies on the left.

Four years later, amid the heat and humidity of Dallas, the New Right demonstrated that there was a changing of the guard in the Republican Party. It dominated the convention. It wrote the platform, controlled the ebb and flow of traffic and hoopla on the floor of the auditorium, and it set the tone for the speeches. Even moderate Howard Baker employed anti-liberal rhetoric and made harsh attacks on the Democrats that he himself would have criticized had they been made by somebody else in private. The Republican platform was a New Right document: it urged the adoption of prayer in school, opposed the ERA, and stipulated that judicial candidates not openly opposed to abortion should be denied appointments. Senator Robert Dole renounced the platform, and President Reagan's daughter, Maureen, refused to sign it, but most delegates gave it their enthusiastic endorsement.

Jerry Falwell led the convention in prayer, and the media were so hot on his tracks, requesting interviews—one would have thought he was a presidential contender. One of the questions most frequently asked was his views on Supreme Court appointments. Walter Mondale and Geraldine Ferarro were claiming that if Reagan were reelected, Falwell would be given the right to veto appointments. Falwell said that he was given no such pledge nor did he ask for one. Many commentators did not think it mattered; it was still true that henceforth, no serious Republican presidential candidate could ignore the new right's wishes.

Notes

1. Lou Cannon, *Reagan* (New York: G.P. Putnam's Sons, 1982), p. 202.
2. Frederick von Hayek, *The Road to Serfdom* (Chicago: University of Chicago Press, 1944).
3. Milton Friedman, *Capitalism and Freedom* (Chicago: University of Chicago Press, 1962), p. 10.
4. *New York Times*, 21 January, 1977.
5. Richard Pipes, "Why the U.S. Thinks It Can Fight and Win A Nuclear War," *Commentary* (July 1977): 21–34.
6. Thomas Powers, "Choosing a Strategy for World War III," *The Atlantic Monthly*, November 1982, p. 103.
7. William Simon, *The Time For Truth* (New York: Reader's Digest Press, 1978), p. 221.
8. *Washington Post*, 23 July, 1978.
9. *Washington Post*, 30 December, 1979.
10. Donella H. Meadows et al., *The Limits to Growth* (New York: Unicorn Books, 1972), p. 27.
11. Robert Nisbet, "The Rape of Progress," *Public Opinion*, June/July 1979, p. 5.

12. Michael Novak, *The Spirit of Capitalism* (Washington: American Enterprise Institute, 1982).
13. Aaron Wildavsky, "Using Public Funds to Serve Private Interests," *Society*, January/February 1979, p. 39.
14. William G. McLoughlin, *Revivals, Reawakenings, and Reform* (Chicago: University of Chicago Press, 1978).
15. The Gallup Organization, "Religion in America," *The Gallup Poll Index* 145 (December 1979).

CHAPTER SEVEN

Taking Stock

Just as the nation is said to be saturated with "conservatism," I am arguing that there are almost no conservatives [in the United States]. — George Will

Insofar as conservatives concede that the American predicament exists, their assumptions about its origins are erroneous. Many of their solutions, therefore, are misdirected or will cause more harm than good. Consequently, if right-wing ideologies dominate policy for the rest of this decade, the U.S. predicament will deepen and perhaps spawn a societal crisis. This grim prognosis is founded on an anomaly. The Reaganite counterreformation is out of step with the main currents of Western conservatism. It is not deserving of the label "conservative" but rather "radical liberal." This irony will be addressed as we take stock of the American predicament in this chapter.

The Sources of Political Gridlock

In assessing our polity, there are two major issues deserving of special attention: the institutional sources of political gridlock, and a political culture that diffuses political authority and celebrates privatism. Because the media have treated political gridlock in detail, we need only underscore its major elements.

The Diffusion of Congressional Power

Comprised of 535 independent political entrepreneurs, Congress is incapable of addressing critical national problems. To a significant degree, the speaker of the House has been stripped of powers to discipline members of his party, to control the flow of legislation through that body, and to make committee assignments. This condition, along with the expansion of the committee system, has diffused power in the House and has made the forging of a comprehensive legislative agenda well nigh impossible. Members of Congress operate like feudal lords. Jealous of their prerogatives and protective of their fiefdoms, they dwell on parochial issues and ignore those of national significance. Consequently, even when the president belongs to their party, they may ignore pleas to set aside short-term considerations for long-term policies vital to the public interest.

Lyndon Johnson was the last strong majority leader in the Senate. After he became vice president in 1961, he was replaced by Mike Mansfield, who made the Senate a more egalitarian body. One example is the expansion of the influence of junior senators, through the allocation of more committee slots to them. Their power was enhanced further in the 1970s when they were allowed larger staffs. By the mid-1980s, Senator Dan Quayle—who was in charge of an in-house study of the Senate—told reporters, "We are witnessing the disintegration of the U.S. Senate."[1] This was not solely the judgment of a relatively junior senator. Even old-timers like Howard Baker, the Republican majority leader, lamented that the Senate was incapable of addressing serious national problems.

Party Disintegration

Because of the centrifugal forces of federalism and our system of checks and balances, we have never experienced the kind of centralized, well-disciplined parties common in Europe. We have fifty Democratic and fifty Republican parties, which only function like national organizations every four years when they select a presidential ticket. Binding primaries and other reforms, calculated to make the parties "more representative," have instead further weakened them. Consequently, they cannot coordinate power between the branches of government when in control of the White House, nor effectively function as a "loyal opposition" when out of power.

PAC Democracy

Political action committees (PACs) now provide most of the money for campaigns. In 1984 they contributed a record $104 million to congressional candidates, a 25% jump over the 1981–82 cycle.[2] Party leaders are less vital to a candidate's election than political consultants, pollsters, and mass-mailing wizards, because television and modern technology are more important in securing votes than party organizations or public gatherings. The ability of parochial interests to dominate the policymaking process through "iron triangles"—congressional committees, executive agencies, and private organizations—has grown enormously. Congresspersons, when confronted with powerful special interests, cannot hide behind the speaker or the party the way their predecessors did. The parochial needs of influential single-purpose interest groups, therefore, are served while those of the public are shortchanged.

Television

Most voters derived political information from television; however, this medium trivializes political discourse by treating issues casually and by playing up personalities instead. This condition is compounded by the fact that Americans are poorly informed about public affairs. They have access to first-rate journals, newspapers, and other relevant material (including some excellent TV programs), but only a small percentage of them, including those with college degrees, make use of this information. It is a mistake to blame television per se for the fact that in comparison with other industrial societies, Americans are poorly informed about political matters. As we shall observe shortly, this condition is a product of our political culture.

Television, however, has contributed to the American electorate's disenchantment with government. Few presidents can pass muster in the face of TV cameras that dog their tracks from morning to night, seven days a week, throughout their term of office. As a consequence, after elections, our presidents are forced to conduct public business as they would during campaigns. This involves obfuscating the facts, distorting their positions, and engaging in public relations gimmicks. This display of "blue smoke and mirrors" is no substitute for the serious business of governing a large, complex society.

Gridlock in the White House

The power of the president has expanded with the rise of the welfare and national security bureaucracies. But newly elected presidents must live with the budget and legislative agendas of their predecessors. Presidents wear many hats and must forge political programs in the face of serious internal and external crises, under severe time constraints and without the kind of access to legislative power enjoyed by a prime minister. The president's job is complicated by the awesome power of the single-purpose interest groups, which have filled vacuums left by the parties and congressional leadership. It is only in the face of palpable crises, therefore, that the president can muster support to deal with problems comprehensively. And even in instances where the nation's security is at stake, he often cannot mobilize support to act quickly and decisively. The huge deficits hovering over the United States are a case in point.

Practitioners and students of U.S. government alike agree that there is a crisis of governance in the United States and that reorganization of our polity is imperative. Political scientists have been urging the strengthening of our political parties for decades; former White House aides, Ted Sorenson and Lloyd Cutler among them, have suggested the fusion of the legislature and executive in the manner of a parliamentary system. Short of such measures, they see no end to political paralysis in Washington. Other commentators urge a revision of our federal system to eliminate anti-democratic anomalies. For example, Wyoming, a state with about 400,000 residents, enjoys the same representation in the Senate as California, with a population exceeding twenty million.

There is no paucity of reforms that could facilitate the governing of our large, complex society, but the climate is not conducive to their adoption. On the contrary, conservatives are bent upon reducing political authority in Washington. This position places them in conflict with conservative thinkers of yesteryear. This is one feature of political gridlock that has been ignored by the media.

In assaulting liberals, conservatives such as William Simon, the former treasury secretary, claim Edmund Burke and the founding fathers as their intellectual mentors. But Burke favored strong government, which he deemed vital to an organic society; the founding fathers believed in a public good, which Simon portrays as a "collectivist myth." Political scientists have called our attention to this irony, but their analysis has been confined to scholarly journals and books not widely read outside academia. Many thoughtful people, therefore, were surprised when George Will, the conservative syndicated columnist, television commentator, and Reagan confidant, wrote in 1983: "My thesis has this perhaps entertaining implication: Just as the nation is said to be saturated with 'conservatism,' I am arguing that there are almost no conservatives, properly understood . . . " in the United States. He urges those who designate themselves "conservatives" to remember that "common sense, reason and history all teach that 'strong government conservatism' is not a contradiction in terms."[3]

Will places the role of government in proper perspective when he cites Edmund Burke's observation that the state involves a partnership with members of society that transcends commerce, and that "it becomes a partnership not only between those who are living, but between those who are living, those who are dead, and those who are to be born."[4] Here, too, is the basis for the organic society that 20th century American conservatives revile.

Americans who fancy themselves conservatives in the Burkean tradition often display a discrepancy between their professions of faith in conservative philosophy and their actions. For example, attempts to preserve tangible links with past generations mean little to so-called conservatives who, in the name of free enterprise, demolish a historic dwelling and replace it with a convenience store. It was this disregard for tradition that prompted 19th century conservatives to view capitalism as a revolutionary force.

Will reminds us that Burke took a dim view of individualism and materialism, and this cannot be a source of solace to those who deem any assault on these virtues as "collectivist." But that's not all. Will strikes at conservative mythology when he says that one cannot draw a line between politics and economics. A free market "economic system," he reminds us, "is a public product, a creation of government."[5]

Will professes, therefore, that conservatives should not denigrate political authority, but instead support affirmative government in order to promote social order and harmony among our people. They need a Disraeli or a Bismarck to show them how the welfare state can accomplish this; it is not inimical to conservatism but necessary to its well-being.

The author's point is that we must go beyond institutional factors in seeking an answer to the question: Why is our polity afflicted by political paralysis? In short, a political culture that distrusts government is a major source of political gridlock, and this impulse is deeply rooted in the American political tradition. Indeed, Ronald Reagan's distrust of government attracted many voters to his cause.

Our privatistic political culture also accounts for the fact that compared to citizens of other democracies, Americans are poorly informed about political matters. In private, politicans frequently discuss the ignorance of their constituents on a range of vital issues, but they are obviously wary of making such comments publicly. This condition is closely tied to our political culture, and it is a mistake to blame it primarily on our education system or media distortions. The fact is that schools everywhere reflect the priorities of society; in the United States ignorance about our history and public affairs in general speaks volumes about our own.

This condition also accounts for the success of the "Teflon presidency" of Ronald Reagan. Years after he was elected, Reagan displayed ignorance of critical issues, frequently distorted important facts, and was unaware of vital developments to a degree that startled even his supporters. One vivid example appeared when it was revealed that he did not know that two-thirds of the Soviet nuclear triad is comprised of ground-based ICBMs—the target of his first proposals in the short-lived Strategic Arms Reduction Talks (START). No wonder Moscow reasoned that Reagan was not serious about negotiating a fair treaty. During his first term, pundits were convinced that his ignorance and bloopers would hurt him at the polls. They were wrong, in large part because so many voters knew even less than he did about these matters and were not interested in them.

Our privatistic political culture also accounts for the conviction that people of substance do not engage in public affairs. Many business leaders are of the opinion that "if politicians and government bureaucrats were really smart, they would be making money," managing the corporate enterprises which are responsible for the country's greatness. Conservatives who write about "privatizing" problems treated by government and who employ business criteria to evaluate public programs, however, are guilty of a serious oversight. Namely, many aspects of our predicament cannot be solved through private solutions because they are public in nature, and government programs cannot be assessed solely on the basis of whether or not they are cost-effective.

One does not use the same criteria to judge the performance of business enterprises and government agencies. The role of government is to achieve social order and to meet the needs of citizens when they cannot be met through the private sector. The ultimate goal of the state is justice, not efficiency. Any thoughtful person deserving of the honorable label "conservative" understands this, but as Will has observed, there are few authentic conservatives in America today.

Government and the Economy

Government intervention in the economy expanded dramatically during the 1930s, because Adam Smith had been wrong about the free market's capacity to operate like a self-regulating mechanism. Herbert Hoover's inaction in the face of economic calamity was consistent with the Scotsman's thinking, but doing nothing had only made things worse. In large part because economic crisis management by the government has prevented postwar economic recessions from reaching the magnitude of the Great Depression, many younger political leaders have forgotten a critical lesson gleaned from the 1930s: in spite of capitalism's impressive performance, it has endemic flaws that necessitate government intervention.

There are two compelling reasons why government must continue acting as society's principal economic manager, and they are as old as capitalism itself.

In the 1930s New Dealers in the United States and economic intellectuals in Britain were grappling with one of capitalism's most enduring problems—how to tame the business cycle. When the Great Depression hit, many thoughtful people concluded that at long last Marx's prediction that capitalism would self-destruct had come true. Some heirs of Smith, such as Lord Keynes, however, were convinced that Marx could be proven wrong if, through fiscal and monetary fine-tuning, the state flattened the curves of the cycles. This entailed deficit financing and the heavy hand of government, but it also meant that capitalism could survive.

For close to twenty-five years after World War II, Keynesian policies helped keep the economies of the industrial democracies on a course of steady growth, dramatically improving living standards in North America, Japan, and Western Europe. Conservative charges that liberal policies would produce an economic disaster were ignored by voters who were enjoying unparalleled prosperity. It was only after stagflation shattered people's confidence in the 1970s that conservative assaults on public spending and government regulation of business were seen as plausible explanations for high unemployment and inflation. Such claims were not always based upon sound analysis, but dismal economic conditions lent them credibility. The anti-business bias of liberal intellectuals, and their propensity to misrepresent our economy, also discredited leftist claims that the right's assessment of the nation's predicament was seriously flawed.

The economy does not operate the way the Chamber of Commerce's Richard Lesher says it does, and John Kenneth Galbraith is correct that segments of it operate more along the lines of corporatism than capitalism. But it is foolhardy to deny that supply, demand, and competition govern most economic activity in the United States. The left's refusal to concede that risk-taking, entrepreneurship, and plain hard work have contributed to the nation's wealth simply conflicts with the facts. Such practices detract from otherwise cogent leftist critiques of our free enterprise system—for example, that it is unjustified for investors and CEOs to reward themselves with huge bonuses when government finances their endeavors or minimizes their risk-taking through protectionist measures. Even worse, the left's past myopia in regard to the dismal performance of collectivist economies discredits programs, such as a national medical program, that deserve to be supported on humanitarian grounds.

The left's traditional misrepresentation of our economy accounts, in part, for the popularity of naive right-wing notions about economic reality. Consequently, many younger Americans who have come of age politically since the 1970s now parrot clichés, half-truths, and outright falsehoods about the free enterprise system that make even some business publicists wince in embarrassment.

In the midst of the country's celebration of Adam Smith's "invisible hand," many Americans have forgotten that only the federal government is capable of coping with major economic crises. The right's success in challenging this lesson of the past has forced public authorities to support hackneyed notions they know are false but cannot disparage, because they fear the political consequences of bucking "the conventional wisdom." Even today there are Republicans and Democrats who know that a tax hike is the only solution to the country's deficit problem, but they continue to chime in with the supply-side chorus of resolution through economic growth.

The second endemic flaw of capitalism, necessitating government intervention, is an inability to distribute goods and services to all segments of society. "Collectivist" programs such as social security, unemployment compensation, and government assistance in a variety of forms have helped offset capitalism's inability to equitably distribute the abundance it generates. The right has opposed these programs and others that have softened the impact of several recessions since the end of World War II. Without them, political discontent would have been widespread, and demands for more government intervention in the economy would have escalated dramatically.

Just consider what the political climate would have been like if workers had been unable to rely on unemployment benefits, the elderly on social security, and young people on public programs that generated jobs or subsidies for a college education. Without the cushion of these programs, business profits would have plunged, bankruptcies skyrocketed, and mortgages defaulted; other calamities would have occurred to foster massive and widespread disgruntlement. European Tories have long understood the utility of the welfare state. Disraeli and Bismarck adopted safety-net programs to undercut the appeal of socialism and to preserve the ruling class's political power a half century before their American counterparts.

Capitalism enjoys the overwhelming support of the American people, but it is incapable of surviving without the welfare state. To speak of returning to a purer form of capitalism favored by the Friedmanites is as utopian as the policies of those left-wing ideologues who still believe communism is a viable system.

Finally, there are problems in the international economy that demand more assertive governmental action. We shall treat these matters in a later chapter, but before moving on, one more internal economic development must be treated. Many commentators refer to it as the "two-tiered society."

We noted earlier that in the postwar years, liberal economic policy undercut the far left when it resolved grievances associated with economic inequality—not by closing the gap between the rich and poor, but by enlarging the pie and enabling all segments of society to move up the economic ladder together. Today most Americans enjoy a high living standard, but while those in the middle-income groups and above are making economic gains, most people below them face stagnation or an actual decline in their living standards—hence the two-tiered society. Evidence for this condition is ample and has been the subject of much discussion. Its source is found in the anomaly that while many sectors of our economy are doing well—high technology, the service industries, and professions—others are experiencing grave difficulties—the smokestack industries and farming, for example. The following items provide more concrete evidence of the uneven development responsible for the two-tiered society.

Item 1: Rising Poverty

In the summer of 1985, the Census Bureau reported that while poverty fell slightly, 14% of the population of the United States—comprising 33,064,000 people—was poor. Furthermore, the rate of poverty was higher in the mid-1980s than at any point in the previous decade. From 1984 to 1985 poverty rates fell for whites 11.5% to 11.4% and for blacks 33.8% to 31.3%. But the rate for people 65 and over rose from 12.4% to 12.6%. The poverty rate for female-headed households was 34% in 1985, a .5% drop from the previous year. Most shocking of all, 27.2% of the country's children were living in poverty.[6]

Item 2: High Unemployment

Over the last decade we have heard a great deal about the "displaced worker"—workers in the smokestack industries who have become victims of joblessness. "Between 1979 and 1984, 210,000 steelworkers lost their jobs; that represented 46 per cent of the estimated 453,000 workers in the industry."[7] And early in 1984, when the U.S. auto industry was reporting record profits, the United Automobile Workers represented 200,000 fewer auto workers than it had in 1978. Tens of thousands of other workers in manufacturing have been displaced and will never get their old jobs back. Ultimately most will find work in service industries but earn much lower salaries.

Unemployment continues to affect minority Americans to a greater degree than others, with black unemployment figures twice those for whites. The most ominous employment trend, however, is that minimum unemployment rates after each succeeding recession have been higher than the previous one. After the 1982 recession, unemployment climbed to 7% where it has remained for several years. If this trend continues, the next recession will produce even higher unemployment figures.

Item 3: Declining Income

The income of most Americans has been declining, while the rich have become wealthier. In 1984, the average income (with adjustment for inflation) was lower than that of 1969. It is unfair to blame the Reagan administration alone for this condition; economic dislocations that first lowered living standards occurred in the early 1970s. But this administration's celebrated tax reduction and spending-cut victories in 1981 have contributed to economic inequality. In his first year, Reagan's reductions in social welfare "eliminated the entire public service jobs program, removed 400,000 persons from the food stamp program, eliminated the Social Security minimum benefit, and reduced or eliminated welfare and Medicaid benefits for the working poor."[8]

Item 4: The Destruction of the Family Farm

Farm defaults are the highest they have been since the 1930s, and a growing percentage of small farmers face a similar fate or, at best, will survive by the skin of their teeth. In face of such problems, alcoholism, child and wife abuse, suicide, and even murders are on the rise throughout the farm belt.

The plight of the family farmer has its roots in many sources: low prices, high interest rates, foreign competition, declining sales of U.S. farm products due to an inflated dollar, declining demand, and huge debts acquired during the 1970s when agricultural prospects were bright. To make matters worse, improved agricultural output by countries that were food-dependent a few years ago is bad news for U.S. agriculture. So even after the dollar declines and prices improve, the American farmer cannot sell as much of his product as he has over the past quarter century. This means more farms going under, banks failing, and entire communities in decline. The family farm that Jefferson deemed integral to our society is fading into history.

The Cultural Contradictions of Capitalism

Conservatives are justified in blaming liberals for abetting radical attacks on our society in the 1960s that undermined the quest for excellence in our schools and assaulted the work ethic, family life, and self-restraint in personal behavior and artistic expression. Today one finds less evidence of this trashing of "bourgeois values" among liberal intellectuals, but we are still experiencing the aftershocks of the 1960s "cultural revolution."

The sad state of U.S. education today is linked to reforms adopted then to rid the schools of "elitism" by eliminating "outmoded" curricula and "oppressive" classroom settings. Under the banner of "relevancy," students were "liberated" from activities that stressed reading, writing, and arithmetic. They were encouraged to freely express themselves and challenge the "bourgeois values" associated with American society.

In most places educators have come to their senses and scrapped these misguided reforms. But the damage has been done, causing many of the problems afflicting education today: serious and widespread disciplinary problems, functional illiterates with high school degrees, and college graduates who have little knowledge of U.S. history, little appreciation for great literature, and a well-developed distaste for study or other activities demanding discipline and perseverance.

The schools alone cannot be blamed for attacks on the work ethic, but for many years they did little to uphold it. Moreover, conservatives have cause to blame those members of the helping professions who characterized the work ethic during the Great Society as a "tool of white oppression," thereby contributing to the economic plight of minority people. A rationalization popular among social workers was: "It's better to remain on welfare than to accept a dead-end job." Since then, black leaders such as Jesse Jackson have endorsed traditional middle-class values—work, excellence, discipline— because they are color-blind avenues to success.

Conservatives make sense when they remind us that many professional criminals, who are responsible for a disproportionate number of violent crimes, are beyond rehabilitation. Generally their victims are the poor, the elderly, and minorities—that is, the most vulnerable members of society. These criminals should not be treated like the perpetrators of victimless crime or be given the light sentences usually appropriate for first offenders. Murderers, rapists, and other violent criminals should not be allowed to exploit permissive bail or parole procedures.

To a very significant degree, neither public nor private community development programs will revitalize inner-city neighborhoods until the streets are made safer than they are today. A war on street crime thus must become a national priority, deserving of a massive and comprehensive effort. This should be a priority of those who are concerned about poor, minority, and elderly Americans, and not be characterized as evidence of "oppression."

The right is also justified in expressing alarm about "youth advocates" who would deny parents the right to inculcate their children with values they cherish, religious and secular alike. Such actions help diminish parental authority and delegitimize the family, the keystone of our culture. Leftists have also occasionally held themselves accountable for the cult of instant gratification. One can cite Christopher Lasch, a prominent left-wing historian, who has attacked countercultural therapists for defining "love and meaning simply as the fulfillment of the patient's emotional require- ments . . ." and for popularizing a concept of mental health that "means the overthrow of inhibitions and the immediate gratification of every impulse."[9]

Finally, the religious right has cause to discredit television programs and films that seek to attract young viewers by subjecting them to displays of violence, sadism, and sexual perversity having no redeeming value. One does not have to be a puritan devoid of erotic impulses, a priest of high culture, or a slave to tradition to be sickened by the vast outpouring of cultural garbage emanating from Hollywood.

However, the neoconservatives and New Rightists who have charged the liberal New Class with a wholesale attack against our most precious cultural values and beliefs have exaggerated its influence. The forces wreaking havoc with our culture could not have been brought about solely by a liberal elite espousing "alien" values; they are also inextricably linked to our business culture and the prosperity it has generated. One of the first writers to bring this anomaly to our attention was a champion of capitalism, not a critic.

Almost fifty years ago, Austro–American economist Joseph A. Schumpeter, wrote in *Capitalism, Socialism and Democracy* that capitalism's "very success undermines the social institutions which protect it, and 'inevitably' creates conditions in which it will not be able to live."[10] Capitalism, he warned, would give rise to an adversarial elite that would work toward its demise. This observation is the basis for the neo-conservatives' claim about the destructiveness of the New Class. It is not altogether groundless: there are intellectuals on the left in this country who dwell only upon our society's flaws, never on its positive aspects. But they are not the source of our cultural disarray.

Thirty years after Schumpeter's inquiry into the matter, Daniel Bell, in *The Cultural Contradictions of Capitalism*, provided a more comprehensive analysis of why many of the values and beliefs prevalent in the United States today clash with our quest for economic growth. The crux of his thesis is that "the Protestant ethic and the Puritan temper were codes that emphasized work sobriety, frugality, sexual restraints, and forbidding attitudes toward life. . . ."[11] These pivotal features of early American culture were congruent with an economic system that stressed hard work, discipline, and thrift. The upshot of this marriage was the development of the world's most productive economy. But over time the "traditional bourgeois value system" began to erode, ironically because capitalism produced the world's highest living standards. This transformation first took form during the 1920s when

> mass consumption . . . was made possible by revolutions in technology, principally the application of electrical energy to household tasks . . . and by three social inventions: mass production on an assembly line, which made a cheap automobile possible; the development of marketing, which rationalized the art of identifying different kinds of buying groups and whetting consumer appetites; and the spread of installment buying, which, more than any other social device, broke down the Protestant fear of debt.[12]

By the 1950s the culture was no longer concerned with how to work and achieve, but with how to spend and enjoy. "Despite some continuing use of the language of the Protestant ethic, the fact was that by the 1950s, American culture had become primarily hedonistic, concerned with play, fun, display, and pleasure."[13]

The charge that our culture is in disarray because of the evil machinations of countercultural liberals is relevant but inadequate. Marshall Berman reminds us that Marx vividly described the destructiveness of "modern bourgeois society" in *The Communist Manifesto*: "All that is solid melts into air, all that is holy is profaned, and men at last are forced to face the real conditions of their lives and their relations with their fellow men."[14] This reflected the fears of 19th century European conservatives who deemed industrial capitalism destructive of the old order; it was by no means a concern of socialists only. In another passage of the *Manifesto*, Marx celebrates the liberal ethos: "The bourgeoisie, in its reign of barely a hundred years, has created more massive and more colossal productive power than have all previous generations put together."[15]

Concomitant with the industrial revolution, however, was the ascendancy of the middle class, which spearheaded the democratic revolution. The old social order European conservatives sought to preserve served a select few at the expense of many. In contrast, the new capitalist industrial order promulgated widespread cultural and social upheavel, but it also paved the way for improvements in the lives of ordinary citizens, expanding their opportunities for economic and social advancement. In contrast to tradition-bound European thought and practice, American liberalism freed the individual from oppressive community obligations and encouraged individual self-actualization. In the United States an individual's self-worth was measured by his or her ability to achieve, albeit principally by the ability to make money, and not by accidents of birth, religion, or formal education.

The liberation of the individual, in turn, set into motion economic enterprise that produced an unrivaled harvest of agricultural and manufacturing output. It spawned scientific discoveries and technological innovations that astounded European observers many decades before an American landed on the moon. The invention of new medical cures and health systems prolonged life and allowed those who lived longer to enjoy aspects of human existence that only a tiny minority was privy to in traditional society. The United States attracted wave after wave of immigrants to its shores because in the New World ordinary folk were given the opportunity to actualize their potential and provide their children with opportunities undreamed of in the Old World.

It was not surprising, therefore, that the children and grandchildren of immigrants from Eastern and Southern Europe who led the neo-conservative movement were outraged in the 1960s by New Left charges that "Amerika" had replaced Hitler's Third Reich as the world's leading fascist power. They were justifiably incensed that some student militants and antiwar activists asserted that there was no difference between the USSR and the USA. They also challenged, with good reason, the simple-minded faith that many of their former liberal/leftist colleagues had in government's capacity to solve society's problems and the hostility toward our economic system that many intellectuals and academics displayed.

Today, however, it is inexplicable why they persist in blistering foes who no longer wield significant intellectual influence or discernible political clout in the United States. Even more puzzling is their turning a blind eye to social and economic inequities still afflicting millions of Americans and their propensity to lash out at those who express concern about these matters.

Through influential journals such as *Commentary* and *The Public Interest* and in papers and conferences sponsored by think tanks such as the American Enterprise Institute, the neoconservatives have enhanced our understanding of the limits of government and the positive aspects of our economic system. But like the Great Society liberals who exaggerated government's capacity to solve many of our problems, they have lent their intellectual prowess to orthodox right-wing claims that if left alone, the private sector will provide remedies.

But many problems afflicting our families, communities, and workplaces are not susceptible to privatistic solutions—they need to be addressed through public initiatives.

Over the past several decades, for example, women with children have been entering the labor force in massive numbers. Between 1945 and 1975 the percentage of working wives rose by 20%—from 6.5 million to 19.9 million. By 1985 almost half of the nation's married women with children one year old or younger worked. Families headed by a single woman or by two breadwinners comprise most of the families in the United States. Eli Ginsburg has said, "This growth in female labor force participation [is] the most significant phenomenon of the 20th century."[16] This may be an overstatement, but some educators and social scientists believe that poor performance at school, juvenile delinquency, and developmental disorders are all linked to situations in which parents have little time for their children. Increasingly public agencies must provide day-care and after-school assistance to American youngsters and help families breaking under the heavy pressures associated with two-breadwinner and single-female-headed households.

As the aged become a larger proportion of our population, more of society's resources must be devoted to care for them. Existing facilities for the very old are inadequate, as are the economic mechanisms necessary to pay for them. To place the burden of providing for the elderly on the back of the American family is to contribute to its disintegration. Here is one area where "throwing money at a problem" will go a long way toward solving it.

Changes buffeting families are accelerating the erosion of viable communities where residents enjoy a sense of place, where most disruptive members of the community are held in check, and where problems afflicting the community are handled informally through voluntary associations. The destruction of these "mediating institutions," which legitimate conservatives such as Peter Berger and Richard Neuhaus celebrate, is, however, also related to the lack of metropolitan planning in the United States.[17] During the tax revolt of the late 1970s, grassroots activists asserted that big government committed to "wasteful" social welfare programs was responsible for the fiscal plight of many communities. But this conclusion was wide of the mark. The real problem was weak government and the inability of local political authorities to control land use, thereby allowing builders to construct developments with little thought about the long-term costs to taxpayers. What we need is stronger local government that can control the way we develop our communities—to reduce expensive capital investment projects, environmental dislocation, and social costs that are a product of nonplanning.

To suggest, as many neoconservatives do, that we follow the advice of the right and seek privatistic solutions to the problems sweeping this country and causing cultural disarray is a flight from responsibility and common sense. There is, of course, merit to the charge made by fundamentalists that many problems afflicting family life in the United States are a result of individual irresponsibility. And it is true that in some cases we have spent too much time stressing citizens' rights instead of their obligations. Moreover, even if one does not subscribe to their religious precepts, all thoughtful and caring people appreciate that there is a spiritual side to life that explains a great deal about the human condition.

Yet even deeply religious thinkers remind us that we cannot ignore the secular aspects of life and the need for government:

> Man is by nature a social being, and cannot live and thrive out of society; society is impracticable without strong and efficient government; and strong and efficient government is impracticable where the people have no loyal sentiments, and hold themselves free to make war on their government. . . .[18]

These are not the words of a 20th century liberal seeking to reaffirm the role of government in our society; they stem from the pen of Orestes Brownson, a 19th century convert to Catholicism who belongs to that small fraternity of U.S. conservatives whose ideas are consistent with those of their British cousins, Burke and Disraeli. The leaders of the American religious right today would deny the merits of these observations and incorrectly label them "collectivist."

There are other puzzling things about the religious right. With the exception of the "right-to-life" movement, the religious right has opposed or ignored the great moral crusades of the 20th century: the quest to empower workers through the labor movement, the campaign to provide blacks with equal status through civil rights laws, and the effort to eliminate sexual discrimination through the women's movement. In spite of preoccupation with the scriptures in making secular pronouncements, many leaders on the religious right ignore Christ's teachings regarding the brotherhood of man, concern for the poor, and other ethical truisms to which both Christians and non-Christians can subscribe. One can make the case, therefore, that the religious right—at least in its secular behavior—is neither Christian nor conservative, but rather espouses ideas akin to the Social Darwinism popular in the 19th century.

It is perhaps glib to say this, but the reason for confusion about our cultural values and beliefs today stems from a simple observation. In the past, the quest for self-enrichment and self-gratification was channeled in a socially productive direction by a religious piety that was part of a communitarian ethos and a strong sense of *civitas* (i.e., civic obligation). Today, however, the cult of the individual is celebrated both by left-wing psychoanalytic theory—which stresses self-fulfillment and denigrates traditional obligations, secular and religious—and the religious Right, which espouses a privatistic vision of society destructive of collective action and public life.

The Future: Unity or Polarization?

Will the American predicament produce a societal crisis similar to the one likely to afflict the USSR? There is a possibility it might, but it is remote for several reasons.

Social order in the United States rests on political authority, not political power. The democratic consensus that denied political extremists the opportunity to exploit the Great Depression will also serve as a bulwark against radical movements in the future. No ethnic group is intent on seceding from the U.S. political community, and newcomers to the country quickly adapt to it. We hold no people in military bondage, so we are not fearful that they will rise up against us and precipitate a conflict capable of spilling over into our society.

The U.S. economy is blessed with abundant and diverse resources, advanced technology, skilled workers, talented entrepreneurs and managers, and a large market affording government and business alike enormous leverage vis-à-vis their competitors. Political stability promotes a climate facilitating economic enterprise. Billions of dollars enter the United States yearly because foreign investors, worried about political conditions at home, know that radical political change will not jeopardize their investments in this country. In the future, they may reduce their investments, but the United States will always be a magnet for capital.

Our culture, though in turmoil, has always thrived on change, flux, and uncertainty. Its central values support the political and economic systems and are celebrated by people from all classes, races, and ethnic groups. Contrary to the fear of nativists, immigrants to our shores quickly embrace our values. Indeed, they often reaffirm those in decline—witness the health of the work ethic among newcomers from Asia and Latin America. Our pluralistic culture and vibrant economy have attracted the most enterprising people from abroad, and they have infused our country with a steady stream of talent, enhancing the welfare of everyone—newcomers and old-timers alike.

Although a societal crisis is remote, two caveats are in order. First, as we shall observe later, our predicament may preclude us from resolving international economic problems capable of harming all the democracies, including our own. Second, the New Right is bent on a course of action that threatens to polarize our society.

Political polarization occurs when large numbers of people move from the center to the right on the one hand, while an equally sizable number move to the left on the other. This is what happened in Europe between the world wars, culminating in the rise of totalitarian movements. As Lipset has observed, the United States escaped polarization during the 1930s (although class conflict was visible) because the vast majority of Americans from all walks of life moved left.[19] In the 1980s the same thing has happened, only this time the movement has been toward the right.

The current political scene, however, is marked by a form of class politics reminiscent of the 1930s. At that time, the American Communist Party sought to organize the "proletariat" into a revolutionary force capable of destroying capitalism and "bourgeois democracy." The communists failed. Over the past decade the radical right has engaged in class warfare with more success. For example, as the media have told us time and again, the conservatives have seriously weakened their liberal adversaries. But the media have ignored another conservative campaign, and it is one of the major stories of our time. It involves a well-orchestrated, well-financed campaign to destroy the labor movement.

Organizations such as the National Right-to-Work Committee claim that they want to eliminate barriers to "voluntary unionism" and to make unions more democratic. Labor leaders, however, believe that their goals are less benign, the primary one being the destruction of organized labor, the only institution in the country whose primary purpose is to represent working people.

Officials in the AFL–CIO concede that there are a number of reasons why unions represent less than 20% of the nonagricultural labor force: a decline in manufacturing and a rise in service jobs, a shift in economic activity from the Snowbelt to the Sunbelt, foreign competition, and labor's own shortcomings. But in the last decade when all of these developments converged, the far right embarked upon a campaign to emasculate the American labor movment, a quest unthinkable a decade earlier. The country's "Reed Larsons" (head of the National Right-to-Work Committee) and CEOs of firms known for their anti-labor policies, such as J. P. Stevens and the Adolph Coors Company, harbored such ideas, but few Fortune 500 executives did. The idea was not unappealing, but labor was strong and had many political friends. As labor's ranks shrunk and its support in Congress declined, however, many business executives decided that unions were vulnerable. It was possible to undercut, if not destroy, them as effective collective bargaining agents. Henceforth workers would have to accept "reasonable" wages and fringe benefits, and they no longer could infringe upon management's prerogatives, such as establishing work rules, job descriptions, etc. Excessive demands on the part of some unions, the Darwinian climate, and the enmity the labor movement earned for discriminating against blacks and women helped minimize the misgivings some business leaders had about attacking it.

Labor's enemies have used a combination of the velvet glove—coming close to but not quite matching the wages and fringe benefits that organized workers earn—and the mailed fist—firing or reassigning employees to less attractive jobs—to keep their firms union-free. It is illegal to fire a worker for joining a union, but many companies have learned it is cost-effective to pay fines and avoid the larger economic penalties unionization entails. To the dismay of labor leaders, skillful and effective law and consulting firms have emerged which specialize in such services, and unions have not developed adequate countermeasures.

The plight of manufacturing and economic uncertainty in general have contributed to the success of union decertification campaigns; in such efforts workers elect to leave an existing union for a company union or choose not to belong to any labor organization. The AFL–CIO blames the Reagan administration for encouraging such campaigns. Reagan's decertification of the 11,000-strong Professional Air Traffic Controllers (PATCO) during his first year in office shocked the labor movement and emboldened its enemies. This unprecedented move sent corporate executives a message that Washington would not interfere with union-busting; on the contrary, it would lend a helping hand to companies so inclined. Labor officials support this charge by citing pro-business rulings of the National Labor Relations Board under Reagan's stewardship.

To make matters worse, many of labor's closest friends in Congress have been returned to private life in face of the conservative tide that has swept the country. Those who have survived the onslaught have begun to employ rhetoric by the U.S. Chamber of Commerce and the Young Americans for Freedom. The appearance of well-heeled corporate trade associations and right-wing PACs like NCPAC have not gone unnoticed by members of Congress who desperately need campaign funding. Those who have turned to these organizations for help tend henceforth to vote "right" on the issues and turn their backs on the unions that formerly helped bankroll their campaigns.

The success of this anti-labor blitzkrieg is shown by occurrences other than labor's failure to organize the unorganized and by the decertification drives. The best example of how well labor's enemies are doing is illustrated by the fact that unions are "giving back" wage increases and fringe benefits wrested earlier from their employers. On the defensive, unions have been accepting wage packages that do not keep pace with inflation. In 1984 wage hikes in major labor contracts were held to 2.5%, "one of the lowest rates on record and well under the rate of inflation." This figure is even more impressive when one considers revelation by the Bureau of Labor Statistics that wage gains in the previous contract period averaged 8.6%.[20]

As labor loses its clout at the bargaining table, nonorganized workers will experience setbacks, too. Wages will plunge, and conditions of employment will deteriorate in those areas of the country where unions have always been weak. The first major objective of those leading the assault on the labor movement, then, is to weaken it as a powerful economic force in the United States. If successful, they will restore the ability of business to dominate the collective bargaining process as it did prior to the 1930s.

The second major objective of those intent on crippling the labor movement is a political one — to turn back the clock on the New Deal. Since the 1930s, organized labor has provided much of the political clout to expand the welfare state, leading the fight for civil rights, education, aid for senior citizens, and other programs to help needy and neglected members of society. Since the Wagner Act was adopted in 1935, it has empowered workers politically. Through unions, workers acquire information and skills that middle-class voters acquire in college, the business world, and the professions. Union members have a better understanding of issues than other workers, and they are more inclined to participate in the political process. By voting, disseminating information, and manning phone banks, they help liberal candidates compensate for inadequate campaign war chests.

In states where unions are strong, therefore, programs for the poor and working people are more generously funded than in those states where they are weak. The same holds true for health and safety laws that protect workers at their place of employment and public support for education and child care. Were unions to double their membership in the Sunbelt, liberal candidates at all levels of government would find it easier to win elections. This is one of the reasons the right has targeted labor unions for destruction.

If it succeeds, the social and political costs will be high. Through unions, workers have achieved both higher living standards and greater economic security. In the process, they have refuted Marx's contention that capitalism is incapable of reforming itself, that workers can only achieve justice with its destruction. By giving working people a stake in society, unions have contributed to political stability. Should the far right destroy the labor movement, working people would have to turn to government to meet needs heretofore met by unions. Conservatives who presently rail against "big government" then will be responsible for enlarging the state's outreach into society. Government is as large as it is today because so-called conservatives in the past refused to deal with the legitimate grievances of workers, blacks, and women through the private sector or at the state and local levels of government.

The prospect that victims of the two-tiered society will become politically aroused and provide the mass base for a liberal revival does not frighten enemies of organized labor or affirmative government. This is largely because of the conservative mood of the country and the disarray of New Deal Democrats. Also, one does not have to be a New Rightist to acknowledge that the political apathy of Americans occupying the lower tier of our society bodes ill for a liberal political revival. There are many reasons why economic hard times have not produced political upheaval among this group.

First, our political culture, which stresses privatism, minimizes discontent associated with economic disruptions. In Europe political authorities express alarm when unemployment exceeds 6%; in Washington, that figure represents "full employment." Similar logic accounts for the United States being the only major industrial society without a national medical system. To most Americans, medical care is not a province of government.

Second, the social welfare programs opposed by conservatives in the 1930s have helped cushion the impact of poverty and provided greater economic security to working people.

Third, while millions of Americans have been stricken by unemployment, declining living standards, and the psychic disorders associated with economic hard times, many of their friends and relatives continue to experience economic and social advances. In other countries, people of ability locked into socio-economic straight jackets turn to radical solutions to break the chains of inequality binding them. They cannot remedy their problems within the system, so they work outside it. But the openness of our society allows bright, energetic, and resourceful people from all races, religions, and regions of the country to "make it." Like Turner's "frontier," socio-economic mobility (or at least the illusion of it) has served as a safety valve, dissipating potentially serious discontent.

A fourth reason for conservative optimism is that the groups Democrats hope to bring together to achieve political success are at odds with one another. Black–Jewish relations were harmed by Jesse Jackson's "Hymietown" remark in the 1984 Democratic primaries and his refusal to disassociate himself from the Reverend Louis Farakkhan, who is known for anti-Semitic statements. But prior to these incidents, both groups had clashed over the use of quotas in affirmative action programs. Hispanic leaders have displayed displeasure with what they claim is the propensity of black spokespersons to speak for them when they discuss "minority issues." Blacks, in turn, complain that Hispanic immigrants are taking jobs from them. Animosity toward unions in many parts of the country is associated with the fact that Jews and Catholics have long played a pivotal role in unions. Racial, religious, and other forms of ethnic divisions have subsided, but they continue to undercut "working-class solidarity" in the United States.

Conservative domination of the public policy debate is a fifth reason why Americans at the lower tier of society have not displayed a "politics of resentment." Conservative thinking has dominated most of the industrial democracies over the past decade; this has been true of West Germany, the United Kingdom, Japan, and even the Scandinavian countries. François Mitterrand bucked the conservative tide early in the decade, but after socialist solutions failed to revitalize the French economy, he turned to capitalist remedies in desperation. The conservative counterreformation has made an imprint on the minds of millions of our most talented and economically adroit citizens, and they will not disregard its teachings soon.

This last observation is linked to a final explanation for political tranquility in the midst of a national malaise—middle-class opposition to economic liberalism. During the 1980 Democratic presidential primary, Walter Mondale attacked Gary Hart for his insensitivity toward the needy. In assessing Hart's programs, he asked, "Where's the beef?" Journalists milked this question to enliven coverage of a long, boring contest, but few of them dwelt on the shocking revelation that Americans who had escaped economic setbacks displayed little concern about those who had not. Large numbers of Americans lived in rural shacks and urban slums, suffered from malnutrition, and did not receive adequate medical care—yet they resided in the richest, most agriculturally abundant, and medically advanced society in the world. Polls indicated that Americans favored social welfare programs but voted for candidates who opposed them or promised to "keep them in check." Many of the young urban professionals who favored Gary Hart in the primaries later voted for Reagan. They feared he was trigger-happy, and were turned off by his opposition to abortion and support for school prayer, but his economic policies had upheld the living standards of middle-class Americans such as themselves.

It is with such observations in mind that the Reaganites have reason to be optimistic about their future prospects. But as Kevin Phillips, one of our most perceptive conservative columnists, has observed, their hubris may be their undoing: "Ideologically committed people who finally obtain real power after being spurned for decades have a tendency to excess—to believe that their particular insights and perceptions can explain and achieve virtually everything."[21]

Hubris contributed to the "month of shocks" that jarred the Reagan administration in November 1986. By late evening on November 4, the TV networks revealed that despite Ronald Reagan's extensive efforts in the last weeks of the campaign to help elect Republicans, the GOP had lost control of the Senate. The Democratic-controlled 100th Congress would make Reagan's last two years in office difficult.

That same day, however, another story surfaced that would eventually prove even more devastating to the administration's fortunes. An Iranian official confirmed that the United States had shipped arms to Iran. Two days later, the president denied this, stating that there was "no foundation" to the story that his former national security adviser, Robert C. McFarland, had traveled to Teheran. After the press reported that a large shipment of arms had been delivered to the Iranians, the President conceded that a delivery had been made, but said it involved only a small amount of arms that "could easily fit into a single cargo plane."[22] When the press proclaimed that the arms deal was a trade for U.S. hostages then being held by Islamic terrorists in Lebanon, the White House responded that the arms transfer was really an attempt to develop rapport with "moderates" in the Khomeini regime.

This was the pattern that characterized press–administration relations over the next several weeks. The press would provide new information about the Iranian arms deal; the administration would deny it, but then concede that something of the kind had transpired. White House spokespersons sought to put a "positive spin" on the revelation: the deal was part of a campaign to restore U.S. influence in Iran, and release of the hostages was something of a bonus.

On November 25, Attorney General Edwin Meese informed a group of incredulous reporters that a small team of NSC people had arranged the covert arms sale to generate an estimated $10 to $30 million for the Nicaraguan contras. Meese said that the two key actors in the operation, NSC aide Lt. Colonel Oliver North and the president's national security advisor, Admiral John M. Poindexter had left their posts—the first was fired, the second resigned. This revelation set into motion a flurry of activity, on the administration's part to minimize damage and on Congress's part to get to the bottom of the story. An independent council was appointed by the White House to determine whether criminal laws had been broken; a review board was established to investigate the NSC's operations; and several congressional committees prepared to investigate the affair in the 100th Congress.

Although the president rebounded from a dip in the polls by the time the new legislative session began, the "Iran-contra affair" clearly had undermined the administration's capacity to conduct affairs of state with the same firm hand the president had displayed prior to the scandal.

In an amazing replay of the last major scandal to rock Washington, Watergate, the pointman in the White House who defended what apparently was illegal activity was Pat Buchanan, President Reagan's principal media adviser. Buchanan had served President Nixon as a speech writer. He appeared on TV, and wrote articles in newspapers, defending Colonel North's misguided but "patriotic" actions, implying that the liberal press was out to destroy the President. This was not the first time that hardliners in the administration sought to defend it by scapegoating liberals, portraying them, on occasion, as subversives rather than as political adversaries.

A good example occurred during the spring of 1985, when the Reagan administration was fighting for congressional support for SDI. George Keyworth, the president's science advisor and a leading advocate of "Star Wars," stated in an interview that the press is "drawn from a relatively narrow fringe element on the far left" that is trying to "tear down America."[23] The next year, Buchanan, wrote an op-ed piece in the *Washington Post*, stating that those congresspersons who did not support the president on aid to the "contras" were actually voting for Ortega, the Sandinista leader.[24]

Attacks of this nature against the media, liberals, labor leaders, and educators are a cause for concern. They remind one of the politics of hysteria that flourished in the aftermath of both world wars. Should the economy falter in the future and the political tide turn against the right, one can expect a hysterical reaction from that quarter. There are extremists on the right, blinded by their recent successes, who are prepared to wage a holy war against the "enemies of the American way of life." They are throwbacks to the 19th century Know-Nothings who blamed Irish Catholics, and later the "wops," "kikes," and "niggers," for urban and labor unrest; they are contemporary analogues of those who manipulated the post-World War I "red scare" to destroy the labor movement in the 1920s; and they are soul mates of those who exploited the McCarthyite hysteria to discredit the New Deal in the 1950s.

This time Catholics and Jews will be spared such purification drives (indeed some of them may be allied with the nativists). The most likely scapegoats will be gays, humanists, feminists, and foreign policy moderates who "revile American values" and "seek to appease Moscow." In this connection, one disturbing feature of the 1984 elections was that when the words "vested interests" were employed by many Reaganites in the South, everyone knew this meant blacks. The New Right conducted a massive and effective registration campaign by warning, in effect, that if white voters did not register and vote for Reagan, Walter Mondale, the captive of "vested interests," would be elected.

Should a new wave of nativism break upon the land, Hispanics and Asians are likely to be priority targets. One unfortunately can argue that when, in seeking to secure support for its Central American policies, the administration warns that communist victories in the region will result in the United States being inundated by immigrants, it is making nativistic appeals. And the Ku Klux Klan has already attacked immigrants from Vietnam in many parts of the country.

The New Right's reaction to a serious and protected recession, then, is bound to divide the nation and not unify it; to exacerbate divisions in our society and not heal them; and to ignite an internal conflagration that will produce a climate of hatred and discord. Even if the good sense of Americans representing a spectrum of political views from both parties prevails, and we avoid serious polarization, a president will be hard pressed to unify the country and quickly resolve its predicament. Once again, the ship of state will flounder, and we shall lurch from one partial solution to another, perhaps precipitating a societal crisis.

Whatever the future holds, one thing is certain: the conservative counter-reformation cannot lead us out of our predicament. It can only deepen the problems afflicting us—political stalemate, economic turmoil, and cultural disarray.

- At a time when we need strong government, leaders of the conservative counterreformation are reaffirming an 18th century liberal view of government distrustful of political authority.
- At a time when economic changes at home and abroad threaten our economy, they counsel us to rely on the market alone to resolve our economic plight.
- At a time when the centrifugal forces of modernity are dividing America, they celebrate individualism and privatism, while rejecting a communitarian ethos that could unite us.

The irony is that the United States has the capacity to cope with its predicament, but may not—because authentic conservatives have little influence in society today.

Notes

1. *New York Times*, 25 November, 1984.
2. *Washington Post*, 3 January, 1985.
3. George Will, *Statecraft as Soulcraft: What Government Does* (New York: Simon and Schuster, 1983), p. 23.
4. Will, *Statecraft*, p. 28.
5. Will, *Statecraft*, p. 123.
6. *Washington Post*, 27 August, 1986.
7. *Washington Post*, 24 May, 1984.
8. Thomas B. Edsall, *The New Politics of Inequality* (New York: W. W. Norton, 1984), p. 17.
9. Christopher Lasch, *The Culture of Narcissism* (New York: Warner Books, 1979), pp. 42–43.
10. Joseph A. Schumpeter, *Capitalism, Socialism and Democracy* (New York: Torchbooks, Harper & Row, 1962), p. 61.
11. Daniel Bell, *The Cultural Contradictions of Capitalism* (New York: Basic Books, 1976), p. 55.
12. Bell, *Cultural Contradictions*, p. 66.
13. Bell, *Cultural Contradictions*, p. 70.
14. Marshall Berman, "All That Is Solid," *Dissent* (Winter 1978): 55.
15. Berman, "All That Is Solid," p. 57.
16. *Washington Post*, 1 January, 1977.
17. Peter L. Berger and Richard John Neuhaus, *To Empower People: The Role of Mediating Institutions in Public Policy* (Washington: American Enterprise Institute, 1977).
18. Orestes Brownson, "Liberalism and Progress," in Russell Kirk, ed., *The Portable Conservative Reader* (New York: Penguin Books, 1982), p. 276.
19. Seymour Martin Lipset, *Political Man* (Baltimore: The Johns Hopkins University Press, 1981).
20. *Washington Post*, 27 October, 1984.
21. *Washington Post*, 16 December, 1984.

22. *Washington Post*, 28 December, 1986.
23. *Washington Post*, 10 June, 1985.
24. *Washington Post*, 5 March, 1986.

PART THREE

International Implications

CHAPTER EIGHT

Domestic Strife: Implications for the Superpower Rivalry

If we can push the Soviets, they will collapse. — Ronald Reagan

In pondering the relationship between the Soviet crisis and Moscow's international behavior, several questions leap to mind. Will the Soviets adopt more aggressive policies abroad to compensate for turmoil in the empire? Or, preoccupied with their crisis and fearing the correlation of forces favors the United States, will they adopt more restrained policies toward the LDCs? What impact will the U.S. military buildup and the Soviet crisis have upon Gorbachev's arms control posture? Will upheaval in the empire spark an East–West confrontation—even if the Soviets seek warmer relations with Washington? And, finally, how might Moscow respond to a United States stricken by its own predicament?

Aggressive Soviet Policies in the Third World

The Soviets will seek salvation from their internal problems by acting boldly on the world stage. This is the view of U.S. hardliners, who believe the USSR has not spent vast sums of money on its armed forces merely to protect themselves against hostile neighbors. According to Secretary of Defense Weinberger, "It would be dangerously naive to expect the Soviet Union, if it once achieves military superiority, not to exploit their [*sic*] military capability even more fully than they are now doing."[1]

Michael Ledeen warns: "The Soviet Empire is driven by its revolutionary ideology and its vision to expand . . ." and the combination of "great military might and a deep domestic crisis" is a dangerous one for us. "The situation may be growing even more dangerous" with "the arrival . . . of a new generation of Soviet leaders."[2] They did not experience the horrors of war firsthand, so they may be more inclined to resort to force than their elders.

Richard Pipes links aggressive foreign policies to the regime's survival. Signs of weakness abroad erode its power base at home; therefore, it is senseless to distinguish between the Soviets' internal and external security requirements. Furthermore, there is a self-fulfilling logic to Soviet imperialism: by making new enemies, the Soviets have a rationale for expanding their borders. Consequently, as long as the dialectics of Soviet imperialism persist, so will the East–West rivalry in the Third World, producing a climate unfavorable to détente.[3]

These views can be dismissed as the ravings of cold warriors. However, scholars with more moderate views of the Soviet threat also see a relationship between Soviet internal problems and aggressive behavior abroad. Dimitri Simes says that modest successes in the Third World have enhanced the Soviet regime's legitimacy: "The periodic establishment of even short-lived self-esteem is perceived as proof of the growing historical relevance of the Soviet Union."[4] Seweryn Bialer writes: "The Soviet notion of what is positive in the Third World is opposite that of the United States and the West. It welcomes ferment, instability and revolutionary upheavals; not equilibrium, stability and orderly change."[5] The Soviets do not think of the LDCs independently of the East–West struggle; rather, they view wars of national liberation as one of many battlegrounds that will determine in the end whether they or the capitalists will prevail.

Bialer says that in the face of rising discontent, the Politburo may resort to oppression to keep the people in line. To justify their actions, the leaders may "seek to re-create the atmosphere of a besieged fortress, to rally around the theme of external enemies, and to foster public xenophobia."[6] Under these circumstances, Moscow would welcome confrontations with foreign powers, including the United States.

This analysis leads us to a disconcerting conclusion: as the Soviets lose ground on the "second front"—on the domestic scene—they will transfer the venue of the competition to the "first front"—the East–West rivalry— even at the risk of war. The military remains Moscow's principal internal and external resource. Nations, like people, rely upon their strengths to get them out of trouble. We can be assured, then, that in an attempt to compensate for serious internal problems, the Kremlin would project its military power to intimidate its enemies, to embolden its allies, and to convince the Soviet people that the regime will endure—whatever roadblocks are strewn in its path.

Reducing Soviet Commitment in the LDCs

The preceding forecast could materialize, but it is unlikely that the Soviets will adopt aggressive policies to compensate for their crisis. It is more likely that mounting problems at home will tame Soviet international behavior and reduce their trouble-making in the Third World. The Kremlin will remain protective of areas close to its border such as Afghanistan but seek to consolidate its position in the LDCs—not expand it. Soviet officials believe they are overextended in the Third World. It is costing them billions of rubles annually to maintain the economies of socialist welfare cases. Assistance to their eleven Third World client states—Cuba, Mongolia, Vietnam, Kampuchea, Laos, North Korea, Angola, Ethiopia, Mozambique, Afghanistan, and South Yemen—costs billions of dollars annually, at a time when the Soviet economy is sagging and Moscow is helping to prop up the economies of Eastern Europe. The burden of helping "fraternal socialist countries" will get heavier as Soviet growth rates fail to match those of the 1960s. As with the British earlier in the century, the viability of the Soviet home economy is being underminded by its colonial commitments.

Although the Soviets will exploit turmoil where they can without high costs or stiff U.S. resistance, they cannot ignore the following truism: the correlation of forces in the Third World—the major battleground in the East–West competition—has shifted in favor of the Americans. Gorbachev is conveying an image of confidence and bluster to the world, but he cannot ignore this disconcerting fact.

In the 1960s many Western intellectuals believed that the LDCs would take the Marxist road to development. Few of the new nations had a democratic tradition, and most of them lacked the entrepreneurial talent, capital, and skilled labor force to follow the U.S. economic model. Democratic capitalism held out the promise of political liberty but had no answers to poverty. The Soviet system, in contrast, could not provide liberty, but it could provide bread. Faced with a choice, the vast majority of the world's poor would choose bread.

Today few commentators anywhere believe the Soviet model offers the LDCs hope. It provides neither freedom nor bread, as the Ethiopian experience has demonstrated so tragically. Even regimes depending on Russian assistance for their survival have voiced displeasure with Soviet economic policy. Not long after the Sandinistas forced Anastasio Somoza to flee Nicaragua, Fidel Castro visited the country and told the Nicaraguans not to get too closely entwined with the Soviet bloc economically. In conversations with the leaders of the new government, the Cubans asserted they had found that a "state distribution system is less efficient than a market system."[7] They also advised the Nicaraguans not to complete a major truck purchase from East Germany, noting that the quality of Soviet-bloc goods is poor. These candid remarks emanated from spokesmen of a country receiving $9 million a day from Moscow, and which had run up a debt to the Soviets of $8 billion.

About this time, African leaders who espoused socialism began to acknowledge the shortcomings of the Marxist–Leninist road to economic development, too. According to a Liberian official, Guinea's Marxist leader, Sékou Touré, told Samuel K. Doe, the master sergeant who had engineered a coup in 1980, to "keep the capitalist system that Liberia has . . . an old system that people are used to and is apparently the best for the country." He added, "Touré also said that he might have done a number of things differently . . . now that he had the benefit of hindsight."[8] To Moscow's dismay, the Marxist regimes in Angola and Mozambique have been eager to develop extensive commercial relations with the United States; they also realize that the West, not the East, has the most to offer their economies.

An analysis of capitalist versus socialist economies in Asia clearly reflects favorably upon those that have followed the capitalist road to development— Taiwan, Singapore, and South Korea. Even with considerable Soviet assistance, the Vietnamese economy is in shambles. Once an exporter of rice, Vietnam is now importing food to feed its people, whose living standards have plunged with communist rule. No economy in the world which emulates the Soviet model is doing well, nor is there one that would not do better were free market practices given greater leeway.

There is, however, one aspect of the Soviet experience that is acutely relevant to Third World leaders: the ability to maintain political power in the face of popular discontent and economic stagnation—factors that have destroyed past regimes. This is what appealed to Castro, and it has attracted the Sandinistas' attention, too. The ability to govern in the face of the populace's hostility is a valued commodity, and we should not underestimate its attraction to those who lust for power. Furthermore, by providing military assistance, and to a lesser degree economic aid (mainly at strategic points), Moscow is deemed a coveted ally by many Third World elites.

Alignment with the USSR does not guarantee that Soviet clients will always receive a helping hand, and the aid may be meager and accompanied by strings. The Ethiopians have discovered this, and so have the Sandinistas— possibly a twelfth Soviet client. Cuba, of course, is a special case. The Soviets have been generous to Castro because they covet Cuba as a Soviet base in the Western Hemisphere. Their presence in the Caribbean is proof that the USSR is a superpower. But even Havana knows that in the final analysis, Soviet interests take priority over those of "fraternal socialist countries." In the spring of 1982, several American foreign policy experts visited Cuba and reported that Castro wanted to reach an accommodation with the Reagan

Administration. Seweryn Bialer, who made the trip, wrote afterwards that the Cubans expressed concern about Soviet support in the event of a showdown between Havana and Washington. They feared "the Soviets would react chiefly with rhetoric and threatening gestures should the U.S. move against Cuba or its revolutionary allies in Central America."[9]

Finally, Timothy Colton rejects the idea that Moscow will try to compensate for its predicament by projecting power abroad. "In the past, hazardous ventures abroad have not been times to ease the mood of the Soviet population."[10] On the contrary, the government hushed up Soviet activities in Afghanistan for years. The Soviet Union may eventually prevail in Afghanistan, but a Soviet victory there is not going to help Gorbachev with his internal problems.

It is precisely because the Soviets are power-oriented that their domestic troubles will convince them of the wisdom of refraining from Third World adventures. Gorbachev realizes that his most serious security problem is a sick economy. Over time, economic stagnation will lead to the deterioration of Soviet conventional and nuclear military power—not to mention serious divisions in Soviet society.

Gorbachev, like Stalin decades ago, may conclude that it is foolhardy to expend scarce resources to promote global communism, and that the Soviets should concentrate instead on building "socialism in one country." This pragmatic policy can be adopted without violating Leninist theory, which holds that revolution cannot be exported but must be a product of internal conditions.

Unless we assume that Gorbachev is a fool, the Soviet leadership has learned something over the past twenty years about the limits to military power and to the influence the superpowers can wield vis-à-vis countries that are comparative Lilliputs. The Soviets invested billions of rubles to court Egypt, Somalia, and several other African countries, but they have nothing to show for their investment. On the contrary, like the United States, they have learned that recipients of military and economic aid do not always march to the tune of their benefactors. Worse yet, small countries that receive such assistance may embroil the superpowers in crises that could precipitate a nuclear war, as the Russians and Americans learned during the Yom Kipper War of 1973.

Slowing Down the Arms Race

When Gromyko was replaced by Shevardnadze, Western pundits wrote that Gorbachev intended to devote less time to relations with the United

States. His actions since then refute that conclusion. The reason is obvious: The United States is the only power capable of destroying the Soviet Union in a nuclear attack. The Soviets are profoundly concerned about the American military modernization program. It challenges Soviet security on both the "first" and "second fronts" of the superpower competition.

Looking at the U.S. threat from the first front vantage point, the Russians no longer appear confident that they enjoy a military advantage, as many Reaganites claim. And contrary to Reagan's detractors, Moscow resumed armed control talks, and Gorbachev met Reagan, at Geneva and Reyjkavik, because he feared modernization of U.S. offensive nuclear forces and Reagan's SDI program.

The Soviets view his military modernization program as nothing less than a quest to secure a first-strike capability. How else can one explain the Americans placing MX missiles in the very silos Reagan contended were vulnerable to a Soviet first strike? Russian officials have an answer, and it is a simple one: the United States has no intention of using the MX in retaliation; it plans to use it in a first strike against the USSR. The same holds true, they say, for the D-5 warhead, a "missile-busting" weapon that will be placed on Trident submarines in a few years.

That's not all. Soviet strategists contend that the Pershing II missiles have been deployed in West Germany to decapitate Soviet command and control centers as part of a U.S. first strike. And measures to upgrade the U.S. C³I (command, control, communications, and intelligence) capability is further evidence that the U.S. buildup is offensive, not defensive, in nature. U.S. defense analysts, moreover, are candid in asserting that the United States scrapped MAD for a nuclear war-fighting capability.

In keeping with their awe of U.S. technology, they see SDI as a potentially viable (though imperfect) defense against ICBMs, and not just the dream of an old man who has spent most of his life in the wonderland of Hollywood. A larger concern is that SDI research will allow the Americans to achieve a new offensive capability and subject the USSR to a first strike. Many Soviet leaders believe that Reagan resumed the summit process to placate his critics at home and in Europe, and to lull Moscow into believing that he was serious about arms control when in fact he was only buying time to deploy his SDI system or offensive breakthroughs associated with it. Whatever doubts Gorbachev may have about the U.S. commitment to arms control, there are compelling military reasons for him to negotiate an agreement with the Americans—one where he trades off heavy Soviet ICBMs for SDI.

In addition to their respect for U.S. technology, the Soviets are impressed by the size and adaptability of the U.S. economy. A strong economy is vital to military preparedness, and they fear that if the Americans are prepared to accept the staggering economic cost and run the risk of destabilizing the nuclear balance, the United States could surge ahead of the USSR in a new arms race. Simultaneously, even if it cannot gain a military edge, Washington might compromise Soviet security on the second front by running the Soviet economy into the ground.

Georgi Arbatov, speaking before a group of scholars in Washington in the spring of 1985, said:

> The arms race has become an unaffordable luxury . . . in the economic sense. Some Americans may take such a statement by a Soviet representative as a vindication of the current strategy of 'wearing down' the USSR and its allies through military competition. Undoubtedly, we are very reluctant to spend money on arms when there are so many economic, social and cultural needs requiring great expenditure and effort.[11]

Moscow would not allow the Americans to surge ahead of the USSR, but would match the United States stride for stride. Arbatov can be taken for his word; nonetheless, the Soviets have cause to be worried about the burden of a new arms race. At a time when their economy is sputtering, they can ill-afford large defense increases. A halt or, at the very least, a slow down of the arms race is vital to the resolution of the Soviet crisis.

The Kremlin is finding it difficult to maintain its bloated defense budget. Indeed, there is evidence that the Soviets have had to curtail defense expenditures to accommodate a sluggish economy. The CIA believes that since 1976, slower rates of economic growth have forced the Kremlin to accept "slower growth in defense spending." Looking at the future, the CIA concludes:

> Certainly the pressure to step up defense procurement must be intense given the state of Soviet–American relations and the recent increases in U.S. spending on military hardware. But a decision on increasing the rate of growth of defense spending has to be a tough one, not so much because of the impact it would have on overall economic growth but because of the implications for Soviet society. Our analysis indicates, for instance, that at current rates of investment, and even with defense growing at our present estimate of 2 percent a year, per capita consumption would grow by only 1–1.5 percent annually during 1986–90. Accelerating defense spending to a rate of 5 percent a year—a rate approximating 4 to 5 percent growth observed during 1966–1976—would jeopardize Soviet prospects for anything but minimal improvement in consumption levels.[12]

The superpowers devote approximately the same amount of money to defense—about $300 billion. But whereas this represents 6% of the U.S. GNP, it accounts for 12% of the Soviet GNP. The Soviets must make a greater sacrifice to maintain their armed forces than the Americans. Consequently, its rhetoric aside, the Kremlin is not as confident as it once was that it can keep up with the United States in an arms competition without paying a very heavy price in the process. If the Soviets are going to revitalize their economy, they must devote more investment to nonmilitary sectors—to meet their people's consumer needs, to be sure, but more urgently to develop a secure economic base, which is capable of sustaining heavy defense spending over many years. In other words, the Soviets must slow down the arms race now so that they may keep up with the Americans in a future arms competition.

Upheaval in Eastern Europe and Superpower Conflict

Even if the Soviets seek more harmonious relations with the United States, upheavel within their empire may heighten East–West tensions and drive the superpowers to the brink of nuclear war. Recall Bruno Kreisky's prediction that it is only a matter of time before one or more of the Eastern European countries openly challenge indigenous communist rule or Russian hegemony, thereby precipitating a Soviet-led Pact invasion. One can envisage the following scenario unfolding in Poland.

Solidarity is resurrected as Jaruzelski's regime suffers serious economic setbacks, the Communist party is badly divided, and the Polish people become bolder in displaying hostility toward communism and the Soviets. A government of reconciliation, including Solidarity, the Catholic church, and elements of the party and army, replaces the general in a nearly bloodless coup. Solidarity requests that it be recognized as a legal entity representing the workers and peasants of Poland, and its demands are met in a special meeting at Gdansk. Western governents promise the new regime a massive injection of foreign aid, and in the meantime the AFL–CIO provides Solidarity with financial resources that allow it to function as a national organization.

After several weeks marked by confusion and alarm in Moscow, Gorbachev orders Warsaw Pact forces to invade Poland, citing the Brezhnev Doctrine as justification. The Soviets lead massive land, sea, and air operations designed to crush resistance quickly. Although Gorbachev recognizes that the invasion will cause him problems with the West, he reasons that the loss of Poland would be a much greater setback than a momentary decline in East–West relations. The Americans will lash out rhetorically and curtail trade for a while, but like Eisenhower in 1956 and Johnson in 1968, the U.S. president will not provide military assistance to the Poles. The Western Europeans will not go beyond a verbal assault; indeed, many of them will argue that the Poles brought this tragedy upon themselves by pushing the Soviets too far.

The invasion does not produce the quick results the Soviets hoped it would. The Poles are not cowed by the show of force but are driven to acts of heroism in resisting the invaders. Units of the Polish armed forces, which had remained neutral, now join the government and train civilians to resist the Soviets. The Soviets prevail, but only after months of bitter fighting and tens of thousands of casualties on both sides. The world views the brutal oppression of the Poles via television and is shocked. Public pressures in the United States terminate arms control talks and commercial transactions with

Moscow. In Western Europe, massive demonstrations protesting the invasion occur in all the major cities. The reaction is more severe than Moscow had anticipated, but worst of all is the expression of outrage in West Germany.

The public there is appalled when Soviet troops put down demonstrations in East Germany after their German comrades refuse to do so. Many civilians are killed and wounded, and some East German units side with the protestors. For the first time since World War II, Soviet and German troops are locked in combat. Developments in the GDR give impetus to more demonstrations in the Federal Republic. They are spearheaded by the newly formed Reunification Party, which has replaced the Greens as the movement most popular with young Germans. Commandos belonging to the party's paramilitary wing stages raids against Soviet forces in East Germany. Incensed, the Soviet commander strikes several miles into West Germany in "hot pursuit" of the Germans. In the process his units encounter U.S. troops, who open fire. This sets off a series of actions and reactions on the part of the Soviet and U.S. forces. No one is sure who fired the first nuclear weapon.

The point here is that a societal crisis in the USSR could lead to a situation that contains all the elements of an international crisis. From the Soviet perspective, the stakes are high. They stand to lose control over a vital part of their empire. Their options are unappealing since they cannot allow the "counterrevolutionaries" to prevail, but if they crush them, they provide ammunition to hardliners in the West. Finally, they do not have the time to defer action, and they must make crucial decisions under circumstances where mistakes and miscalculations can lead to drastic consequences. As von Clausewitz, the German philosopher of war, wrote, during war "friction" or unanticipated developments frequently occur in spite of one's best laid plans. In the face of a crisis in the Soviet empire that could plausibly lead to its disintegration, and at a time when East–West tensions are high, the Soviet leaders may make miscalculations that lead to a nuclear war.

The Soviet Response to a U.S. Crisis

How would the Soviet Union respond to a United States stricken by crisis? The initial Soviet reaction will be upbeat: Gorbachev will think of the advantages to be derived—U.S. leadership preoccupied with domestic turmoil, pressures to spend more on domestic programs and less on defense, a "loss of nerve" in international affairs, and so forth. Upon reflection, however, his optimism will be superseded by Marx's warning that the capitalists will not surrender prerogatives of wealth and power without a fight.

Hardliners will blame Moscow for a U.S. crisis, just as they have in the past. Soviet writers contend that Nixon's program to reach an accommodation with the Soviet Union was sabotaged by American "cold warriors," who used Watergate as a pretext to eliminate Nixon because he acknowledged the

USSR was a superpower and was prepared to negotiate with the Kremlin. The invasion of Afghanistan served the same function during the Carter administration when it was cited as cause for the Senate to reject SALT II.

Since the 1985 Geneva summit, the Soviets have softened their public attacks on Reagan, but privately they still believe he represents those in U.S. ruling circles who oppose an accommodation with Moscow. Soviet officials make an interesting distinction between Richard Nixon's anti-communism and Ronald Reagan's antipathy toward the Soviet Union. Nixon, they claim, was a staunch anti-communist, but he was not "anti-Soviet." Reagan, by contrast, does not distinguish between his hatred for communism and his hostility toward the Soviet Union. Soviet visitors to the United States still remind their hosts about Reagan's "evil empire" remarks and similar harsh rhetoric.[13]

The Soviets are less concerned about hostile words than threatening actions, although in the case of SDI they apparently do not make a distinction between the two. Gorbachev has said, "Talk about its alleged defensive character is, of course, a fairy tale for the naive. The plan is to try to neutralize Soviet strategic weapons and to secure a possibility to deliver with impunity a nuclear strike at our country."[14]

Even Soviet officials who do not subscribe to this worst-case scenario believe that Reaganite defense policies represent a security threat to the Russians. But it is no consolation that they are designed to disrupt the Soviet economy and deny the USSR superpower status. One told journalist Robert Kaiser, "Of course Reagan's program is not war. He is trying to beat us down, to damage us politically and economically after we have worked so hard to establish equality. We can't let him get away with that, and we won't."[15] As long as Ronald Reagan is president, Soviet officialdom will harbor such fears.

Given their deep-seated distrust of Reagan, his followers in the GOP, and like-minded people in the Democratic party, they will deem a United States wracked by recession, political upheaval, and social discord to be a very dangerous antagonist. The U.S. ruling classes, fearing for their political lives and economic treasures, will deflect the people's anger toward the "communist menace." Washington will depict Soviet support for progressive governments and movements in the Third World as evidence that Moscow is on the march and adhering to its timetable to conquer the world.

Under these circumstances, the Soviets will take costly precautions as the "reactionaries" in the United States, desperate to save themselves, conduct a massive military drive to surge ahead of the USSR. It will mean putting Soviet strategic nuclear forces on a higher state of readiness and bringing conventional forces up to full strength. Workers numbering in the hundreds of thousands, and badly needed to keep the economy humming, will be called up from their reserve units and put into uniform.

Because the costs of mobilization will be astronomical and especially damaging to an economy in crisis, the Soviets may decide to rely more upon their nuclear forces and less upon conventional ones. Strategists who question the wisdom of this action should not forget that there is a precedent for relying primarily on "nukes": the West has not matched the WTO's conventional capabilities—even though it has the money, manpower, and technology—because conventional forces cost more than nuclear arms.

In addition to the security and economic risks associated with an America in crisis, the Soviets will encounter political risks in their own society. Economic dislocations associated with mobilization will compel the government to reduce the flow of consumer goods to the people, and perhaps to impose food rationing. To assuage popular discontent, propagandists will blame the Americans for the sacrifices the Soviet people have to make. This will prove effective for a while, but over time belt-tightening will fan the flames of mass discontent among the minorities perhaps, if not the Russians. The Kremlin will have to worry about divisions within the ruling elite, too; after a period of unity they could have a falling-out over the proper response to the American threat.

If the United States is stricken by recession, one must assume that there will also be a global economic crisis, because the U.S. market for goods and services is the world's largest. Consequently countries in the communist bloc, as well as those in the capitalist world, will be economically damaged. The USSR is less dependent upon the ebb and flow of international commerce than the United States, but this is not true of its satellites. After all, one of the causes of Solidarity's rise in the early 1980s was the beating the Polish economy took in the face of the worldwide recession. It had become so entangled with capitalist economic interests that it ran a high fever when the West caught a cold. Future international economic calamities may, therefore, deepen the plight of the satellite economies, and force Moscow to provide assistance to them or run the risk of insurrection or economic collapse.

Finally, Gorbachev's reformist campaign may be undercut by the plight of his capitalist enemies. The crisis will give new credibility to the Marxist claim that capitalism will eventually self-destruct. Opponents of reform will exclaim, "Why adopt reforms that ape capitalism, when it is in decline?"

One does not have to search far for the lesson from this analysis: in much the same fashion that Americans must look to a Soviet crisis as a mixed blessing, so too must Moscow look upon a U.S. predicament as a double-edged sword. The prudent policy for Gorbachev to follow, then, would be to avoid a confrontation with a "cornered" U.S. leadership and wait with the expectation that Washington's predicament will be transformed into a societal crisis. Moscow could sit back, devote its energies to its own crisis, and watch the Western alliance slowly unravel. As we shall observe in the next chapter, this scenario is not as far-fetched as most Americans think it is.

Before looking at this disconcerting prospect, we must assess what bearing the American predicament will have upon U.S. relations with the USSR in an era of austerity. Four critical questions must be addressed: can the United States achieve a military edge over the USSR?; can Washington use its economic prowess to force the Soviets into making concessions?; what impact will the U.S. predicament have upon arms control negotiations?; and finally, what are the problems and prospects of resurrecting détente?

U.S. Economic Problems and Defense Capabilities

On his return from the 1985 Geneva summit, Ronald Reagan addressed Congress and declared that the United States neither sought military superiority nor a first-strike capability. These pledges were greeted with skepticism in many circles, at home and abroad. Reagan had stated categorically in his first term that he sought military superiority, although he backed away from this stance after it spawned protest in Europe and the United States. Second, as we have observed, the Soviets are convinced that the United States is seeking a first-strike capability. Like their counterparts in the Pentagon, Soviet strategists focus on an adversary's capabilities, not his intentions. Many American arms control advocates believe the United States is acquiring this capability — or, at the very least, our force structures suggest this — even if Washington has no intention of attacking the USSR. The Americans want to use this edge to contain Soviet international aggression, and to have a strong hand at the bargaining table and there are American officials who have no faith in arms control and détente. They believe that the only way to guarantee U.S. security is to achieve military superiority.

Policymakers of this opinion ignore some important facts. The United States cannot regain the edge in nuclear weapons it enjoyed during the Cold War. The Soviet economy is half the size of ours, and our technology is superior to theirs, but the Soviets can squeeze rubles out of their people to match us missile for missile, weapon system for weapon system, even if the arms race is carried into space. The United States has the means to conceivably exceed the Soviet Union in nuclear capabilities, but the American people will not make the economic sacrifices to accomplish this task. Large defense outlays are possible even in the face of economic hard times, but if the economy falters, voters tightening their belts will demand defense cuts.

Wall Street fears that the Pentagon's search for dollars will "crowd out" the capital requirements of business people and consumers. Heavy defense spending will drive up interest rates, reignite inflation, and prevent U.S. firms from matching the Japanese in the race for the high-tech market. It is no secret that the Japanese economic miracle is associated with a small defense budget, and with the opportunity to channel money directly into civilian research and development programs.

The business community believes there is little prospect of reducing the deficit as long as defense expenditures are high, so the Reaganites may rue the day they decided to keep a rein on liberal "big spenders" in Congress by confronting them with enormous deficits. David Stockman made this claim during the first Reagan administration, and it surfaced again in the summer of 1985 when he announced his resignation as director of the Office of Management and Budget. Even liberal members of Congress would think twice about funding their favorite social welfare program in the face of soaring deficits. Stockman subsequently denied making this statement, but Friedrich von Hayek wrote in a Viennese journal that year that "one of Reagan's advisors told me why the President" permitted such a huge increase in the deficits. He continued: "Reagan thinks it is impossible to persuade Congress that expenditures must be reduced, unless one creates deficits so large that absolutely everyone becomes convinced that no more money can be spent."[16]

But this argument has been used against bigger defense budgets, and it will be used to good effect in the future—especially if the economy experiences difficulties. An economic slump could drive up the deficit figure from $200 billion to $300 billion. Under these circumstances, even the staunchest supporter of the Pentagon would have trouble justifying massive defense outlays.

There are technical and strategic hurdles in the way of a U.S. drive for nuclear superiority, too. William Perry, a DOD official under Carter and a Reagan appointee to the Scowcroft Commission (which evaluated the MX basing mode), has observed that our technological superiority only allows us a five-year edge in the deployment of strategic nuclear systems. This should be kept in mind when assessing SDI. The Soviets may be incapable of building their own system, but they are capable of overwhelming our own.[17]

Many prominent scientists with defense-related expertise contend that SDI will not work the way the president first told the American people it would— that is, to protect them against a nuclear attack. They claim it will not accomplish the more modest military objective either—making our ICBMs less vulnerable. Furthermore, it cannot prevent cruise missiles from reaching targets in the United States, and the Soviets are rapidly catching up to us in this technology.

Even though there are doubts about its effectiveness, there is one thing SDI will accomplish: It will destabilize the nuclear balance, years before it is fully deployed. SDI means terminating the ABM treaty, and this move will poison arms control negotiations and overall East–West relations. The Soviets will interpret deployment of its first stages as an attempt to "break out" of the present situation of nuclear parity in a U.S. drive for superiority. Moscow's offensive countermeasures will hamper arms control talks and foster a new round of accusations, thereby heightening East–West tensions and bringing us closer to a nuclear war.

Finally, former defense secretary James Schlesinger estimates that—at a minimum—a multilayer Star Wars system will cost about $1 trillion. A major portion of the defense budget, therefore, will be devoted to this system, in the process compromising efforts to make our offensive systems less vulnerable. But modernizing our offensive systems is more feasible than SDI, and it should be accomplished in concert with arms control talks to reduce these dangerous weapons.[18]

Meanwhile, the drive to modernize U.S. conventional forces will be hampered by SDI expenditures. With new technology, such as "smart bombs" and other lethal conventional weapons, NATO planners believe that the West can deter an attack from the East. In other words, it may soon be feasible to safeguard Western Europe against a WTO assault without relying upon nuclear weapons, as is envisaged under our existing policy of flexible response.

There are, however, two drawbacks here that are directly related to the U.S. predicament. The first one is cost. The United States has relied on nuclear weapons to deter the Soviets for almost forty years because they are cheaper than conventional forces. Our European allies, who occassionally accuse us of being "nuclear mad," have chosen the same course for the same reason. They have the economic resources, manpower, and technological capability to match, if not exceed, the conventional capability of WTO—without U.S. help. They have not done so because large defense increases would ignite a firestorm of political protest in their countries. In an environment of economic austerity, voters in the democracies will resist efforts to modernize conventional forces, favoring reliance on cheaper, albeit more dangerous, nuclear weapons.

The second requirement for a conventional deterrent involves the availability of manpower with the education, skills, and discipline to operate modern weapon systems. The military, in private, makes no secret of the fact that it needs middle-class youngsters once provided by the draft. It is noteworthy that Martin Anderson, a Reagan brain-truster for years and the president's domestic affairs adviser in his first term, has been a leading opponent of the draft. He argues, as Reagan does, that the draft violates basic conservative principles, such as political liberty.[19] This laissez-faire approach to national security is further proof that 20th century conservatism is incapable of providing a philosophical or practical basis for our security requirements. Without a draft, development of a conventional Western deterrent is well-nigh impossible.

The United States must continue to devote a large portion of government revenues to national defense—even if arms control talks bear fruit. But, while making legitimate improvements in its armed forces, the United States must not feed Soviet paranoia by leading Gorbachev to believe that we intend to drive him to the wall. Like all bullies, the Soviets are especially sensitive about being bullied by someone else, and because their internal crises may cause them great anxiety, they may respond irrationally to real or perceived threats from abroad. Of course, military power cannot be divorced from East–West relations, and the Soviets must pay a price for a shift in the correlation of forces in much the same way that they thought we had to during the 1970s. Although, as Dimitri Simes reminds us, "having the Soviets on the defensive for a change feels good and opens new options for U.S. diplomacy," we must be careful less we forget that "insecure but still-powerful regimes" have the means to flex their military muscle and to engage in risky adventures.[20]

The Limits of U.S. Economic Power

Among U.S. hard-liners there is a propensity to overestimate both Soviet military might and the West's ability to wage economic warfare against the Soviet Union.

Richard Pipes has made the most comprehensive case for economic warfare against the USSR. He says that because the Soviet Union is in "the throes of a serious systemic crisis," the United States can compel Moscow to adopt far-reaching reforms. Soviet Russia, like tsarist Russia, is run by conservative leaders who only change things when they have no other recourse. "Changes for the better that one can expect in the nature of the Soviet government and in its conduct of foreign relations will come about only from failures, instabilities, and fears of collapse and not from growing confidence and sense of security."[21]

Pipes is confident that "the key to peace lies in an internal transformation of the Soviet system in the direction of economic decentralization, greater scope for contractual work and free enterprise, national self-determination, human rights and legality." Pipes concedes that "the obstacles to such reforms are formidable. The nomenklatura will resist changes as long as it can and that means, in effect, as long as it is able to compensate for internal failures with triumphs abroad."[22] Nonetheless, if resolute the United States can modify internal Soviet behavior by employing its economic and technological resources.

Pipes is too sanguine by far. It is against the nature of democratic/capitalistic countries to manipulate their abundance in a comprehensive campaign to modify internal Soviet behavior. Jimmy Carter imposed a grain embargo on the Soviets after they invaded Afghanistan, and while it caused Moscow some difficulty, it hardly crippled the Soviet economy. The Soviets purchased grain from other capitalist countries that were delighted to sell it to them. Reagan lifted the ban because it was politically unpopular in the farm states. It deflated farm profits at a time when agriculture prices were already low, and U.S. farmers protested loudly.

Although Reagan bowed to his farmers, he urged the Europeans not to cooperate with the Soviets in the construction of the Yamburg pipeline enabling them to sell Siberian gas and oil to Western European customers. Reagan said this would leave the Europeans open to blackmail in the event of another energy shortage and allow the Soviets to use their profits to sustain their military buildup. But the Europeans had good reasons to cooperate with the Soviets: they needed the jobs and profits associated with the massive construction project, they needed Soviet petroleum to reduce their dependency on OPEC, and they saw little difference between the U.S. sale of grain to the USSR and their sale of equipment to Moscow.

Washington was forced to give in on the pipeline, but the Pentagon has taken a hard line against selling high-tech equipment to the Soviet bloc. The allies have agreed to proscribe such sales, but they differ with the Americans over what constitutes "strategically relevant" equipment. U.S. high-tech firms, therefore, complain that they are being denied the opportunity to sell their products to the Soviet bloc while their foreign competitors are filling the orders. Our allies are not greedier than we are; their circumstances are different, however. Some European economies are not doing as well as our own, and the Japanese economy is more dependent upon exports than ours.

The bottom line is that the very factors accounting for the success of the free enterprise system—ingenuity, enterprise, and the quest for profits—prevent capitalist countries from using their economic prowess in a calculated, coordinated fashion in their competition with the Soviet bloc. Pipe's recommendation that we wage economic warfare against the Soviet Union may be based upon solid knowledge of Soviet society but a flimsy understanding of capitalism and U.S. society. If the democracies had the unity of purpose to use their awesome economic resources at the Soviet's expense, this would be a big plus for them. Unfortunately, they are incapable of doing so. Except under unique circumstances, there is little prospect that the West can wage economic warfare against the Eastern bloc.

U.S. policymakers must keep this in mind when considering how they can exploit U.S. economic and technological resources in the superpower rivalry. These can be exploited, but modestly—not as a powerful stick capable of beating the Soviets into submission, but as a carrot. For example the United States can engage Moscow in the commercial transactions it covets, in exchange for political concessions or acts of good faith, such as permitting greater autonomy on the part of the satellites or allowing more people to emigrate. We should neither provide capital nor know-how as a gesture of goodwill if we get nothing in return, nor bribe the Soviets with economic and technological lucre in the expectation that we can get them to make fundamental changes in their system. However, if occasions arise when expanded trade or technological transfers promote liberalization in the USSR, we must make the effort. Confrontationists have good reason to be cynical about gestures of goodwill making the Soviets more humane at home and tractable abroad. But the opportunity may arise when such gestures will help, although modestly, proponents of liberalization in the USSR, or may induce Moscow to cooperate with Washington in reducing conflict in a Third World nation. We should not assume, a priori, that past Soviet behavior will always be a guide to Moscow's future actions.

There may be times when the United States uses its economic resources as a stick—for example, when the Soviets engage in such behavior as the invasion of Afghanistan or the destruction of Solidarity. A unilateral action of this kind cannot gravely harm the Soviets, or force them to desist or take rectifying actions, however, in the short run, it may rile the waters for Moscow and embolden other countries to follow the U.S. example. Gorbachev has been manipulating the Western media to shape opinion in the European and Asian democracies, in the process becoming more vulnerable to a backlash from these sources.

The long-run consequences of U.S. displays of anger vis-à-vis commercial relations may have greater impact upon the Kremlin. The economic costs alone may be insufficient to deter the Soviets from engaging in aggressive behavior, but when considering these along with other costs—political, ideological, and so on—Moscow may decide it is imprudent to commit such acts.

In most instances, economic retaliation will be symbolic, but such measures are crucial to the health and welfare of our society. Among other things, they sustain cherished values unifying the nation, and enhance the self-esteem of the people, and secure respect from foreign observers, friends and enemies alike.

In assessing the relationship between economic developments and the superpower rivalry, two things are clear. First, at a time when they are reluctantly facing the limits of military power, factors other than martial prowess will play an increasing role in international security affairs. We should welcome the opportunity to compete with the USSR in the economic arena, because in this venue we enjoy a decided lead. Recall that the economic achievements of the capitalist countries are the primary reason for the apparent shift in the correlation of Third World forces in a direction favorable to the West.

Second, the ability of the United States to use economic leverage to influence Soviet behavior must be placed within a larger framework. We must integrate U.S. economic policy, along with political and military initiatives, into a global national security strategy. Our economic and technological capabilities are powerful weapons that we can bring to bear in defending our vital global interests. But they must be employed purposively and in a comprehensive and directed fashion, not on an ad hoc basis or only during crisis periods. This can be accomplished without mobilizing our society behind the kind of neomercantilist strategy that undermines political liberty and our free enterprise system. It would be an enormous undertaking to be sure, and we should not minimize the difficulties involved; but as we address the superpower rivalry on the Second Front, we must be prepared to assess our national security from nonmilitary perspectives that have not heretofore received the attention they deserve.

The U.S. Predicament and Arms Control

The arms control record to date is no cause for optimism. Since the Hot Line Agreement of 1963, many arms limitation accords have been signed, yet the superpowers have more nuclear weapons today than they had then. Even with a 50% reduction, they would still have enough weapons to devastate each other's society.

And time is not on the side of the arms controllers. The problem of verification will become more difficult as new weapons are deployed. Currently cruise missiles carry both nuclear and conventional warheads, and it is impossible to determine which without inspecting them. The deployment of smaller missiles with single warheads may foster greater strategic stability—because they make a first strike more difficult—but may also complicate the problem of verification. The Soviets have indicated that they may accept on-site inspection, but we have reason to be skeptical about this pledge.

It will be years before fears of a first strike subside, but the superpowers must continue arms control talks. Future prospects are even grimmer than existing ones. Harold Brown and Lynn Davis claim that without progress on arms control, "the resulting balance in 1990 would show each side with approximately 15,000 strategic nuclear weapons, or about 5,000 more than today." The United States would maintain its lead in strategic nuclear warheads, those on SLBMs and bombers, but "the Soviet Union would increase its advantage in missile throw-weight. . . . Each side would have sufficient warheads to threaten the other side's ICBMs, even in a mobile or some other alternative basing mode."[23] After years of heavy defense outlays, we would be no better off than when we started—perhaps worse off. William Perry says we are approaching the point where the accuracy of offensive missiles will be close to 100%.[24] Under these circumstances, will either side feel more secure?

The Russians will be tough negotiators even if they occasionally make unexpected concessions. Gorbachev will try to cut a deal that leaves Moscow with an edge and to exploit the talks to divide the West. The Brown/Davis scenario, however, cannot be ignored. The precarious nuclear balance dictates that we pursue arms control agreements with Moscow whatever the difficulties.

The impact of a new arms competition upon the U.S. economy is another incentive. Ours is larger than the Soviet economy, but the "crowding out" problem is a real one. And unlike Mr. Gorbachev, his U.S. counterpart must contend with free people who expect high living standards and are prepared to punish politicians who cannot provide them. Circumstances may develop in the future, moreover, where the Soviets are capable of maintaining their high level of defense spending while political opposition prevents U.S. leaders from doing so. The Gramm-Rudman-Hollings law has already contributed to such pressure.

In spite of many incentives for arms control negotiations, there is strong opposition to them in Washington. As Strobe Talbott documented in his *Deadly Gambits*, many defense analysts argue that U.S. security cannot be safeguarded though arms control treaties. They claim that the Soviets have cynically manipulated arms control talks to undercut support for the U.S. deterrent, in order to divide the Western allies and enhance their own military prospects at our expense. In this connection, Talbott mentions Richard Perle and Fred Iklé as two of the strongest advocates of this position in the Reagan administration.[25] They were not unhappy when the Soviets discontinued arms control negotiations late in 1983, as the Western allies began to deploy Pershing II and cruise missiles in Europe; they were not pleased with the Soviets' return to the negotiating table in 1985. But pressure both from the allies and within the United States prevented opponents of arms control in Washington from blocking the resumption of arms limitation talks and the Reagan–Gorbachev summit which took place in Geneva that year.

The anti-arms control faction within the Reagan administration, however, can take some comfort in, and, perhaps some credit for, the failure of the "pre-summit" which occurred in Reykjavik, Iceland, October 11–12, 1986. Soviet and American officials provide conflicting accounts of what happened at Reykjavik, but several facts are clear. According to Democratic Senator Albert Gore Jr.,

> during the fourth and final negotiating session, both sides, tentatively agreed to reduce all offensive strategic nuclear weapons by 50 percent over five years, and that President Reagan then formally offered to continue those reductions down to zero in a second five-year period for ballistic missiles only. That would have left each side with bombers and cruise missiles, both air- and sea-launched. There is no dispute that General Secretary Gorbachev rejected this offer and counterproposed that during the second five-year period we reduce all strategic nuclear weapons to zero.[26]

If the United States were to agree to this proposal, the Soviet Union would, according to the Pentagon, enjoy an advantage in conventional forces.

What was subsequently agreed to is the subject of dispute. Secretary Shultz said in Iceland that "all offensive strategic arms and ballistic missiles would be eliminated," but later remarked that it was "unclear" what weapons would be eliminated. The President told Senator Sam Nunn that the tentative agreement included all nuclear weapons, but afterwards administration officials denied this.[27]

The Soviets, meanwhile, "released direct quotes from President Reagan based upon their translator's notes that indicates he did agree tentatively to eliminate all nuclear weapons."[28] If true, did the President make this proposal out of ignorance, or did he do so because he believed Gorbachev would never accept it, and that he would score propaganda points for the United States?

To complicate matters further, Soviet and American officials disagreed on a range of other questions; for example, whether or not U.S. negotiators agreed to a freeze on INF weapons—U.S. cruise and Pershing II missiles and Soviet SS-20s—which would have left the USSR with an advantage in intermediate-ranged nuclear systems. This prospect is especially unnerving to NATO's European members.

Since it appeared that Gorbachev had agreed, prior to Reykjavik, to resolve the INF issue in a manner which would leave both sides with equivalent INF weapons, even if the SDI issue was unresolved, the Soviets must take blame for the pre-summit's failure, too. If the meeting had produced a limited breakthrough—that is, an INF agreement—it would have been a significant step forward toward the ultimate resolution of differences over heavy Soviet missiles on the one hand, a special concern of the United States, and SDI on the other one, a system which concerns the Soviet Union.

Meanwhile, arms control detractors have persisted in their opposition, charging that the Soviets have cheated in the past and will do so in the future. Specifically the Russians have violated provisions of the SALT I ABM treaty and the SALT II ban on building more than one new ICBM; consequently the United States is no longer bound by them. The ploy, however, that they hope will serve as the greatest barrier to fruitful arms control negotiations is "linkage." They contend that there can be no progress on arms control as long as the Soviets are threatening U.S. security in other venues.

Presidents Nixon, Ford, and Carter adhered to the principle that linkage should not be applied to the SALT process. It was in the nation's interest, they contended, to achieve an arms control accord with Moscow even if the Russians were misbehaving in other venues. Many arms control advocates support this position today, but it has been undermined over the past decade. Congress, and the public, first turned against SALT in the mid-1970s when the Soviet and Cuban presence in Africa escalated. Public opinion in opposition to SALT II was mounting prior to the Soviet invasion of Afghanistan, and that action clearly killed any prospect that the Senate would ratify the treaty.

The plain truth is that progress on arms control is unlikely as long as superpower relations are cool. Furthermore, acts of Soviet imperialism will stop the process altogether. For example, there will be a firestorm of protest if the Soviets use force to crush dissidents in Eastern Europe. Under these circumstances, it would be easy to muster the one-third-plus-one vote needed in the Senate to kill an arms control treaty.

Gorbachev can negotiate with the United States whatever the status of East–West relations; the same does not hold for his counterpart. If either one of the superpower leaders ignore this fact, there is little hope for arms control. In other words, an arms control breakthrough is nearly impossible without an overall improvement in U.S.–Soviet relations — in a word, détente.

The Prospects for Détente

The November evening in 1985 that President Reagan returned to Washington from Geneva and addressed Congress, Senator Jesse Helms was being "roasted" at the capital's Hyatt Regency Hotel. The conservative stalwarts — politicians, television preachers, and grass-roots activitists — who gathered in the hotel ballroom shared their feelings with reporters about the summit. They were mixed. All of them took comfort in the fact that, hoopla and hype aside, nothing substantive had transpired. Others, like Howard Phillips, lamented that the summit had created "an environment that could make the arms buildup more difficult." Still others groaned when the president revealed that he had invited Gorbachev to the United States the following year. When the cameras set upon George Shultz, Richard Viguerie whispered, "There's the real villain." Viguerie told liberal columnist Mary McGrory, "Conservatives feel he is soft on communism."[29]

Since SALT I, the Right's litmus test for determining "softness on communism" has been one's orientation toward détente — only "appeasers" or statesmen who have lost their nerve, such as Nixon and Kissinger, its U.S. architects, support it. Shultz, who was Nixon's treasury secretary, encouraged Reagan to respond favorably to Gorbachev's call for reaffirming détente. He "flunked" the conservatives' test!

As previously noted, one of the hard-liners' major criticisms of détente is that it allowed the Soviets to surpass us in nuclear firepower and, therefore, is responsible for the window of vulnerability. A second major complaint is that Moscow pledged cooperation in resolving conflicts in the LDCs — capable of precipitating a superpower clash — and promised not to seek unilateral gains in the Third World. However, during the Arab–Israeli "October War" of 1973, the Soviets violated the spirit and letter of détente when they failed to warn Washington about the Egyptian and Syrian attack, provided the Arabs assistance throughout the conflict and, on one occasion, even threatened military intervention if Israel moved against the Egyptian Third Army, which it had surrounded in the Sinai. Soviet incursions into black Africa and the invasion of Afghanistan in 1979 were further evidence that Moscow deemed détente a one-way street.

A third indictment of détente alleges that it has served as a "Potemkin village," masking the real and enduring differences separating the superpowers — human rights, political liberty, and intellectual freedom. These are the sources of the East–West rivalry, not nuclear weapons. Nuclear weapons are symptomatic of these conflicts. Failure to understand this accounts for the accommodationists' naive belief that tensions will fade with a reduction in nuclear weapons.

Defenders of détente must address these objections, which are the basis for widespread opposition to a significant thaw in U.S.–Soviet relations. We have treated the first, but the second and third need more attention.

Critics of détente, who complain that the Soviets have neither lived up to the letter nor the spirit of détente, overlook several observations. Nixon and Kissinger oversold détente to the American people, leading them to believe that the rivalry would grind to a halt with the signing of SALT I. But neither they nor the Soviets perceived détente as an end to the arms race; they saw it rather as a means to place the competition within a framework that would reduce the prospects of a superpower confrontation.

Brezhnev interpreted détente in terms of a change favorable to Moscow in the correlation of forces. Washington, he reasoned, had to treat the USSR as a superpower capable of wielding influence on a global basis. For years the United States had had a nuclear advantage and superior power-projection capabilities in the Third World. Consequently, it engaged in "nuclear blackmail" to prevent Moscow from helping progressive Third World movements. By Nixon's second term, however, the Americans no longer could intimidate Moscow. Henceforth, U.S. territory was threatened with the same kind of devastation that the Soviets had had to live with since the late 1940s. Now the Soviets would support "progressive" movements in the LDCs, in the same fashion in which Washington supported pro-Western governments there.

By proclaiming that the global balance of power had shifted in their direction, and by their deeds — Afghanistan, for example — the Soviets helped destroy the legitimacy of détente in the eyes of many Americans; however, they were still serious about avoiding confrontations in the LDCs that could embroil them with U.S. forces. Indeed it has been suggested that during the Yom Kippur War, the Soviet Union was unhappy with the Arabs' attack and tried to discourage its initiation. The USSR bowed to Arab demands for arms, however, because it feared losing face in the region if the arms were withheld. Moreover, publicity surrounding Brezhnev's threat to intervene overshadowed his cooperation with Nixon in trying to bring a quick ending to the hostilities.

Some scholars contend that if Kissinger had consulted with the Soviets about their intentions in Angola and had expressed U.S. concerns, the dispute might have been settled at the negotiating table and not been pursued on the battlefield. Here we see one of the pitfalls of détente in the 1970s: the failure of both sides to discuss their ideas about potential trouble spots on an ongoing basis.[30]

For his part, Nixon did not perceive détente as terminating America's rivalry with the Soviet Union. Months before the May 1972 summit in Moscow, he ordered the bombing of Hanoi and Haiphong, even though

Soviet ships were in the harbor of the latter. Kissinger, moreover, has publicly taken credit for squeezing the USSR out of the Middle East peace talks after the 1973 war. The Nixon administration perceived SALT I primarily as a device to slow down the Soviet nuclear buildup, while hoping the antidefense climate in the United States would soon change so that Washington could forge ahead with new nuclear weapons programs. Like the Soviets, then, the Americns adhered to the letter and spirit of détente when it was consistent with vital U.S. interests, and ignored it when those interests were perceived at risk.

In spite of détente's checkered record, the superpowers must improve their overall relations and strive, in particular, to negotiate a code of conflict that reduces U.S.–Soviet confrontations in the Third World. In working toward this end, U.S. policymakers must keep several things in mind:

First, where the Soviets do not encounter stiff resistance, they will fill power vacuums. However, as Henry Kissinger has stated, Moscow does not have a "master plan for world conquest."[31] And according to Bialer, the Politburo's Third World experts "do not hide their skepticism both about the degree of control which the Soviet Union possesses in such countries as Angola or Ethiopia and about the degree to which such control as they possess can endure."[32]

The point is not to dismiss the Soviet capacity to exploit unrest in the Third World but to place their capacity to do these things in perspective. The claim that the Soviets are behind most of the world's coups, civil wars, and border conflicts gives them greater credit than they deserve, and evokes inappropriate policy responses. The basis for most of the world's discord is historical and communal: Hindu versus Muslim in the Indian subcontinent, Chinese versus Vietnamese in Southeast Asia, Jew versus Arab in the Middle East, and black versus white in South Africa. Those hard-liners in the United States whose choose to see these regional conflicts in global terms are guilty of a serious intellectual error that must lead to flawed policies. For example, opposing the black resistance movement in South Africa because the African National Congress (ANC) has some communists in its ranks and Moscow has provided some support to the ANC. This posture threatens to alientate blacks and convince them that Moscow, and not Washington, supports their just cause.

Second, because political change is a given in the Third World, a critical question U.S. policymakers must address is, How do we treat the diversity of regimes that will replace the existing ones? Several answers come to mind. Robert Rothstein reminds us that instability may foster revolutionary rhetoric but not "very much revolution. There is no need to panic every time a corrupt and repressive regime is overthrown by 'revolutionaries.'"[33]

In addition, Donald Schultz has recommended, "We must be ready to support a wide range of regimes, from conservatives to Marxists from authoritarians to democrats—providing they can maintain some semblance of order and legitimacy and refrain from interfering in the internal affairs of their neighbors."[34] The United States should not turn its back on those LDCs controlled by Marxist regimes, even those aligned with the Soviet Union. We should get them to adopt postures that are Titoist in nature, and we should be careful lest our distaste for their social systems result in policies that push them into the arms of the USSR.

A caveat, however, is in order. Those governments that help promote Soviet hegemony and/or engage in free-lance military adventures on their own, such as the Cuban, Vietnamese, and Libyan, have chosen to become embroiled in the superpower competition. They have placed themselves in a position where, in effect, they are operating in a bipolar context, and they should be treated accordingly.

Third, the United States should engage the Soviet Union in discussions on the fundamental political issues that are most likely to lead to an international crisis. Surveys of the Soviet press indicate, for example, that "the Soviets are . . . worried about the Middle East—presumably not only as a result of overlapping security interests, but also [because] of the unpredictability and bellicosity of regional clients and the consequent possibility of being propelled into unsought confrontation."[35]

Defense analysts in Washington agree with Moscow's contention that the Middle East is the area where a direct U.S.–Soviet clash is most likely to occur. For over a decade, however, the United States, while seeking to stabilize the region, has excluded the Soviets from the peace process. This policy has been justified by citing several fears about welcoming the Soviets back into the process. All of them are irrelevant: they include the fear that Moscow will gain a foothold in the area (it already has one), the fear that the Soviets will disrupt the process (the Arabs and Israelis are capable of reaching a settlement even with Soviet disapproval), and, finally, the fear that U.S. strategic interests will be jeopardized (they are already in jeopardy, even though the Soviets have been kept out of the negotiations).

U.S. policymakers have reason to fear Soviet duplicity in the Middle East, but this is not sufficient reason to bar the Soviets from peace talks. Studies of Soviet behavior in the region indicate that the USSR has cooperated with the United States to prevent crises there. Also, the prospects of war with the Soviets override other vital U.S. interests in the area—indeed, the worst possible setback U.S. foreign policy could suffer would be war with the Soviet Union. This is not an argument in favor of appeasement; there may be instances where we have to resort to force to protect our vital interests. But with the exception of preventing the Soviets from wresting control of friendly countries in the area by military actions, there is no justification for the United States risking a U.S.–Soviet military conflict over disputes in the Middle East.

This is one part of the world where the superpowers must strive to achieve a formal crisis-prevention regime. It is large and complex, and there are many sources of conflict in the region—Arab–Israeli, Sunni–Shiite, Iraqi–Iranian, just to mention a few. Therefore, even if they collaborate, the superpowers cannot expect to achieve stability. Nonetheless, the risk of conflict, which one day may drive them to cross the nuclear threshold, is so great they must both make a concerted effort to avoid crises there. In spite of opposition from within the United States, from Israel, and from moderate Arab states, the U.S. government must reassess its policy of excluding the Soviet Union from Middle East negotiations.

The primary reason for breathing new life into détente is to avoid a nuclear war. Progress will be halting and irregular, not linear, but because the stakes are enormous, we must persist in the endeavor. A balance of terror has safeguarded the peace for over forty years, and the prospects of a nuclear war between the superpowers is remote, but if a war occurs, the outcome will be the most monstrous bloodletting in history. There is no rationale, then, whatever the provocation, for the superpowers to cease searching together for ways to minimize the risk of a nuclear exchange.

A secondary reason for achieving a thaw is that détente may allow us to modify Soviet behavior, albeit modestly. "Détente did open Soviet society to an unprecedented degree," Kaiser writes. "It pushed the Soviets for the first time into the international (capitalist) economic system. It made Solidarity possible in Poland."[36] Colton goes even further: "No one—certainly no one in Moscow with whom I have ever discussed the issue—doubts that an easing of international relations, and especially a thaw in relations with the U.S., would lighten the political task of moderate Soviet reformers."[37] We cannot expect to wield great influence, but we should not forego even the slightest opportunity to encourage liberalization in Soviet society, that is, to enhance the prospects of leaders who will rule by political authority at home while avoiding aggressive behavior abroad.

Détentists, however, cannot ignore the confrontationists' third criticism—that fundamental differences are the basis for the superpower rivalry, not nuclear arsenals. Statesmen who remind us of this unpleasant fact cannot be dismissed merely as cold warriors. One can question the propriety of a U.S. president publicly proclaiming that the Soviet Union is an "evil empire" that thrives on lying, cheating, and deceiving. There is ample cause to attack Reagan's approach to the USSR, his misguided quest for military superiority, his penchant to credit the USSR for most of the upheaval in the world, etc., but his "evil empire" remark is based on fact, not fiction. The USSR is the last authentic empire, one which rules a vast area of Europe and Asia, subjugating peoples from over 100 nations by brute force, lies, and deceit. Tens of thousands of people have been imprisoned, incarcerated in psychiatric hospitals, forced into exile, and murdered for actions that are not proscribed under Soviet law. Millions have had their human rights violated—even though Moscow is party to the UN Declaration on Human Rights and Basket Three of the Helsinki Agreement, which guarantees, among other things, the right to travel freely and emigrate.

The United States, of course, must take some blame for the Cold War and current East–West tensions. Raymond L. Garthoff urges us to look at the competition from the Soviet perspective to appreciate why they have cause to doubt our declarations of goodwill. The Soviets contend that since 1917, the United States has sought to destroy the USSR; indeed, U.S. troops were sent there in 1918 and 1919 to bring down the Bolshevik regime. During World War II politicians such as Senator Harry Truman of Missouri proclaimed that we should support the Soviets if it looked as if the Nazis were on the brink of victory and support the German forces if it appeared that the Soviets were about to win the war.[38]

William Appleman Williams and other revisionists argue that Washington's refusal to acknowledge legitimate Soviet security requirements in Eastern Europe and efforts to impose a global capitalist economic order on Moscow contributed to the Cold War.[39] Moreover, many political scientists claim that U.S. presidents, not their Soviet counterparts, have spurned efforts to resolve outstanding differences. Eisenhower refused to meet with Stalin's immediate successors and Reagan did not meet with Gorbachev until his fifth year in office.

These observations aside, the basis for U.S.–Soviet enmity rests on the fact that the USSR is an oppressive society, ruled by men who violate their own laws at home and resort to force to maintain their hegemony abroad. Stalin murdered tens of thousands of his comrades, and his policies were responsible for the deaths of millions of people. Only Hitler's campaign to rid Europe of Jews and other "subhumans" matches Stalin's crimes. To equate the mistakes and misdeeds of U.S. leaders with those of Stalin is a moral outrage.

Conditions have improved in the Soviet Union since Stalin's death, but his successors have given us little reason to be optimistic about the future. Khrushchev, Brezhnev, Andropov, and Chernenko avoided the same degree of systematic terror that was a hallmark of Stalin's rule, but their actions in Hungary, Czechoslovakia, Poland, and Afghanistan and their monstrous, repressive behavior within the USSR itself proved they were despots of the first order. And how can we forget that Mikhail Gorbachev's two most prominent mentors, Mikhail Suslov and Yuri Andropov, supported the bloodbath in Hungary, the first from his post at the Kremlin, the second from the Soviet embassy in Budapest, the same year that Khrushchev denounced "Stalin's crimes"?

The highly publicized release of Andrei Sakharov in December 1986, after he received a phone call from Gorbachev, has puzzled Western human rights observers. The significance of Sakharov's release will be treated in the concluding chapter, but it is noteworthy that in spite of his pledges for reform,

Gorbachev clearly does not include intellectual freedom, freedom of religion, or other fundamental human rights in this category.

On the basis of the Soviet record, the West has reason to believe that if the Soviets were to acquire a military edge and conclude that they could devastate the United States in a first strike without fear of retaliation, they might take the risk. At the very least, they would engage in a diplomacy of terror with the hope of emasculating the West's security, and they certainly would engage in adventures in the Third World beyond those to which they presently are party.

Because the Soviets have weapons of mass destruction, we must build weapon systems of comparable destructive power to deter them from attacking us or victimizing our allies. Possession of those unspeakable weapons undoubtedly contributes to East–West tensions, but they are symptoms of an even more intractable condition—concrete differences between free peoples and those who are subjects of a reactionary empire. Unless the Soviet leaders scrap their oppressive policies for ones consistent with an open and pluralistic society—even if they are only partial—many of the differences separating the superpowers will be irreconcilable. This is a bleak view of U.S.–Soviet relations, but unless Gorbachev makes a greater effort to rule by dint of political authority and not political power, this is the only conclusion that one can reach.

The list of Soviet crimes is long and well documented, so how can one account for the fact that so many honorable people who have spoken out against human rights violations in other countries have remained silent in the case of the USSR? The answer is simple. None of the other countries have the means to destroy the United States in a nuclear holocaust. In the face of the spectre of nuclear war, then, they deny that there are myriad, profound reasons for East–West tensions and choose to believe that the nuclear arsenals are the cause of the rivalry. Like the advocates of nuclear superiority, these people are looking for a quick fix. They are mistaken—there is no quick fix. We must continue to reside in a world that is indeed MAD. To deny the basis for this situation will neither make the world safer nor promote a resolution of the rivalry.

But commentators who cite these observations as reasons not to negotiate with the Soviets are avoiding reality also. Their skepticism is well founded, and their abhorrence of doing business with a reactionary regime that oppresses entire nations and violates its own laws understandable. Nonetheless, the prospect of a nuclear war compels us to negotiate with the Soviets. One thing we know is that they want a nuclear war no more than we do. To avoid one, we must talk to them and reach agreements that minimize the prospect of a confrontation of any kind. It is irresponsible and immoral not to do so.

Finally, we can take comfort in the fact that if the West can resolve its problems, time is working in its behalf. The Soviet system and empire may survive for several more decades, but there are political, economic, and socio-cultural forces that will eventually destroy them.

Notes

1. *New York Times*, 5 March 1981.
2. Michael Ledeen, *Grave New World* (New York: Oxford University Press, 1985), pp. 199–200.
3. Richard Pipes, *Survival is Not Enough: Soviet Relations and America's Future* (New York: Simon and Schuster, 1984), pp. 49–110.
4. Dimitri Simes, "The New Soviet Challenge," *Foreign Policy* 55 (Summer 1984): 126.
5. Seweryn Bialer, *Stalin's Successors* (New York: Cambridge University Press, 1981), p. 220.
6. Seweryn Bialer, "The Harsh Decade: Soviet Politics in the 1980s," *Foreign Affairs* 59 (Summer 1981): 1019–20.
7. *Washington Post*, 11 November 1980.
8. *Washington Post*, 28 December 1980.
9. Seweryn Bialer, "Cuba, the U.S. and the Central American Mess," *New York Review of Books*, 27 May 1982, p. 87.
10. Timothy J. Colton, *The Dilemma of Reform in the Soviet Union* (New York: Council on Foreign Relations, 1984), p. 87.
11. Georgi Arbatov, "On Soviet–American Relations," *International Studies Newsletter* May 1985, p. 3.
12. Robert Gates, "The Allocation of Resources in the Soviet Union and China in 1984," statement before the U.S. Joint Economic Committee (November 21, 1984), pp. 37–8.
13. *Washington Post*, 25 September 1984.
14. *Washington Post*, 27 June 1985.
15. *Washington Post*, 25 September 1984.
16. Daniel Patrick Moynihan, "Symposium," *Commentary*, November 1985, p. 67.
17. William J. Perry, "Technological Prospects," in Barry Blechman, ed., *Rethinking the U.S. Strategic Posture* (Cambridge, MA: Ballinger Publishing Co., 1982), p. 130.
18. James Schlesinger, "Rhetoric and Realities in the Star War Debate," *International Security* 10 (Summer 1985): 10.
19. Martin Anderson, ed., *Military Draft: Selected Readings on Conscription* (Palo Alto, CA: Hoover Institute Press, 1982).
20. Simes, "Soviet Challenge," p. 43.
21. Pipes, *Survival*, p. 263.
22. Pipes, *Survival*, p. 207.
23. Harold Brown and Lynn Davis, "Nuclear Arms Control: Where Do We Stand?," *Foreign Affairs* 62 (Summer 1984): 1147.
24. Perry, "Technological Prospects," pp. 130–1.
25. Strobe Talbott, *Deadly Gambits* (New York: Alfred Knopf, 1984).
26. Albert Gore Jr., "Stability For Two," *The New Republic* (November 17, 1986), pp. 19–20.
27. Gore, "Stability For Two," p. 20.
28. Gore, "Stability For Two," p. 20.

29. *Washington Post*, 11 November 1985.
30. Larry C. Napper, "The African Terrain and U.S.–Soviet Conflict in Angola and Rhodesia," in Alexander George, ed., *Managing U.S.–Soviet Rivalry* (Boulder, CO: Westview Press, 1983), pp. 155–85.
31. Henry Kissinger, *Years of Upheaval* (Boston: Little, Brown & Co., 1981), p. 15.
32. Bialer, *Stalin's Successors*, p. 277.
33. Robert Rothstein, *The Third World and U.S. Foreign Policy* (Boulder, CO: Westview Press, 1982), p. 55.
34. Donald Schultz, "The Strategy of Conflict and the Politics of Counterproductivity," *Orbis* 25 (Fall 1981): 52.
35. S. N. MacFarlane, "The Soviet Conception of Regional Security," unpublished paper, p. 12.
36. *Washington Post*, 14 November 1982.
37. Colton, *The Dilemma of Reform*, p. 87.
38. Raymond L. Garthoff, *Detente and Confrontation* (Washington: The Brookings Institutions, 1985).
39. William A. Williams, *The Tragedy of American Diplomacy* (New York: Dell Publishing Co., 1972).

Global Economic Disorder and the American Predicament

I believe in the free market, but I am a pragmatist. Reality dictates that something more than the free market is going to be necessary in a crisis.
—Congressman Mike Synar

Declining U.S. Hegemony

The United States emerged from World War II as the premier global power. By 1947 the spectre of another Great Depression, which had haunted U.S. leaders during the war, had faded. The economy was operating near full capacity, and like a powerful locomotive it pulled the economies of Europe and Japan from the rubble of the war. With the exception of the Soviet empire, U.S. political power was felt everywhere. The void that the Europeans had left in the Third World was filled by the United States, which gave birth to new governments and toppled old ones in Asia, Africa, and Latin America. Although the United States dismantled its military machine, it enjoyed a nuclear monopoly, which compensated for the Soviet Union's massive conventional forces.

Without diminishing the importance of the U.S. deterrent, the global economic order the United States established provided a firm underpinning for Western security. The threat of communism, in turn, played a pivotal role in forging unity. It established the basis for multilateral cooperation that was unique in history.

Robert O. Keohane has observed that the U.S. international economic order rested on three interrelated regimes:

1. A stable international monetary system, designed to facilitate liberal international trade and payments. This implied that the United States would manage the monetary system in a responsible way, providing sufficient but not excessive international liquidity.
2. Provision of open markets for goods. The United States actively worked to reduce tariffs and took the lead in pressing for the removal of discriminatory restrictions, although it tolerated regional discrimination by European countries and permitted the Europeans to maintain temporary postwar barriers during the period of dollar shortage.
3. Access to oil at stable prices. The United States, and American companies, provided oil to Europe and Japan from the Middle East where U.S. oil corporations held sway, and in emergencies such as 1956–57, from the United States itself.[1]

The international monetary regime evolved from the Bretton Woods Agreement of 1944, which established the International Monetary Fund and the International Bank for Reconstruction and Development, better known as the World Bank. The representatives of forty-four nations who met at the New Hampshire estate were convinced that "economic nationalism—competitive exchange rate devaluations, formation of competing monetary blocs, and the absence of international cooperation—had contributed greatly to economic breakdown, domestic political instability, and international war."[2] The goal of Bretton Woods, therefore, was to stabilize the international political order through economic growth and thereby avoid another war.

Classical economic theorists, however, were unhappy with the agreement because it postulated that the free market was incapable of achieving international monetary stability. Henceforth the responsibility of managing the international monetary system rested with several governments operating through multilateral institutions. Because these economists represented a minority view, their objections went unheeded.

But the Bretton Woods Agreement did not guarantee economic revitalization. By 1947 it was apparent that the Western Europeans could not generate sufficient capital on their own. They would need a massive injection of dollars to revitalize their economies. This knowledge prompted the Truman administration to promulgate the Marshall Plan. Congress initially balked at the president's request, but he overcame resistance on Capitol Hill by skillfully exploiting fears then rampant in Washington about Stalin's aggressive policies. Also, many observers feared that economic chaos would allow communists to gain power in Western Europe through free elections, especially in France and Italy, where they typically have garnered 25% to 30% of the vote.

Within a decade the Bretton Woods monetary system began to operate as it was meant to. "European currencies became formally convertible into dollars, and the IMF became the central international organization in a par-value international monetary regime." Of critical importance, "the dollar was linked to gold at a fixed price of $35 per ounce, and the currencies of other countries" associated with the regime were "pegged to the dollar at fixed rates of exchange."[3]

The free-trade regime that would parallel its monetary counterpart was originally postulated on the formation of an International Trade Organization, or ITO. But Congress, under pressure from the business community, rejected it. Conservatives were put off by provisions calling for economic planning and state-regulated trade, which would be managed by the ITO. The instrument that was designed as a provisional device until the ITO was established—the General Agreement on Tariffs and Trade (GATT)—eventually became a permanent one, and provided the rules for a free-trade system. "GATT reflected the prevailing agreement on free trade: the economic consensus that open trade would allow countries to specialize according to their comparative advantage and thereby achieve higher levels of growth and well-being, and the political consensus that a liberal trading regime would promote not only prosperity but also peace."[4] Over time, the principles of nondiscrimination, liberalization, and reciprocity were expanded through the Kennedy round of discussions, which was completed in 1967, and the Tokyo round, which ended in 1979.

In the case of oil, "the United States had so many resources—economic, political, and military—that it was able to attain its essential objectives even without a formal multilateral regime." Unlike money and trade, these "arrangements were less explicit and less comprehensive, since the rules and practices had not been agreed upon at international conferences but had been constructed largely by the major oil companies, supported by the U.S. and Britain and acquiesced in . . . by the still weak producing countries."[5] The availability of abundant, inexpensive petroleum contributed enormously to the success of U.S. economic hegemony.

Today, the global economic order is in disarray. The Bretton Woods Agreement has been scrapped, Third World debt threatens the economic viability of many major LDCs on the one hand and the financial community in the developed countries on the other, and an overvalued dollar, in the first half of the 1980s, precipitated a major import/export imbalance for the United States. Protectionism is on the rise, and fears of bitter economic warfare promulgating disunity in the Alliance are well founded. With the collapse of the OPEC oil regime, which replaced the U.S. regime in the 1970s, news on the energy front is good, but disagreement within the ranks of the democracies over an acceptable response to a third shock is cause for concern.

The Death of Bretton Woods

Joan Edelman Spero writes, "August 15, 1971 marked the end of the Bretton Woods period, and the history of the international monetary system since that date has been one of attempts to reimpose an order on the system."[6] On that day, President Nixon, faced with the spectre of stagflation, announced his New Economic Policy (NEP), which had a profound impact on the global monetary system: henceforth, the dollar no longer could be converted into gold. Although the industrial democracies made an effort later that year to stabilize the monetary system through the Smithsonian Agreement, they had only partial and short-lived success. By March 1973, all major currencies were floating, and the market was left to manage the international monetary system.

A number of developments presaged the system's collapse. A decade before Nixon's NEP, the flow of capital was facilitated globally by the return of Western European and Japanese currencies to convertibility, by the proliferation of Eurodollars, by the massive flow of capital held by multinational banks and corporations, and by inflationary conditions associated with the Vietnam War. As the Europeans and Japanese flexed their economic muscles, they became dissatisfied "with the privileged role of the dollar as the international currency."[7] Washington, in effect, was determining the direction of their domestic policies. The ire of America's allies grew apace with détente, as improved East–West relations undercut Western solidarity on monetary matters.

In 1972 the Committee on Reform of the International Monetary System and Related Issues was established within the IMF. What was to become known as the Committee of Twenty agreed upon the general principles of reform, but it failed to translate them into concrete measures. Meanwhile, "the system of fixed exchange rates collapsed, and the float began. Double-digit inflation erupted.... The boom of the 1970s created commodity shortages that reinforced the inflationary trends already in progress." The price of commodities would plunge later in the decade, but these developments underscored a bitter truth: "global inflation demonstrated that in an interdependent system, management depended on the coordination of economic policies heretofore considered strictly national prerogatives."[8]

The first petroleum shock of 1973 to 1974, which precipitated a fourfold increase in the price of crude oil, exacerbated the monetary crisis and produced a further one—massive Third World debt. Banks were inactive in the LDCs until the late 1960s, when economic activity began to lag in the advanced countries and to surge in the Newly Industrialized Countries, or NICs. After the first oil shock, the flood of petrodollars enabled the banks to dramatically increase their loans to the LDCs. Here, many analysts reasoned, was the answer to the petrodollar problem that was wreaking havoc with the international financial system. Moreover, flush with borrowed cash, the LDCs were purchasing goods from the advanced countries, thereby softening the impact of the oil shock.

But the second shock of 1979 forced the industrialized countries to curtail their purchases of commodities from the LDCs. Simultaneously, the Third World economies were whiplashed by soaring energy prices. To make matters worse, as interest rates took off, the problem of serving their debts grew enormously. From 1978 to 1981, for example, the debt service of the LDCs rose by more than 70%, primarily because of rising interest rates. Nonetheless, they continued to look for more loans, and the banks eagerly complied with their requests.

In August 1982 the Mexicans "initiated" the debt crisis when they announced they were unable to service their debt. By the end of the year, Mexico was joined by Argentina, Brazil, Chile, and Venezuela, which along with Mexico had collectively run up loans exceeding $250 billion. Overcoming its ideological predilections against intervention, the Reagan administration took the lead and provided a $2 billion emergency loan and induced the IMF to provide the Third World debtors with new funds. The IMF, in turn, pressured private lenders to do the same. Two years later analysts were claiming that Third World debt was under control—all the major debtors had to do was to follow Mexico's example and adopt a policy of austerity. But the leaders of Argentina, Brazil, and Peru balked. If they adopted draconian policies, they risked fomenting revolution in their countries. If they had to choose between reneging on their debts or political upheaval, they would choose the former.

Today the debt crisis is depressing global economic activity. In spite of efforts on the part of the U.S. government, the IMF, and private banks to rescue the indebted LDCs, the debt of the Latin American countries has risen, not diminished. In large part this is because the political leaders fear social upheaval and political discord should they force further belt-tightening measures on their people. Leaders in the United States, Europe, and Japan deem this justification for avoiding stringent fiscal policies unacceptable, but their behavior is deserving of criticism, too. Their failure to prevent the disintegration of the global trade regime is a case in point.

Protectionism

In 1985, protectionist sentiment in the United States took a dramatic leap forward. The Senate voted 92 to 0 to allow the president to retaliate against Japan's allegedly unfair trade practices. The House, meanwhile, was considering 300 bills designed to retaliate against countries that discriminated against U.S. goods. The bills' supporters claimed that America's trading partners were primarily responsible for the need for bills. The European Community, they said, had been discriminating against U.S. products for years—for example, through its Common Agriculture Policy, the EC blocked U.S. products while subsidizing those of their less efficient farmers, and these subsidies had created huge food surpluses in the United States. As a consequence, the Europeans were violating the principle of comparative advantage, and it was hurting U.S. farmers. Prior to the adoption of their Common Agricultural Policy—for example, during the period 1965–1966—the United States exported $708 million worth of grain and rice to the EC; but from 1969 to 1970, after its adoption, U.S. export of these commodities slumped to $325 billion.[9]

The Europeans also have protected their economies through nontariff barriers (NTBs). A primary example here is the national industrial policies that exist in many of their countries—for example, government assistance to private steel and shipbuilding firms. Consequently, although Margaret Thatcher has proclaimed herself an advocate of supply-side economics, she has subsidized British steel enterprises to hold down unemployment. As a result, U.S. companies have discovered that they are incapable of competing with the British Steel being dumped on our shores at prices below U.S. production costs.

Japan, however, has been singled out by Congress as the greatest practitioner of protectionism and the most serious threat to U.S. high-tech products. The American people are convinced that the Japanese have been engaging in a multiplicity of unfair trade practices. How else can one explain that in 1985, when the worst U.S. trade deficit ever was announced—$148 billion—Japan accounted for one-third of that figure—$49.7 billion.[10]

In the early years after World War II, the United States encouraged the Japanese to discriminate against U.S. imports, to help them revive their economy. By the late 1960s Japan was the world's third largest economy, yet it "remained highly protectionist. Quantitative restrictions remained on many items, including infant industries such as computers, heavy electronic generators, large heavy machinery, and automobiles."[11] Japan continued to undervalue its yen in order to enhance its exports, and with government assistance U.S.-dominated markets were identified and targeted. One of the first great successes of this business–government partnership was Japan's impressive gains in the sale of cars. In 1968 the United States produced approximately 48% of the world's automobiles, the Japanese 2.6%. By the time Ronald Reagan was sworn into his first term in 1981, the U.S. share had fallen to 25% and the Japanese share had soared to 28%. The fact that Japan is now the world's largest producer of cars represents a blow to American pride and self-esteem, and the psychological pain Americans feel is as politically important as their economic loss.

During the 1984 campaign Walter Mondale courted voters whose jobs, businesses, and communities were endangered because other countries—the

Japanese in particular—"were not playing by the rules." Americans were angered with Japanese representives who, when pressed on their country's failure to buy U.S. agricultural products, responded that if Japan did so, "Japanese farmers could be ruined," yet were indifferent to the plight of U.S. auto workers and communities being ravaged by Japanese auto imports.

While Japanese goods were allowed to penetrate our rich market, U.S. products confronted stiff protectionist hurdles, especially when they were equal or superior to those of their Japanese competitors. In 1984, for example, "Japanese telephone equipment sales in the United States totaled more than $2 billion . . . compared with Japanese purchases of $195 million in comparable U.S. equipment."[12] AT&T's divestiture accounted, in part, for this imbalance, but Japanese protectionist policies also contributed to it.

Mondale's attempt to exploit widespread discontent about these matters failed because of Reagan's appeal, the economic recovery, and the country's upbeat mood. In the future, however, if the U.S. suffers a recession equaling that of the 1980–1982 setback, the American people—fearing a protracted crisis and blaming it on "unfair" foreign competition—will seek revenge. Strident nationalistic impulses will be bolstered by economic decline, and a mass populist movement will be waiting for a leader to forge it into a powerful political weapon. One can envisage auto workers from Detroit who manned phone banks for Mondale and ranchers from Texas who helped bankroll Reagan's campaign locking arms in a backlash against the "alien threat." Editorials will declare that "if we are going to avoid a second Pearl Harbor, we must get tough and teach those Japs a lesson." In this connection, a corporativist strategy may become one of our major pedagogical tools. Kevin Phillips speaks for many in the business community when he recommends:

> We need to assert our national self-interest. The government must play a more active role in promoting U.S. exports—running interference for companies that are blocked from selling their products in other countries, matching the subsidies that other nations routinely give to their export industries, cutting away regulatory red tape and getting tough with other governments that steal our patents and ideas.[13]

To European and Japanese analysts, the Americans have no right to play the role of injured party, for they have conveniently ignored U.S. protectionist practices. In addition to the outright adoption of discriminatory legislation, the most effective U.S. protectionist instrument has been "voluntary export restraints" (VERs). Here is how VERs work. Washington, through allegedly noncoercive negotiations, induces one of its trading partners to voluntarily limit exports with which U.S. products are noncompetitive, such as Japanese cars. Since direct measures are not taken against Toyotas, Nissans, and such, this action is not a de jure violation of free-trade principles. But, of course, it is a de facto violation because it is not truly voluntary. If Japan refuses to comply, it faces de jure measures denying its products access to the world's richest market.

The U.S. business community's position is that even if one concedes the merit of these charges, the United States is still less protectionist than its major trading partners. Also, the U.S. has helped keep those partners' economies humming by pressing the fiscal accelerator when, fearing inflation, they were reluctant to do so. From 1982 to 1984, for example, the U.S. economy ran a deficit that cost the United States 4 million jobs; in 1984, 20% of every dollar spent in the United States went to imports.[14] Moreover, this does not take into account the U.S. defense burden. To charge, as the Japanese do, that the U.S. trade deficit is a byproduct of poor management and high wages and to ignore the harmful effect of defense outlays is a convenient form of myopia.

One thing is apparent. The American people believe they are suffering more from protectionist practices than the allies are. In the United States, 69% of the people believe that foreign trade is costing U.S. jobs, 70% say it is a good idea to limit imports, and 60% assert that it is a good idea even if it means reduced product choices for them. Turning to the U.S.–Japanese trade gap, 60% attribute it to Japan discriminating against American goods, and 78% link it to lower pay scales in Japan—that is, the Japanese are underselling us because they deny their workers a decent wage.[15]

This brief discussion of the collapsing monetary and trade systems leads us to an important conclusion. It is imperative that the democracies adopt multilateral policies to revitalize the global monetary and trade regimes. If they fail, their security will be placed at grave risk, and the LDCs will be at even greater risk. Unfortunately, looking at their inept and unruly response to the oil shocks, we cannot be optimistic about their capacity to display the foresight and political will to achieve this objective.

Coping with a Third Oil Crunch

The oil shocks of the 1970s signified the collapse of the U.S.-dominated oil regime. In its stead a new one monopolized by OPEC emerged. But the cartel's success in driving up oil prices led to energy conservation, exploration for new oil, transfers to other sources of energy, and most important of all, a global recession. This combination of developments led to OPEC's collapse by the mid-1980s. One may ask, therefore, why discuss the oil regime at all since the market has reasserted its control over this vital commodity? The answer is twofold.

A third oil shock could occur in the near future, sometime in the early 1990s. A number of factors could produce one—a strong and enduring global economic recovery, dwindling oil reserves, wars, or accidents that could cut off supplies, to mention several of the most plausible ones.

There are compelling reasons, then, for the United States to join other oil-importing countries in minimizing the damage of a future shock. First, our allies remain dependent upon foreign oil. Another shock would harm them and eventually cause a contraction in our own economy. Second, an energy shock would do the LDCs grave economic damage and foster political upheaval of disastrous proportions, including coups d'état, civil wars, and revolution. U.S. economic and strategic interests in the Third World would both suffer. Finally, a price spike following a constricted oil inventory would have an inflationary impact upon our country. High oil prices affect the overall price of energy, whatever form it takes. Inflation would set in motion a series of economic disruptions—high interest rates, declining consumer demand, etc.—that would deal the U.S. economy a serious blow.

The other reason for looking at the vagaries of the oil regimes is that the democracies did not do well in responding quickly and decisively to the previous energy shocks. A third crisis, or similar international economic disruption, therefore, may have a devastating impact on their societies.

Henry Kissinger, in *Years of Upheaval*, writes: "The hesitant reaction of the consuming nations [after the Arab embargo] compounded their difficulties. Their reluctance to cooperate with one another perpetuated their vulnerability, virtually guaranteeing a permanent crisis." Kissinger chastises French president Georges Pompidou in particular for trying to sabotage a unified approach to the crisis. But "no European government took up our offer of private exchanges on energy cooperation. [Moreover,] the European nations refused to share oil supplies even with their embargoed partner, the Netherlands, for fear that the producers might in retaliation extend the embargo to them."[16]

In spite of French resistance, the twenty-one oil-consuming countries formed the International Energy Agency after the 1974 crisis. IEA made plans to deploy an emergency scheme to reduce the harm done to the organization's membership in the event of another crisis and tested the system on several occasions. The first time was under the Reagan administration in the summer of 1983, and the results were disturbing. That exercise assumed a curtailment in Persian Gulf petroleum output that threatened IEA's members. (This was at a time when OPEC still appeared to have the capacity to operate as an effective cartel, and government spokespersons publicly expressed concern about a third shortfall.) The administration, however, refused to cooperate; rather than circumvent the free market, it "allowed" the market to cope with the crisis. Although this meant the price of crude oil jumped from $28.63 a barrel to $98 a barrel, Assistant Energy Secretary William A. Vaughan characterized the test as "a significant achievement," and he said, "It reaffirms the validity of President Reagan's market-based approach to energy emergency preparedness."[17]

State officials who participated in the exercise disagreed. The Vermont State

Energy Office asserted: "The administration's refusal to deviate from its allocation-by-price scenario transformed the petroleum crisis into an economic disaster. . . ." A Florida official said much the same thing. A Dutch spokesperson, meanwhile, expressed the consensus of IEA foreign members:

> The whole idea behind the IEA is to keep emergencies from resulting in vastly higher prices. This can't work if the other 20 countries are trying to restrain demand and hold down prices and the United States allows the price to go through the ceiling.[18]

The Reagan administration came under heavy fire from critics on Capitol Hill. Under questioning from Congressman Mike Synar of Oklahoma, chairman of the House Government Operations Subcommittee, Vaughan defended the administration's reliance on the market. He said industry and farm cooperatives, among other groups, should purchase and stockpile crude oil in anticipation of an emergency: "We believe that is the kind of rely-on-yourself, prepare-for-emergencies-yourself that makes sense rather than looking to Uncle Sam to solve your problems." Congressman Synar's comments on the test were brief and to the point. "I believe in the free market, but I am a pragmatist. Reality dictates that something more than the free market is going to be necessary in a crisis."[19]

At that time, representatives of the oil industry said that the president would cooperate with the IEA if a real crisis struck—even if that meant circumventing the free market. But we cannot take comfort in such an observation. Multilateral policies must be in place prior to any crisis, if they are going to protect the consuming countries from serious economic harm and political discord.

Global Depression and International Political Discord

A global economic depression is more likely to materialize than the nuclear war we have spent vast sums to avoid. If an economic crisis occurs, it will precipitate serious political upheaval and regional conflict worldwide.

Political Turmoil in Western Europe

Few governments will survive, the prospects of extremists will escalate, and a sulphuric political climate in the European Community will preclude the level of cooperation needed to resolve the crisis. Democracy may not endure in countries that recently have cast off authoritarianism—Spain, Portugal, and Greece—and age-old enmities may spark new conflicts, such as a war between Turkey and Greece over Cyprus.

The Collapse of Democracy in Japan

There has been a synergistic relationship between political and economic growth in Japan, and there is reason to fear that democracy will not survive a major economic crisis there. A deep and prolonged depression will subject it to monumental social upheaval, and under immense pressures, existing inequities will transform Japanese society into a cauldron of political turmoil. Desperately seeking social order, Japan may return to traditional forms of authoritarian rule.

Upheaval in the Third World

People who have experienced economic prosperity become politically volatile when they are forced to accept lower living standards than those to which they have become accustomed. Therefore, we must be pessimistic about the prospects of the NICs that have made great economic progress over the past decade—South Korea, Brazil, Singapore, etc. The crisis will sabotage the Aquino government's attempt to bring democracy and prosperity to the Philippines, and while India may ride out this storm as it has previous ones, its sibling, Pakistan, is more vulnerable, as are other countries in Asia.

It is doubtful that the oil-rich but politically unstable Persian Gulf states will survive. Some of the countries in the region will resort to aggression to compensate for internal problems or take the opportunity to even the score with traditional foes. In this climate, the prospects rise for another Arab–Israeli war.

Closer to home, internal war will break out in many parts of South America, including major countries such as Brazil, Argentina, and Chile, not just the smaller nations in Central America. Mexico will experience widespread political and social strife, and a Marxist-style revolution will overwhelm its conservative government.

Sino–Soviet Rapprochement

Under Deng Xiaoping, China has developed close ties with capitalist powers in the belief that the PRC's economic development is inextricably wedded to growth in the Occident. With a Western crash, Chinese confidence in capitalist economic prowess will collapse, the pragmatists in Beijing will lose face, and the PRC will move closer to Moscow as the new Chinese leaders reaffirm their faith in Marxism–Leninism.

A Protectionist/Isolationist Backlash in the United States

An international economic crisis will fuel both protectionist and isolationist sentiment in the United States. An economic slump will increase dissatisfaction with the huge U.S. defense burden in particular. This possibility is elaborated further below.

After the 1985 Labor Day recess, Republicans and Democrats alike returned to Washington reporting that their constituents were angry over foreign economic competition. Across the country, jobs were being lost, profits were plunging, farms were being foreclosed, and entire communities were being ravaged by an influx of foreign goods and shrinking U.S. exports. The Japanese were singled out for special criticism, and there clearly was a racial aspect to this phenomenon. How else, Bernard K. Gordon observed, can one explain the fact that in 1984, when Japan-bashing came back into vogue, the United States was importing more from Canada ($67 billion) than from Japan ($60.4 million)?[20]

The Japanese have helped fuel sentiment against them, of course, by limiting access of U.S. agricultural products to their market even when they are much cheaper than Japanese equivalents (for example, citrus and beef products). Even worse, they have refused to import U.S. high-tech products superior to Japanese alternatives, such as Cray supercomputers. Also, many Americans believe that Japanese economic hegemony is a more palpable threat to their security than Soviet missiles: We have an answer to the Soviet military menace, but not to the economic one emanating from Japan. Statements from Tokyo belittling U.S. economic prowess—for example, assertions that "the U.S. has lost the economic race and should get out of Japan's way"—do not sit well with Americans whose self-esteem has been badly bruised by having lost their jobs to Japanese competition.

Whatever the relations between the United States and its allies, pressures to reduce defense spending will rise in Washington as the economy falters. Secretary of Defense Weinberger denies that there is a negative correlation between defense spending and economic growth, but most analysts outside the administration disagree with him. Wall Street researchers have found that "high levels of defense spending correlate with low economic growth for the seven advanced industrial states." Indeed, "military spending diverts the resources and distorts their allocation, thereby hindering growth and contributing to inflation." Furthermore, the Council on Economic Priorities found that "among advanced industrial states in the 1970s, economic growth, growth in productivity, and gross domestic fixed-capital formation were strongly and negatively associated with military spending."[21] Today on Main Street and Wall Street alike there is a consensus that the United States must dramatically reduce the defense budget if the country is going to avoid a serious economic crisis. Sentiments of this kind, not Soviet pressure, represent the greatest threat to SDI.

Economic austerity will heighten pressures to reduce foreign commitments and, in some instances, forge alliances between supporters and opponents of Ronald Reagan's interventionist policies. Christopher Layne, who rejects the Reagan Doctrine as a "quixotic" overextension of U.S. power, notes that Washington's influence has diminished in relationship to growing European and Japanese economic might, "yet the distribution of military responsibilities in Western Europe and Japan still reflects the conditions of 40 years ago." Approximately 56% of the U.S. defense budget is devoted to NATO, while "Japan, the world's second-ranking economic power, spends a mere 1% of its GNP on defense and depends completely on the United States for its security."[22] Layne contends that "deficits and strategic overextension really are two sides of the same coin. Taken together, they indicate that America's aspirations at home and abroad have outstripped its ability—or willingness—to pay for them."[22]

Neoconservatives such as Irving Kristol, who applaud Reagan's interventionist policies nonetheless agree with Layne that America's presence in Europe should be reduced. In this decade, they note, we have been maintaining over 300,000 troops in Europe at a cost exceeding $150 billion annually. But Europe has the manpower, the economic base, and the technology to match the Warsaw Pact in either conventional or nuclear forces. It does not need U.S. assistance of any kind. Why, many interventionists ask, should we continue to bear this burden when Europe refuses to join us in containing communism in parts of the Third World vital to U.S. interests, such as Asia and Latin America?

In face of the scapegoating that an economic crisis will provoke, the allies will defer decisions on controversial defense and arms control policies. They may even have a falling out over a common approach to the Soviet military threat. In this climate, the Japan–NATO alliance will become a hollow shell: each country seeking unilateral solutions to its problems, none prepared to make the sacrifices necessary to rectify the alliance's drift toward self-destruction.

At the same time, the security of the United States will suffer another devastating blow. It is quite likely that a global economic calamity will transform the American predicament into a societal crisis approaching that threatening the USSR. Fortunately, this grim prospect can be avoided, but it will involve extensive U.S. intervention in global economic affairs and unparalleled cooperation on the part of the allies.

Averting a Global Economic Crisis

In *A Grand Strategy for the West*, Helmut Schmidt, the former West German chancellor, writes: "If the world is to be kept in overall economic, social and military equilibrium, the West needs internal cohesion in its European, North American and Japanese alliance." Above all, "the West needs a coherent concept of its own economic development."[24] No such concept exists. It is a vital national security priority that this situation be rectified.

What is needed is a global economic regime akin to that which produced a quarter century of economic growth after World War II. Toward this end, three objectives must be accomplished:

Monetary Stability

Steps must be taken to achieve the stability that the Bretton Woods Agreement produced. Politically, it may be impossible to achieve a comprehensive system, but a partial one that involves the world's major currencies will be sufficient. Since the mid-1980s, the Group of Five—West Germany, France, Japan, the United States, and the United Kingdom—have demonstrated that they can bring order to the global monetary system and have the capacity to resolve the Third World debt. In the fall of 1985 the Plaza Agreement, initiated by Treasury Secretary James Baker, led to a devaluation of the dollar. The next January in London the Group reduced interest rates to ameliorate the burden of Third World debt, and another Baker initiative, first announced in Korea in 1985, materialized in 1986 when the U.S. Treasury and multilateral lending institutions provided Mexico with a multibillion dollar rescue plan.

These actions prompted Washington observers to conclude that the pragmatists in the White House, who had been arguing for intervention, had won the day. This conclusion may have been premature, but Baker's initiatives clearly bolstered the claim that the Group of Five can sustain a monetary system that fosters growth and stability.

A Free Trading System

Ideally we should strive for a multilateral system governed by the most-favored-nation and non-discrimination principles. Practically we may have to settle for a system in which multilateralism covers most trade, but bilateral and regional agreements (some that violate free trade principles) thrive as well. The British political economist Susan Strange says too much has been made of the international economy's difficulties: "Trade experience in the early 1980s tells us that protectionism in fact poses no great threat" to the global economy. She states that bilateral arrangements involving "governments or governments and multinational companies have kept world trade expanding in spite of protectionism. . . . world trade fell only in 1982, after nearly a decade of mounting protectionism, and by 1 percent, a trivial amount compared with the 28 percent fall in world trade in 1926–35."[25] Like many economists, she believes that if the international monetary system can be put right, we need not worry about the status of free trade.

Stable Oil Prices

The best economic news of the 1980s was the plunge in oil prices and OPEC's inability to prevent this windfall to the oil-consuming countries. The U.S. economy's 1986 performance would have been truly dreadful without it. With a plunge in energy costs, interest rates fell, and housing and auto sales soared in the first quarter. The present glut buys us time to develop policies to overcome a future price spike or shortfall in oil. We must exploit it because inflated petroleum prices and the revitalization of OPEC may not be many years ahead of us.

The prospect that OPEC will reemerge as a powerful global economic force is just one of many barriers to multilateral cooperation. There are numerous other barriers, of course:

- The economic health of the "summit seven" countries, (Japan, France, Italy, West Germany, Canada, and the United States) depends on growth in the rest of the world, but this underscores a serious problem. Game theorists tell us that the larger the number of players, the poorer the prospects that they will achieve multilateral cooperation.
- Larger and more powerful LDCs, such as India and Brazil, believe that their economic interests are best served by bilateral deals, not multilateral schemes.
- Since the 1960s the expectation of citizens in the democracies have risen dramatically, and to a greater degree than at any time in history, the legitimacy of political authorities is "based on their ability to deliver jobs, maintain relatively stable prices, distribute wealth equitably, enlarge the economic pie and provide a better quality of life."[26] Their existing economic difficulties have made them even more aware of this fact. Consequently they will avoid economic policies that require greater international cooperation, if such policies cause hardships at home.
- It may be beyond our technical capacity to manage the global economy even if we have the political will to do so. Peter F. Drucker has observed that most economic theory rests on "the macroeconomies of the nation-state," not the international economy.[27] Our models, therefore, are outmoded and frequently irrelevant to our economic problems.

Finally, many observers claim that with declining U.S. power, the world is fated to live with an unpredictable international economy. But other students of international affairs are more optimistic. Lester Thurow, in *The Zero-Sum Solution*, acknowledges U.S. power is slipping but that "while the United States is no longer strong enough to dictate economically to the rest of the world, as it did at the first Bretton Woods Conference, it is still the strongest country in the industrial world. As a result, it still needs to play the role of manager of the international trading system."[28]

A growing number of politicians, with their eyes on the White House, support this observation. They realize that the world is entering a new era, and awesome changes, creating such great disruptions, provide statesmen with unique leadership opportunities. But here is where the American predicament may become the most serious barrier to multilateralism: our polity and political culture are poorly designed to engage in the long-term multifaceted strategic planning that multilateralism demands. Ambitious and farsighted members of Congress appreciate the need for such planning, but institutional and cultural constraints dictate that they lurch from crisis to crisis.

Notes

1. Robert O. Keohane, *After Hegemony* (Princeton, NJ: Princeton University Press, 1984), p. 139.
2. Joan Edelman Spero, *The Politics of International Economic Relations* (New York: St. Martin's Press, 1985), p. 35.
3. Keohane, *After Hegemony*, p. 149.
4. Spero, *The Politics of*, p. 95.
5. Keohane, *After Hegemony*, p. 140.
6. Spero, *Politics of International*, p. 55.
7. Spero, *Politics of International*, p. 52.
8. Spero, *Politics of International*, pp. 57–8.
9. Spero, *Politics of International*, p. 105.
10. *Washington Post*, 31 January 1986.
11. Spero, *Politics of International*, p. 106.
12. *Washington Post*, 10 January 1985.
13. *Washington Post*, 16 December 1984.
14. Lester C. Thurow, *The Zero-Sum Solution* (New York: Simon and Schuster, 1985), p. 333.
15. *New York Times*, 9 June 1985.
16. Henry Kissinger, *Years of Upheaval* (Boston: Little, Brown & Co., 1983), p. 896.
17. *Washington Post*, 19 September 1983.
18. *Washington Post*, 19 September 1983.
19. *Washington Post*, 23 September 1983.
20. Bernard K. Gordon, "The Truth in Trading," *Foreign Policy* 61 (Winter 1985–1986): 98.
21. *Washington Post*, 23 September 1983.
22. Christopher Layne, "The Real Conservative Agenda," *Foreign Policy* 61 (Winter 1985–1986): 80.
23. Layne, "The Real Conservative," p. 80.
24. Helmut Schmidt, *A Grand Strategy for the West* (New Haven, CT: Yale University Press, 1985), p. 63.

25. Susan Strange, "Protectionism and World Politics," *International Organization* 39 (Spring 1985): 223–24.
26. Edward L. Morse, "The New Economic Nationalism and the Coordination of Economic Policies," in Werner Link and Werner J. Feld, eds., *The New Nationalism* (Elmsford, NY: Pergamon Press, 1979), p. 66.
27. Peter F. Drucker, "The Changing World Economy," *Foreign Affairs* 64 (Spring 1986): 770.
28. Thurow, *The Zero Sum Solution*, p. 379.

Conclusions

The Soviet Union

The Soviets will be preoccupied with the Brezhnev legacy of stagnation for the remainder of this century. It "has become . . . the official code word for the Brezhnev years, in much the same way as 'hare-brained schemes', used to stand for Khrushchev's rule and the 'personality cult' for Stalin's."[1] Paradoxically, the symptons of stagnation—a chronically sick economy and technological backwardness—are a byproduct of one of Brezhnev's greatest accomplishments on the "first front," that of obtaining superpower status coequal with the United States. Gorbachev's principal security goal, therefore, must be to protect the USSR on the "second front" just as Brezhnev did on the first front. This will entail policy revisions in Soviet foreign and domestic affairs.

In the first instance the USSR must reduce its international commitments. Gorbachev knows that the Soviet Union is badly overextended abroad, and— his speeches to the contrary—he realizes that the correlation of forces is not in its favor. U.S. global hegemony is declining, and Washington is suffering setbacks in the Third World, however, contrary to right-wing claims, these do not automatically translate into Soviet gains. The most successful LDCs are those following the capitalist road to development.

Meanwhile, developments in Western Europe are no cause for glee in Moscow. The Western Europeans have been voicing displeasure with U.S. policies, but the NATO alliance remains intact. The EC is the world's most powerful economic union; consequently, the spectre of Eurocommunism has become something of a historical curiosity. Today the communist parties of

217

Western Europe are the weakest they have been since World War II, and Marxism–Leninism as a powerful intellectual force is at its lowest ebb since the 19th century.

The Chernobyl accident has caused the Soviets a profound loss of face. It demonstrated that while militarily powerful, the USSR is sadly backward in other respects—a bumbling Leviathan incapable of managing dangerous technology and not to be trusted by civilized neighbors.

All of these developments provide an incentive for the Soviets to reduce their profile abroad, to calibrate their commitments to the real world, and not to be sidetracked by ideological fantasies.

Secondly, the Soviets need an arms control treaty with the United States to release funds for modernization. Reluctant to appear too anxious, Gorbachev may feign indifference toward negotiations or seek propaganda points by citing U.S. recalcitrance as evidence that Washington, not Moscow, is holding up the talks. But in doing so, he runs the risk of abetting those U.S. officials who oppose arms control and are seeking military superiority. They will cite Gorbachev's "half-hearted" efforts in order to justify their own obstructionist policies.

Moreover, time is not on his side. Although an arms control treaty is in the interest of both camps, pressing domestic problems make it even a greater priority for the USSR. As long as there is no progress on the arms limitation front, Gorbachev must pump billions of rubles into defense, rather than into activities capable of resolving his economic crisis. Yet this, and not a U.S. nuclear strike, is the most imminent threat to Soviet security.

Finally, there are developments looming on the international horizon that are both cause for alarm in Moscow and incentive for Gorbachev to resolve his internal problems as hastily as possible. There is, for example, the PRC. A common border almost 5,000 miles long, historical enmity, and ideological differences guarantee cool Sino–Soviet relations indefinitely. Consequently about 25% of the USSR's armed forces are stationed along the Soviet–Chinese border. Moscow's fear of China will grow as the PRC reaps the fruits of its modernization drive. Over time, given the PRC's immense population (bordering on empty Russian territory) and its vast economic, political, and military potential, the Soviets will gradually lose political control of areas of Soviet Asia that abut China.

A similar diminution in Soviet influence is likely to occur in Muslim areas of the USSR in the face of assertive Islamic neighbors who border the Soviet Union's soft underbelly in the Middle East. The greater safeguard against this threat is not Soviet tanks, but economic prosperity that meets the expectations of Soviet Muslims.

By reducing his foreign commitments and achieving an arms limitation accord with the Americans, Gorbachev will approach resolution of his crisis. But more importantly, he must address his internal difficulties, which are far less tractable than his problems abroad. Most Sovietologists are convinced that Gorbachev is serious about reform but say he will move slowly lest he arouse powerful defenders of the status quo. This proviso presumably explains why Gorbachev's actions have not, as yet, matched his bold rhetoric. But even assuming he makes fundamental changes in the Soviet economy (providing for greater monetary incentives, decentralizing decision-making, keying pay scales to productivity, and so forth), their ultimate success rests on adopting reforms in the intellectual and political realms, as well. In brief, to match the West economically and technologically, the Soviet Union must become a freer, more open society.

In this connection, the release of celebrated dissidents in 1986, among them Anatoly Scharansky and—the most celebrated of them all—Andrei Sakharov is encouraging. Indeed, letting Sakharov appear before U.S. television audiences soon after he was allowed to return to Moscow from exile in Gorky indicated that perhaps Gorbachev has adopted a new, more permissive policy toward dissent. There are two schools of thought on this matter.

Optimists link this development to Gorbachev's commitment to "openness" in the USSR. Like the communist leadership in Beijing, Gorbachev and his associates realize that Soviet society cannot modernize as long as the brightest and most innovative elements in the Soviet Union are afraid to express themselves.

Other commentators are more guarded in assessing the significance of Sakharov's release; that is, it is a propaganda ploy that Gorbachev hopes will earn him points in the West. In short, it will facilitate the commercial contacts with the West that Gorbachev needs so badly to revive the moribund Soviet economy.

At this point one must stick with the pessimistic interpretation, at least until there is further evidence that the Soviets will permit dissidents to freely express their displeasure with the regime's policies, and to have a voice in political, economic, and cultural decisions that the party heretofore has monopolized.

It is significant, however, that since Gorbachev's ascendancy, the Soviet press has dealt with problems of Soviet society in a more forthright fashion than in the past. Although its treatment of the Chernobyl nuclear disaster did not meet Western standards, the openness Moscow did display was noteworthy. The same holds true of the frequent press conferences conducted with Western journalists by Soviet officials.

There is no mystery as to what is going on here. Gorbachev believes that he can recast Soviet society without profoundly affecting the regime or the CPSU's domination of the USSR. He will permit heated and open debate of matters that fall into the category of "low politics"—the availability of goods and services—but not "high politics"—the right of citizens to have a voice in the political process, to freely express views about the flaws of communism, to form truly independent labor unions, and the like.

But whatever his preferences, modern societies cannot actualize their potential while repressing people and circumscribing intellectual inquiry. At some point, Gorbachev must allow his scientists, academics, technocrats, and managers greater intellectual freedom and, yes, a voice in the political process, too. What's more, truly significant changes in the economic system will necessarily lead to greater access by citizens to power centers presently dominated by the party elite. In other words, Gorbachev some day will have to make a choice—economic stagnation or political pluralism.

Although the Soviet crisis is serious and enduring, it would be foolhardy to predict the imminent demise of the Soviet regime and Russian empire, certainly if we think of the word "demise" as being definitive, final, total. But over the long pull, the Soviet Union will be transformed from a quasi-totalitarian society into a pluralistic one. The Soviet regime as we know it will not survive this transition.

The empire will survive for decades, but ultimately the centrifugal forces of ethnicity in the USSR and nationalism in Eastern Europe will deny the Russians the hegemony they presently enjoy. Gorbachev then is faced with a truly revolutionary situation; ironically, many Westerners do not acknowledge this because they do not think dialectically.

What policies should the United States adopt toward the Soviet Union as it struggles with serious internal upheaval? The following observations may provide guidance to U.S. policymakers.

- The United States cannot bring down the Soviet Union through economic warfare or by withholding the technology it needs to modernize. The world food glut has destroyed, probably forever, the U.S. manipulation of its grain surplus at the Soviets' expense, and Moscow can purchase most high-tech products from America's allies. Misguided efforts to wage economic warfare against the Soviets will heighten East–West tensions and, perhaps of larger importance, divide the democracies.

- In the short run, the Soviets will make concessions to undercut support for U.S. defense hikes, to achieve favorable terms of trade, etc. But opportunities to influence Soviet policy will be few and far between, and then we can only expect to have a modest impact upon their actions. The Soviets cannot be forced to institute liberal policies; the ruling elite must decide to do so. Over time, however, the Soviet bloc will become so entangled with the capitalist-dominated global economy that it will become increasingly more vulnerable to external pressures. Some U.S. officials oppose Soviet membership in GATT, but should they become part of that organization, they may become more subject to Western pressures, not less.

- The West, moreover, can employ its economic clout to influence developments in some satellite countries. For example, the wholesale pardoning of Polish political prisoners in September 1986 was linked to Jaruzelski's quest to resume full economic relations with the United States.
- If Gorbachev succeeds in his modernization drive, he must reduce defense spending, but the United States cannot then achieve military superiority bydefault. Moscow will take every measure necessary to keep up with Washington, and besides, economic troubles will force the U.S. government to significantly reduce its defense budget in the remainder of the 1980s. The best way to achieve superpower nuclear stability is through the maintenance of a second-strike capacity and the pursuit of arms control accords.
- It is imperative that the superpowers reach crisis prevention agreements; for example, establishing nuclear risk reduction centers, arranging agreements that reduce the prospect of a clash in the Third World, etc.
- Finally, whatever it is called—détente, peaceful coexistence, constructive competition—the superpowers must improve overall East–West relations if they are going to make progress on the items discussed above. Pressing domestic problems are incentives for them to develop a relationship based on restraint, accommodation, and at times, cooperation. We have good cause to be wary of the Soviets, but there are areas of common interest, such as avoiding a nuclear war and preventing nuclear proliferation, that offer the opportunity for fruitful agreements with them.

The United States, then, has reason to be optimistic about the future of the superpower rivalry, but it has cause to be concerned about its own predicament. If it is to be resolved, nothing less than a new social contract must be forged by the country's leaders and its people. In this connection, the following conclusions are in order.

The United States

The founding fathers understood that a nation's security rests on a strong, stable, and effective government. They feared the Articles of Confederation were incapable of providing strong government, so they hatched a plot to replace them with a new basic law. They did not, however, meld the states into a unitary system or fuse legislative and executive power into a single body as in a parliamenetary system. Today, therefore, federalism and our system of checks and balances are responsible for the diffusion of political authority in Washington—that is, for the crisis of governance.

Big government is not the problem—weak government is. The failure of Washington to resolve the deficit crisis is rooted in a political system designed to make it difficult for a majority to act quickly and boldly. The inability of the United States to take the lead and work with other democracies to resolve international economic problems also has its roots in outmoded political institutions and a political culture that disparages political authority. As a growing number of observers in academia, Washington, and the media realize, the time has come to restructure our political system, to empower the parties, and to foster greater fusion between Congress and the president than presently is the case. The objective here is to create a situation in which the combined power of Congress and the presidency can be mobilized and directed to resolve national problems.

To muster the political power necessary to change national policy, citizens on the lower tier of society must be empowered. Wide-scale citizen participation is not merely consistent with democracy—it is vital to the resolution of the American predicament. Leaders who favor fundamental readjustments cannot mobilize a national constituency around a reformist agenda without the collective power of society's least privileged citizens. If conservatives in the United States subscribed to an ethos of noblesse oblige, an infusion of mass-based political protest into the political bloodstream perhaps would be unnecessary. Unfortunately, this honorable principle has not been part of the American conservative ethos for over a century. And contrary to the claims of liberal pluralists, our nation's elites do not "anticipate" the needs of society's underprivileged members or make grassroots activism unnecessary.

Finally, the conservative counterreformation is responsible for widespread confusion about the role of government. Contrary to the claims of 20th century American conservatives, government is not a necessary evil, but intrinsic to civilized society. Through government, a nation safeguards its security abroad and achieves justice at home. Conservatives acknowledge that the first goal cannot be achieved through private initiatives but claim somehow that the second one can. This idea was first fully developed by 18th century liberals and is based upon the flawed proposition that individuals, in promoting their parochial interests, enhance the public interest. This is, of course, to confuse the private and public realms and to offer private solutions to public problems. Our predicament is public rather than private in nature and to resolve public problems through private initiatives is to engage in a form of social pathology.

Contary to the claims of Marxists, however, a capitalist society can be both prosperous and just. It can sustain a culture in which individualism and communitarianism coexist. To achieve these vital objectives, government must be strong and the political community unified. This brings us to the second component of a new social contract, closely linked to the first one. It involves economic growth and economic equality.

The security of the United States rests on economic abundance. Economic growth has served as a social adhesive. It has enabled our pluralistic society to achieve unity out of diversity, and to build and sustain a mighty military deterrent. To avoid the pitfalls of the business cycle, however, the federal government must continue to serve as economic crisis manager. Only the federal government has the capacity to grapple with this socially destructive byproduct of capitalism. As the U.S. economy becomes more entangled with the global economic system, the government must play a similar role internationally. A major challenge before the United States and its trading partners, then, is to develop multilateral policies capable of restoring the monetary and trade regimes, which have declined with U.S. hegemony, and to adopt fiscal measures to keep the global economy humming.

The United States no longer has the hegemony it had twenty-five years ago, but it remains the premier democratic power, and it must take the lead in building a new economic order. If the international monetary regime is restored, a number of measures must be adopted: the central banks of the advanced countries must keep short-term interest rates low; exchange rates should be stabilized through "target zones" or similar anti-fluctuation measures; and a coherent long-term strategy must be formulated to deal with Third World debt. Over the long pull, the LDCs possess markets the democracies need, to absorb the surplus products and services Marx predicted would lead to their demise. The economic health of the Third World, therefore, closely influences the economic welfare of the First World.

A new trading system must be established that reflects the changes that have occurred since GATT was first created. If a new system promoting the principles of nondiscrimination, liberalization, and reciprocity is not established soon, the world will once again be engulfed by economic warfare. As Lester Thurow has observed, there are many economic elements at work today that were nonexistent or unimportant years ago when GATT was esablished—such as nationalized industries, industrial policies, subsidized interest rates, and multinational companies. The democracies and their major trading partners in the Third World must develop new rules that treat all these factors.

Thurow reminds us, however, that new trade rules alone will not restore a liberal free-trade regime: "While new trading rules are needed, they are not the heart of the problem. The heart of the problem is being able and willing to run the major industrial economies at full employment without inflation. If that cannot be done, no new set of rules is going to rescue the current system."[2] Here again the United States has a large role to play, but so do the other democracies, Japan and West Germany in particular. They must adopt fiscal policies that facilitate economic growth. They have been reluctant to do so because they fear inflation and political backlash at home, but they must increase their economic output. The U.S. economy will slow down at some point, and world trade will stagnate. The resultant economic crisis will be far more damaging to their societies than inflationary disruptions. Of course, it will be easier for politicians in Bonn and Tokyo to adopt such policies if their counterparts in Washington actively demonstrate that they are committed to a comprehensive set of multilateral programs and are prepared to take measures unpopular with the U.S. electorate.

Although economic growth rests on international cooperation, economic equality—vital to unity within the United States—is primarily a domestic matter. Ronald Reagan has helped resolve our predicament by helping the American people to restore confidence in themselves and their country. This is no small achievement, but it is a short-term accomplishment, and pales in significance before the long-term legacy of his policies—a two-tiered society. Much of the progress we had been making in reducing economic inequities, prior to his election, has been dashed under his stewardship. The Reaganites contend that their economic policies terminated the 1980–1982 recession, and set the economy on the course of recovery—a course that may experience occasional difficulty, but is a true one.

The record tells us a different story. On the macro level, the huge deficits that have the potential to devastate our economy will be with us well into the next decade. Even more to the point is the situation at the micro level. The story line here can be stated succinctly: Americans on the upper tier are doing well, but those on the lower one are not. Many face bleak economic futures.

For most of this decade the unemployment rate has been over 7%, but the figure is higher because government undercounts joblessness. For example, those who have stopped looking for work are excluded from the count. The living standard of the average American family has slipped. This hold true for many middle-class Americans who earn less than their parents did at a similar age and today cannot afford to purchase the home their elder brother or sister could in the 1970s. Black Americans are falling behind whites in the race for economic equity, because black poverty is on the rise. Furthermore, the number of blacks attending college and medical and law school is declining.

Poverty is increasing throughout the United States. Organizations that provide food to the hungry and shelter to the homeless report that they are unable to meet the demands for their services. Some needy Americans are victims of economic change, but others—the deinstitutionalized mentally ill who cannot care for themselves and have become street people, for example, and youngsters who no longer get school lunch programs—are suffering because of budgetary cutbacks. In spite of enormous food surpluses, it is estimated that 8.5% of our people go hungry, and 15.5 million live below the poverty line but are denied food stamps. Finally, how can we forget that a disproportionate number of children living in poverty reside in female-headed households—that is, 13 million, which accounts for 40% of the population in poverty.[3]

We need not dwell on this data. Our newspapers and electric media have been recounting this information to us throughout this decade. But as yet there is little protest, either from the people who are being afflicted or by those of us who are more affluent but should be outraged by their plight. Political observers are confused by this situation. No doubt the factors we cite in chapter 7 provide some plausible explanations. Lester Thurow, however, is unquestionably correct when he says: "At the moment there are no political countersurges on the horizon to counter the economic surge toward inequality that is now underway. If history is any guide, however, there soon will be."[4]

The proponents of laissez-faire economics who allege that the free market can resolve these problems are clearly mistaken. The free market cannot eliminate such economic inequities, even in a rich society like our own; thus, public actions must be taken to reduce them. Before going further, however, we should acknowledge that there are certain things that government cannot do and that there are many things healthy individuals should do for themselves. Everyone capable of working should be gainfully employed, not living on welfare or relying upon public assistance alone for their income. Individuals must take responsibility for their actions. For example, fathers—married or unwed—must be compelled to care for their children, and so should mothers. In an era of austerity the American people will, and should, demand that public assistance be provided only to the truly needy.

But the Friedmanites and other champions of laissez-faire economics must acknowledge that if the private sector cannot provide jobs, government must do so, either directly through job programs or indirectly through incentives to private employers. Whatever the mechanism, government must act. This holds true for all the other problems mentioned. Many of the public programs will be inefficient, but the purpose of government is to achieve social order and to promote justice, not efficiency. The deficiencies of many public programs are evidence of government ineptness and the pitfalls of large bureaucracies, but they reflect the flaws of our economy, too. Nonetheless, these flaws are acceptable, because capitalism creates wealth better than any other economic system and its deficiencies can be ameliorated through social welfare programs.

This brings us to a conclusion unappealing to most Americans. Growth alone cannot achieve economic justice. It is, of course, essential to the nation's economic welfare, but we must raise taxes if we are to reduce economic inequities that foster disunity in our society. Economic reality dictates that we acknowledge the merit of Oliver Wendell Holmes's observation that "taxes are what we pay for civilized society."

In contrast to political and economic policies, it is more difficult to link cultural values to the forging of a social contract, but such values are vital to collective behavior. The United States is a society in which the business ethos thrives and is closely woven into the culture. Yet leaders on the religious right are impervious to the connection between an ethos that stresses instant gratification, individual enterprise, and greed, and drug abuse, juvenile delinquency, and other forms of social pathology about which they rightfully complain. This linkage does not mean we scrap our free enterprise economy, but in looking for the roots of many of our cultural problems, we should remain aware of it.

Business leaders who tie the country's economic problems to fractious labor/management relations fail to see that the U.S. business ethos, which places competition and individualism above cooperation and community, may have something to do with the problem. Here the problem is not capitalism per se, but an American variant of it. In West Germany, for example, a larger percentage of the labor force is unionized than in the United States, yet relations between workers and their bosses are more harmonious there than in our country. To a large degree this stems from employers believing that unions are legitimate economic institutions. The security workers derive from their unions, in turn, predisposes them to work harmoniously with their employers.

Japan, like the United States, is a highly competitive society, but there is a major difference between the two countries. The Japanese employee–employer relationship stresses cooperation rather than competition, "groupism" not individualism. In our society, Darwinian impulses dominate economic life, and labor/management relations are perceived in terms of a zero-sum game. We cannot adopt the measures that are unique to Japanese culture, but there are things we can copy that will reduce tensions at the workplace—for example, a reduction in the wage differentials between workers and managers. In Japan they are not as wide as in the United States, and the high performance level of Japanese executives gives lie to the claim of their U.S. counterparts that money is the overriding factor in spurring managers to excellence.

Erazim Kohak presents us with a disturbing thought. American culture, as it is manifested in our living patterns, more closely resembles the Third World than Europe. He writes that "in the decades since the suburban dispersal, the U.S. has effectively abandoned the European civilization pattern in favor of a Third World one." In Europe the pattern of growth:

> has been one of a purposeful use of communal resources to sustain an attractive urban environment—basically a walking-distance community—capable of generating and sustaining trade and culture, amid an agriculture countryside. By contrast, in the Third World urban sprawl swallows up cities and spills over the countryside, resulting in a pattern that is no longer urban or rural. The sprawl is too extensive to sustain a culture—that requires a community—or to make a public transport system viable. What remains is a mass of dispersed individuals fostering individual opulence amid social disintegration. Public services crumble, communities with them. What remains is the faceless sprawl.[5]

Kohak says that while Europe was rebuilding its cities with Marshall Plan help, the United States in the 1950s was dispersing funds to individuals—for example, through the Veterans Administration housing program—to encourage suburbanization: "By 1960 the erstwhile cities had become decaying slums amid faceless sprawl, their inhabitants dispersed too widely to support theaters. The trains stopped running; there were no more streetcars as the motor car, breathing noxious fumes, reigned supreme." This transformation spoke volumes about our nation's policy priorities:

> The true villain, as throughout the Third World, was the decision to boost individual affluence by abandoning social responsibility. America's post-war taxation did not keep pace with inflation, and the proportion of tax resources devoted to the commonweal rather than to boosting individual affluence plummeted.[6]

It is in this context that the Reaganites' policies must be interpreted, for they hold before us a vision of the "frontier" where individuals are free to pursue material gain. It is a compelling vision, one that has enthralled generations of Americans, but it is a flight from social responsibility, a fanciful voyage that could have ominous consequences for the country. It is an ethos that leads to the excesses of an Ivan Boesky.

History instructs us that a societal vision unifying a people around a common political agenda cannot be legislated. A religious covenant served that purpose when the Puritans first colonized the country, and a secular one inspired a later generation of Americans to fight for their independence. The United States was stricken by a civil war when that common bond was broken in the 19th century. During the 20th century, the Great Depression and World War II unified the people and inspired them to act decisively.

Americans have shared a vision of the public good throughout their history, although sometimes it has been more widespread and compelling than at others. Circumstances—economic, political, and social—have had a lot to do with the form it has taken and the impact it has had upon our people. Circumstances will provide the opportunity to forge a new social contract in the near future. On the basis of past performance, we have reason to be optimistic that the American people and their leaders will embark upon a new course of reform, just as their forebearers did in the 1930s. But this outcome is not preordained. We must make it happen.

Notes

1. David Holloway, "State of the Union," *New York Review of Books*, 12 June 1986, p. 18.
2. Lester C. Thurow, *The Zero-Sum Solution* (New York: Simon and Schuster, 1985), p. 18.
3. *Washington Post*, 27 August 1986.
4. *New York Times*, 19 November 1985.
5. Erazim Kohak, "A Letter from Europe," *Dissent* (Fall 1985): 407.
6. Kohak, "A Letter," p. 408.

About the Author

Richard J. Krickus is professor of political science at Mary Washington College, Fredericksburg, Virginia. He has published numerous articles for academic journals, national newspapers and journals of opinion. His previous publications include *Pursuing The American Dream* (Anchor/Doubleday and Indiana University Press, 1976). He has served as a consultant to the Office of Economic Opportunity, the Defense Department, the U.S. Arms Control and Disarmament Agency, the U.S. Army and the U.S. Joint Economic Committee. Dr. Krickus has worked as a political consultant and co-founded the National Center For Urban Ethnic Affairs, located in Washington, DC. He lives in Fairfax, Virginia, with his wife, Mary Ann, and his two children, Anthony and Alexandra.

Index

Also by Sarah J. Harris

The Colour of Bee Larkham's Murder